# Micro-moth Fi

## A Guide to Finding the ~~Early Stages~~ in Lancashire and Cheshire

2nd Edition

A Chronological Guide
from January to December

# Ben Smart

# Lancashire & Cheshire Fauna Society

Registered Charity 500685
Publication No. 125
2018

ISBN 978-1-9997312-4-3

Smart, B. 2018. Micro-Moth Field Tips. (2nd Edition)
Lancashire & Cheshire Fauna Society, Rishton.

I am grateful to the Lancashire and Cheshire Fauna Society for providing the opportunity to publish this book and their very generous assistance in co-funding and administering the project. The society plays an important role in recording and publishing data on local wildlife.

More information can be obtained at the society's website at: www.lacfs.org.uk

## Butterfly Conservation

Thanks also to the Lancashire branch of Butterfly Conservation for their very generous assistance in terms of the co-funding of this publication. The charity is dedicated to the conservation of butterflies and moths.

More information can be found at the website of the Lancashire branch at: http://www.lancashire-butterflies.org.uk

First printed in 2017, the book's overwhelming success demanded a reprint so we have taken the opportunity in this second edition to correct an oversight and add a few extra pages for a foodplant index. We've also made some minor corrections.

# Introduction

The purpose of this book is to encourage moth recorders to get out into the field and take more notice of the often fascinating feeding signs of micro-moths. As written descriptions of what to look for may seem slightly vague, photographic illustrations are provided to assist the finding of each of the species described. Whilst the book focuses on moths found in Lancashire and Cheshire, the field tips within will hopefully be of use to people in other localities who wish to study the early stages of the microlepidoptera.

There are various reasons to look for these early stages.

*   Some of these moths are much more easily recorded in this way. Many of the adult moths will be highly unlikely to venture into a mercury vapour light trap.
*   Recording the moth on the basis of feeding signs and evidence of habitation means that the moth's presence can be recorded for much of its twelve-month life cycle, rather than just the few days when the adult moth may be flying. This should enable us to develop a more accurate idea of each species' true distribution and ecological needs, facilitating the formulation of management plans, if needed, to ensure the survival of vulnerable species.
*   As moth recorders, such study can add to the interest of the hobby and means the hobby can be maintained, even on those days in winter when very little is flying. It is certainly possible to record at least ten species in good habitat, even on the darkest mid-winter day. It is for this reason that the book has been arranged in a chronological order, to describe some of the signs likely to be found in any given month. Of course, some of these signs may be present for a number of months. There may also be regional variability as to when these signs appear. Some of this will be clarified in the text of species accounts.

## County recording

The counties of Lancashire and Cheshire contain quite a wide variety of habitats from moorland to lowland mosses; from coastal sand-dunes and pine forests to extensive farmland. There are also a number of species to be found in more urban and suburban environments, in areas of municipal planting. Even town and city gardens can provide suitable habitat for many of the species mentioned within this book.

The recording of Lepidoptera is usually geographically based upon Vice-County lines. The Vice-counties were a biological recording concept established in the mid-19th century (Watson, 1852). Continued use of these ensures stable boundaries, unaffected by local government reorganisations.

**VC58** is Cheshire, including Wirral and Greater Manchester south of the Mersey, and extending into Derbyshire to include land north of the River Etherow and west of the River Goyt.
**VC59** is south Lancashire including Merseyside and Greater Manchester north of the Mersey.
**VC60** is north Lancashire, north of the River Ribble.

Each of the three vice-counties has a county micro-moth recorder. Cheshire and Lancashire also have County Moth Groups. Their websites contain further information about recording moths in VC 58, 59 and 60.
Cheshire - http://www.record-lrc.co.uk/c1.aspx?Mod=Article&ArticleID=G00040001
Lancashire - http://www.lancashiremoths.co.uk

# How to use this book

Following the introductory section, there are twelve chapters, one for each month. Each month contains 10-18 species accounts with text and photographs to aid location of the feeding signs. The photo details for each species account relate only to the feeding signs seen in the top left image, unless stated otherwise.

Alongside each species entry a code number has been added. These are taken from "A Checklist of the Lepidoptera of the British Isles" by Agassiz, Beavan & Heckford (2013). An example is *Taleporia tubulosa* with a code number of 11.006. The number 11 relates to the family, in this case Psychidae. The number 006 relates to the taxonomic position of this moth within the family.

A guide is also given to the national and local distribution. However if the species does not seem to be present in your Vice-County, do not be put off. Looking for field signs can sometimes demonstrate that a species is more common than records of trapped adults alone would indicate.

Following each chapter is a single page containing ten larvae, larval cases or leaf-mines, useful to compare to the species contained in the main accounts. Due to limited space, the larval stage is the only one documented and is done so in numerical terms. For instance 10-4 is October to April.

# Acknowledgements

The photographs are mine unless stated. I am very grateful to Rob Edmunds, Willem Ellis, Chris Manley, Tymo Muus, Tina Schulz, Jenny Seawright, David Shenton, Ian Smith and Oliver Wadsworth for allowing me to use their photos. All are credited fully on the relevant pages.

Sources used within this book are acknowledged on p.213. In particular, Tutt (1901-1905) was a great influence in the calendar year format of this book. The information within Emmet's Field Guide to the Smaller British Lepidoptera 2nd ed. (1988) was also essential, as my battered copy can attest. I am very glad to say that a third edition of this wonderful book is in preparation.

The accounts contained within this book are based on my own findings within Lancashire and Cheshire over the last fifteen years or so. There are a number of people I would like to thank for their assistance, company and friendship during this time. Kevin McCabe, Steve Palmer and Steve Hind have all provided lots of support and knowledge, and in a number of cases advised on sites to explore. Ian Smith was particularly instrumental in influencing my interest in the early stages of micro-moths, and he has also helped in providing detailed information related to a number of the species.

Steve Palmer was also kind enough to read the text prior to publication and made very many helpful corrections and suggestions. I am extremely lucky to have benefited from Steve's support and expertise during the development of this project.

Thanks to Dave Bickerton for his assistance in getting this book published and in helping with the design, printing and distribution.

Finally I would like to thank my wife, Katherine, and my children for their support, and their tolerance of my hobby, even as rearing pots threaten to take over kitchen cupboards!

# Rearing micro-moths from the early stages

In many cases, it is necessary to rear the early stages through to confirm the identity of the moth. Even when not essential, most will find that it is of interest to do so. It will hopefully also result in the emergence of a perfect specimen which will be an ideal subject for macro-photographers. When freshly emerged, most micro-moths will be more likely to sit still for their photograph, at least in comparison to the often ragged specimens that may be fished out of the bottom of the light trap or netted in the field.

A few general principles in relation to rearing should be noted. For all species it is essential to avoid larvae or pupae drying out. For those species that will feed up quickly and pupate a week or two later, with adult emergence following shortly after, keeping the larva within an air tight plastic pot of about 7cm x 7cm is sufficient. Ensure the pot is kept in a cool, dark environment such as a garden shed. Provide fresh foodplant every three or four days whilst the larva is feeding.

Equally it is essential to prevent undue moisture accumulating in the rearing pot and the development of mould. Only add small amounts of foodplant at a time. Ensure frass (droppings) is removed every two or three days. Adding a small piece of tissue paper into the container can help absorb some of the circulating moisture. It is also helpful to open the pot every day or so to allow the contents to 'breathe', again reducing the moisture level within the pot. As soon as the larva has pupated, ensure all excess foodplant is removed. If the larva has wrapped itself in plant material prior to pupation then obviously leave this in place.

Those species that have a prolonged developmental period, particularly those overwintering as a larva, require special attention. This will be described in more detail in the species accounts. Essentially, aim to replicate the conditions the larvae would experience in the wild, and try and minimise interference with their life cycle as much as possible. This may mean placing the full-fed larva into a netted pot with soil and other vegetation (preferably sterilised to ensure no predators are present), and leaving outside in a sheltered spot. A partially fed larva may need placing in a similar spot but should have some of its foodplant growing within the pot. Take care when adding any further vegetation that other larvae are not also present as this may significantly confuse the results of the rearing. Alternatively, securely tying netting material (such as stockings or pop socks) around the inhabited foodplant can be an effective way of reducing intrusion upon the insect's natural lifecycle.

For leaf-mining species passing the whole of their larval cycle in one leaf, wrapping the petiole in damp tissue or keeping a stem in water may help keep the leaf viable and allow the larva to complete its development.

Sphagnum moss and soft rotten wood are also good to add to the larval container as these will often provide a desirable medium for the larva to enter and proceed to pupation.

When putting a number of larvae in containers to rear through, particularly when overwintering, ensure you have kept accurate records as to which larva is in which container. Also be cautious about putting a number of species in the same container. It may make it difficult to link the emerged adult to a particular larva, thus reducing the value of the record. Also be aware that some larvae have cannibalistic tendencies, although this seems more prevalent amongst the macrolepidoptera.

Finally, never forget to check your containers regularly to ensure that you do not miss the moth's emergence. This should ideally be on a daily basis at the period when emergence is expected. Be aware also, that emergence may be somewhat premature if the larva has been reared indoors in warmer conditions than would have been the case in nature.

# Variability of typical micro-moth larvae from selected families

**Eriocraniidae** (*Paracrania chrysolepidella*)
The typical Eriocraniidae larva is white (or grey in the case of *sangii*), with variable marking on the head and prothoracic plate. The larvae, which do not possess legs, are well adapted to leaf-mining.

**Nepticulidae** (*Stigmella hybnerella*)
Nepticulidae larvae are white, yellow or green. The epidermis lacks markings and is quite transparent, often showing the gut within. Legs are vestigial as befits its leaf-mining nature.

**Tischeriidae** (*Tischeria ekebladella*)
Another leaf-miner, the larvae typically have a flattened head, a broad thorax and an abdomen tapering towards the anal end. It has rudimentary thoracic legs, but no abdominal prolegs.

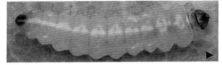

**Tineidae** (*Morophaga choragella*)
The larvae are found using a number of unusual foodstuffs including fungi, rotten wood and stored products. A few larvae from this family will feed on textiles. Some form cases.

**Bucculatricidae** (*Bucculatrix nigricomella*)
The larvae of this family commence feeding as leaf-miners. Typically after a few instars they will switch to external feeding on the same foodplant. The larvae possess thoracic legs and prolegs.

**Gracillariidae** (*Parornix anglicella*)
*Parornix* larvae undergo hypermetamorphosis (p.194) separating the leaf-mining stage and the later instars feeding within leaf folds. The larvae share distinctive prothoracic plate markings.

**Gracillariidae** (*Phyllonorycter tristrigella*)
*Phyllonorycter* larvae spend their entire feeding stage in a single mine and pupate within, usually in a cocoon. As with all Gracillariidae larvae, they also demonstrate hypermetamorphosis.

**Ypsolophidae** (*Ypsolopha ustella*)
These species are external feeders, often creating spinnings between the leaves of their foodplant. The larva is broadest in the middle of the abdomen, tapering towards both ends.

**Oecophoridae** (*Tachystola acroxantha*)
Typically larvae of this group appear quite narrow and elongated. They are generally quite featureless, lacking distinctive pinaculae or dorsal stripes. The prothoracic plate is relatively large.

**Chimabachidae** (*Diurnea fagella*)
The three British species of this family feed on the leaves of trees, shrubs or herbaceous plants. They have distinctively shaped swollen third thoracic legs, similar to a pair of boxing gloves.

**Depressariidae** (*Agonopterix arenella*)
The larvae of this family feed within spun shoots, leaves or stems. Some will mine during their early instars. Like many other micro larvae they can be quite lively, wriggling away if disturbed.

**Gelechiidae** (*Mirificarma mulinella*)
Many Gelechiid larvae show a degree of tapering with well-demarcated segments and a relatively narrow head. *Apodia bifractella* is atypical, lacking thoracic legs or prolegs.

**Elachistidae** (*Elachista argentella*)
The larval stages of most of this family are spent mining grasses, sedges and rushes. The head is markedly flattened. Unlike many leaf-miners, the larvae have thoracic legs and prolegs.

**Momphidae** (*Mompha locupletella*)
Many Momphidae larvae feed on willowherbs utilising a variety of techniques. Some are leaf-miners, some feed within spinnings, some within the seedpods, and some within the stem.

**Pterophoridae** (*Oidaematophorus lithodactyla*). Many plume moth larvae are covered in setae (long bristles). *Adaina microdactyla* feeds within a stem, whereas most others, such as *O. lithodactyla*, feed externally on leaves.

**Choreutidae** (*Anthophila fabriciana*)
The larvae feed within spinnings of the foodplant. They generally have fairly prominent and numerous pinaculae, and relatively long thoracic legs and prolegs.

**Tortricidae** (*Pandemis cerasana*)
Tortricid larvae are numerous and frequently encountered. Many feed in spinnings on the leaves of trees and herbaceous plants. Others feed within stems, roots, seed-pods and fruit.

**Crambidae** (*Crambus lathoniellus*)
The typical crambid larva has long setae, large pinaculae and relatively elongated prolegs. They feed in a wide variety of settings. A few are aquatic in the larval stage, some with gills.

7

# Other lepidopterous and non-lepidopterous larvae

**Geometridae larvae**, such as this Early Thorn (*Selenia dentaria*), will usually have only one pair of prolegs as well as the anal claspers. A few other species, such as the Scalloped Hazel (*Odontopera bidentata*), may have a small, second pair of prolegs.

**Noctuidae larvae**. When small these may easily be mistaken for micro-moth larvae. Most have four pairs of prolegs. Exceptions include the Plusiinae which only have two pairs, such as this Burnished Brass (*Diachrysia chrysitis*), and the Snouts, with three pairs.

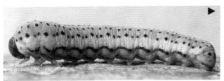

**Sawfly larvae**, such as this *Zaraea fasciata*, a honeysuckle feeder, are often mistaken for lepidoptera larvae. However careful examination reveals the typical larva of the sawfly group of Hymenoptera to have more prolegs than the four pairs possessed by most moth larvae.

A commonly found **sawfly larva** is the Alder Sawfly *Eriocampa ovata*. Its penultimate instar larva is white with a distinctly fluffy appearance, thought to mimic a bird dropping. Careful examination of the prolegs should again confirm that this is a sawfly.

**Fly larvae (Diptera)** differ from moth larvae in having no obvious head capsule or legs. The larva photographed here is a hoverfly. This can be identified as such by the flattened body shape and the pair of posterior breathing tubes. These can just be seen on the right of the photo.

**Beetle larvae (Coleoptera)** may sometimes be similar to lepidopterous larvae. Typically they have an obvious head capsule and thoracic legs. The thoracic legs are generally longer than in lepidoptera, and they lack prolegs.

**Caddisfly larvae (Trichoptera)**, such as this *Limnephilus lunatus*, feed within a case and in the majority of instances live an aquatic lifestyle in their larval form. The case-bearing larvae bear superficial similarities to the Coleophoridae and the Psychidae families of microlepidoptera. Unless the larva itself is checked, they can also be mistaken for the aquatic larvae of the China-mark moths of the Crambidae family.

# The micro-moth larva

Many macro-moth larvae will feed in the open on the foodplant. Such behaviour is rare amongst the microlepidoptera, where larvae will usually feed within an enclosed area, thus offering some protection from predators. This may involve methods such as feeding within leaf-mines, spinnings or within cases.

Micro-moth larvae share a characteristic tendency to wriggle backwards at speed if the slightest touch to the head is made. On the whole, macro-moth larvae do not demonstrate this feature. Once its presence has been discovered, the larva itself can be examined and this can help to confirm the identity of a particular species.

The larval structure, as in the adult, is comprised of the head, thorax and abdomen. In the majority of instances the head has small antennal structures and stemmata (primitive eyes). Plates are present just behind the head (the prothoracic plate), and at the rear end of the larva (the anal plate).

The thorax will usually bear three pairs of thoracic legs. The abdomen usually has four pairs of prolegs as well as a pair of anal claspers. Any deviation from this, such as with the gelechiid moth *Apodia bifractella*, can help to determine identification of a larva to a particular species or family. The presence, size, position and number of pinaculae (spots) can also help identification. Setae are also present in a number of larvae. These are hair-like structures that vary in length depending on the species. They are thought to be sensory in role.

Each larva will pass through a number of instars prior to pupation. The larval appearance may change significantly from one instar to the next.

*Agonopterix heracliana – a typical larva of the Depressariidae family*

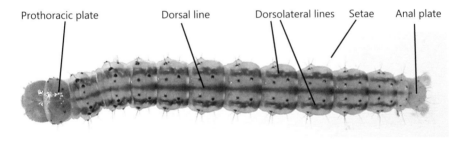

Prothoracic plate    Dorsal line    Dorsolateral lines    Setae    Anal plate

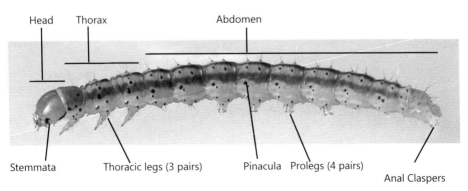

Head    Thorax    Abdomen

Stemmata    Thoracic legs (3 pairs)    Pinacula    Prolegs (4 pairs)    Anal Claspers

9

# Larval feeding methods

Many different feeding methods are utilised by micro-moth larvae. Some feed under bark, on detritus or within dead wood. Others feed within owl pellets, fungi, dead animals, hymenopteran nests, birds' nests and textiles. More common feeding methods are described below.

### Leaf folds

The later larval instars of the *Parornix* group of the Gracillariidae family feed on a leaf from within the safety of a leaf fold. The feeding can be very apparent as the leaf fold turns brown. The larvae make a number of folds, moving on to another when they have derived what nutrition they can from the fold. The photo shows feeding signs of *Parornix anglicella* on hawthorn. The fold on the left contains the pupal cocoon.

### Leaf cones

These are typically made by larvae of the genus *Caloptilia* (Gracillariidae), all of which have a sap-feeding phase followed by a tissue-feeding phase. The feeding signs pictured indicate the presence of *Caloptilia rufipennella*, which feeds on sycamore leaves. The early instar larva forms a small epidermal mine. In the tissue-feeding phase two or three successive cones are rolled, often on the same leaf, as pictured.

### Spinnings

*Anacampsis blattariella* is one of a number of larvae that spin leaves in a characteristic manner (right). In this case the leaves of birch are spun along the midrib to form a tube. Other species form dense spinnings of leaves, within which a number of larvae may feed communally. These include the pyralid larva *Acrobasis consociella* (p.112). The *Yponomeuta* larvae, spin large numbers of leaves together within a web.

### Cases

The Coleophoridae larvae, such as *Coleophora otidipennella* on field wood-rush (right), use cases to protect themselves whilst feeding. The case may be made from pieces of leaf, seed-cases and silk. Adelidae and Psychidae larvae also use larval cases. Psychid cases may contain sand, lichen, even dead insects. Other examples include the Tineid *Tinea pellionella*, whose case may be made from wool, fur or feathers (p.200).

## Feeding in stems and roots

Many species feed internally within the plant. Root feeders include many tortricid larvae from Cochylidae and most of the *Dichrorampha* genus, such as *Dichrorampha simpliciana*, pictured here within mugwort roots. Root feeding larvae are, unsurprisingly, difficult to locate. Stem feeders may leave more conspicuous signs of their presence, such as visible frass (e.g. *Gypsonoma aceriana*, p.91), galls and exit-holes (e.g. *Mompha bradleyi*, p.139).

## Feeding in fruit, nuts, seedpods, seed-heads

Other internal plant feeders use seed-heads (e.g. *Endothenia gentianaeana*, p.53), seedpods (e.g. *Grapholita lunulana*, p.24), nuts (e.g. *Cydia splendana* in acorns, p.24) and fruit (e.g. *Cydia pomonella*, p.144). *Grapholita tenebrosana* larvae feed in rose-hips, causing brown stripes to appear on the fruit. I hoped that had caused the stripes in the spun rose-hips (right). Instead it turned out to be the polyphage *Blastobasis lacticolella* (p.24), which may feed on any of these (and other) pabula.

## Leaf-mines

Many of the smaller micro-moths, and a few of the larger ones, spend part or all of their larval stage between the upper and lower epidermis of a single leaf. Some are able to switch from leaf to leaf. Some miners pupate within the leaf; others leave the leaf when full-fed. Their feeding will usually produce a mine that is typical for that species, thus making identification a simpler business than examination of the adult moth might be. Locating the egg at the start of the mine and whether it is on the upper or underside is helpful. Even the technique of leaving is worth recording as it can help identification. For instance, the larva of *Stigmella lemniscella* makes a slit on the upper surface to exit the elm leaf, whereas *S. ulmivora* leaves the elm leaf via the underside.

Be aware though that not all leaf-miners are lepidopterous. Sawflies, beetles and flies may also mine leaves in ways that are superficially similar to those of the micro-moth larvae. Fly mines in particular are very numerous, so it can help to look for certain characteristics that suggest they are not lepidopterous. Fly mines may consist of a dirty grey blotch mine, with untidy frass. They may alternatively be of a gallery mine type, but usually with a double line of frass. If the larva is visible this should be closely examined. Fly larvae have no obvious head capsule.

## Gallery mines

As the larva feeds, it leaves behind a trail of frass, which may be green, reddish, brown or black. It may form a narrow line, it may be spread to fill the whole of the mine, or it can be laid down in arcs within the mine. The pattern of frass may change within a single mine. All these factors can help in identification of the species, even after the larva has left the mine to pupate.

A common example of this type of mine is the rose miner *Stigmella anomalella* (right).

### Blotch mines

The adult moth lays its egg somewhere on the leaf. On hatching, the larva enters the leaf and begins feeding on the parenchyma within. There may be an initial gallery mine before the blotch mine phase. There is then a large whitish patch within the leaf. Frass may be untidily spread, as with the *Mompha langiella* mine on enchanter's nightshade (pictured), or may be piled up in one section of the mine, as with *Ectoedemia albifasciella* on oak (p.186).

### Blister mines

These mines are made by moths of the Gracillariidae family. The mine pictured right is *Phyllonorycter sorbi* on rowan. The larva enters the leaf after hatching. Its feeding activity causes the leaf to pucker on the upper surface, whilst there are usually creases (the number may be significant) on the underside of the leaf. A few species have their mine on the upper surface of the leaf. *Phyllonorycter* species pupate within the leaf.

## Non-lepidopterous leaf-miners

**Sawfly mines.** Sawfly leaf-miners have much reduced thoracic legs and absent prolegs. Blotch mines are typical, e.g. *Fenusella nana* on birch.

**Fly mines.** May contain a double frass line, such as *Aulagromyza hendeliana* on honeysuckle. Larva lacks head capsule and legs. (photo Rob Edmunds)

**Beetle mines.** Larvae lack abdominal prolegs. Some, e.g. *Orchestes rusci* on birch (below), make a blotch and then cut out a case, similar to the larvae of *Heliozela* spp and *Phylloporia bistrigella* (p130).

# JANUARY FIELD TIPS

At the start of a new year, the prospect of butterflies and moths may seem a long way off. However all species are present in some form throughout the year; whether it be as egg, larva, pupa or adult. Of course finding them at this time of year may be a little difficult as a variety of hiding places are used, such as inside stems, old seed-heads etc. One may also find feeding signs that remain even after the species concerned has moved on.

Whilst January is unsurprisingly one of the less productive months for recording microlepidoptera species, there are enough species out there to make it quite possible to record ten or more species in this month. Many of the December to February selections can be found in any of the winter months.

14. *Coptotriche marginea*
15. *Bucculatrix thoracella*
16. *Esperia sulphurella*
17. *Depressaria radiella*
18. *Metzneria lappella*
19. *Apodia bifractella*
20. *Coleophora alticolella*
21. *Adaina microdactyla*
22. *Epinotia immundana*
23. *Pammene regiana*

*Chorlton Water Park, Manchester, 11 January 2016*

# Coptotriche marginea

| | |
|---|---|
| Tischeriidae | 10.003 *Coptotriche marginea* (Haworth, 1828) |
| Foodplant | Bramble (*Rubus* spp.). |
| Life cycle | Larva: September to March, July. Adult: May to June, August. |
| Distribution | Common in England, Wales, southern Scotland and Ireland. Common in VC58, 59, less so in VC60. |
| Photo details | Feeding signs from Chorlton, Manchester VC59; 04.01.15 (BS). |

Mines of this species are found on bramble throughout the year. The larva within feeds over much of the winter period, although stops eating in the coldest weather. The mine begins as a white gallery, leading to a broader, pale brown funnel-shaped blotch. A hole is made in the lower epidermis of the leaf to allow frass to be ejected. The larva creates a silk-lined tunnel within the mine. Contraction of this silk may cause the leaf to fold around the mine as it develops. First generation larvae pupate within the mine in April; the second generation in July. If attempting to rear it is probably best to defer collecting the mine until later in the season, to prevent the leaf drying out before the completion of larval feeding. Once mines are bought inside into warmer conditions, the adults may emerge somewhat early.

Where present, the mine is easy to detect, and to separate from the more common *Stigmella aurella* (p.202), which forms a long, gallery mine. If there is any doubt, hold the mine up to the light and the relatively large, black-headed larva of *marginea* can be seen within the mine.

A similar species and fellow bramble feeder, *Coptotriche heinemanni*, is much more localised, being found at just a few sites in southern England. The mine of *heinemanni* is much less contracted than that of *marginea*. The adult differs too, having plain brown forewings.

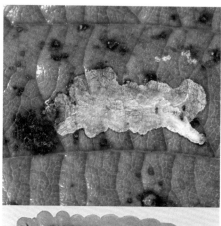

# Bucculatrix thoracella

Bucculatricidae   14.009 *Bucculatrix thoracella* (Thunberg, 1794)
Foodplant       Lime (*Tilia* spp.).
Life cycle      Larva: July to October in two generations. Adult: May to June, August.
Distribution    Locally common in Eng. Few records in Wales/Scot. Absent from Ireland.
                Common in VC58, 59, 60.
Photo details   Cocoon on lime trunk from Chorlton, Manchester VC59; 10.01.15 (BS).

The larva of this moth feeds internally, and later externally, on the leaves of lime trees. In autumn the pale yellow larvae descend from the leaves, often in some numbers and hang suspended by silken threads. They may be taken away on the clothes of some unsuspecting passer-by, or may be more successful and land on the trunk of the lime or nearby wall or fence. Once it has found a suitable surface, the larva constructs an elaborate cocoon. The completed work varies from white to buff-coloured with distinctive longitudinal ridges. The larva then pupates within the cocoon and spends the winter in this stage.

Even after the adult moth has emerged, the vacated cocoon can still be seen and allows this species to be recorded at any time of year. When looking for the cocoon in spring you may be lucky enough to see the distinctive yellow and brown adult moth nearby, resting on the trunk or perhaps on the underside of a leaf.

The leaf-mining stage sees the larva commence feeding in an irregular gallery. This may fuse to form a blotch. The gallery then continues, usually following a vein, and often making angled turns as in the image below. Many mines may be found in a single leaf. When the larva leaves the mine it continues to feed on the underside of lime leaves.

# *Esperia sulphurella*

| | |
|---|---|
| Oecophoridae | 28.019 *Esperia sulphurella* (Fabricius, 1775) |
| Foodplant | Decaying wood and fungi (e.g. *Daldinia concentrica*). |
| Life cycle | Larva: June to April in a single generation. Adult: April to June. |
| Distribution | Common throughout British Isles. |
| | Common in VC58, 59, 60. |
| Photo details | Feeding signs from Chorlton, Manchester VC59; 22.01.06 (BS). |

*Esperia sulphurella* larvae can be found feeding on decaying wood of trees, gorse bushes, stacked timber and also wooden structures, such as old fence posts. In 2014 I found a colony of *sulphurella* pupae cocooned in the rotten wood of a bird table, with each cocoon covered in frass.

Where the larvae are present, good numbers of them can be found in the same location. There is a marked preference for relatively dry wood for their feeding-site. The larvae photographed were located in the dry, dead stump of an old holly tree. The larval presence was demonstrated by large quantities of silk and frass. Copious amounts of frass can also be produced by wood-lice and by beetle larvae. However the presence of silk suggests lepidopterous larvae are present and that further investigation is warranted.

As there are similar, rarer Oecophoridae larvae with similar feeding habits (such as *Oecophora bractella*), it is worth being cautious about identification, and trying to rear the adults. This is reasonably easy as the larvae will be quite happy dining on a piece of dry, rotten wood.

The resultant adults are unmistakable with a marked sexual dimorphism. The female moth (below) has a longitudinal yellow stripe from the base of the forewing almost reaching the yellow triangle at the tornus of the wing. In the male, the stripe extends only a short distance from the base.

# Depressaria radiella

| | |
|---|---|
| Depressariidae | 32.036 Parsnip Moth *Depressaria radiella* (Goeze, 1783) |
| Foodplant | Hogweed (*Heracleum sphondylium*), wild parsnip (*Pastinaca sativa*). |
| Life cycle | Larva: June to July. Adult: August to May. |
| Distribution | Common throughout British Isles. |
| | Common in VC58, 59, 60. |
| Photo details | Pupal signs from Chorlton, Manchester VC59; 11.01.15 (BS). |

The adult of this species may be found by beating gorse and other vegetation during the winter months. It is also be attracted to light on mild evenings. An easier way to look for the presence of the species is by looking for the larval and pupal signs on its main foodplant, hogweed.

Pupal signs can be looked for at any time during the winter, even though the adult moth will already have emerged. The dried stems of the foodplant will bear the tell-tale signs of a 2-4mm hole in the stem. Opening up the stem should reveal a vacated pupal exuvia not too far away from the hole. Other larvae may also be found overwintering in hogweed stems. For instance, I found a Small Magpie (*Anania hortulata*) larva in such a stem in January 2015.

The larva of *radiella* can be found in June and July in a dense and discoloured spinning within the heads of hogweed as it feeds on the flowers and seeds of the plant. When fully-fed the larva descends, makes a hole in the side of the stem, and enters the stem through this. Once inside the stem the larva pupates over summer. The adult moth emerges through the previously created hole in late summer prior to hibernation.

More than one larva may enter a single stem; hence there may be more than one hole in the stem, as in the photograph below.

# Metzneria lappella

Gelechiidae    35.056 *Metzneria lappella* (Linnaeus, 1758)
Foodplant      Greater burdock (*Arctium lappa*).
Life cycle     Larva: August to April. Adult: June to July.
Distribution   Common in England; local in Scotland and Wales. Absent from Ireland.
               Local in VC58, 59, 60; likely to be found wherever the foodplant occurs.
Photo details  Larva in burdock cocoon from Chorlton, Manchester VC59; 25.01.15 (BS).

Collecting old burdock seed-heads during the winter months will often produce a good number of *Metzneria lappella* adults in early summer. Ideally, keep the seed-heads outside, bringing them indoors in April-May. Adult emergence should follow shortly after. Alternatively, if wishing to record the presence of the moth prior to this time, one can break open the seed-heads and look for the larva. The species seems to be common wherever the foodplant is found.

The larva of *lappella* feeds on a number of seeds, spinning a few together. The hibernaculum (the overwintering habitation) is a tube of white silk within spun seeds. On breaking open a seed-head, look for groups of seeds that are spun together. Gently opening these up may reveal a *lappella* larva protruding from one of the seeds. Pupation occurs within this hibernaculum.

Burdock seed-heads are often also tenanted by the fruit-fly *Tephritis bardanae*, so one may find small white bardanae larvae in late summer. These can be differentiated from *lappella* by the lack of a clear head. The *bardanae* larva then forms a black pupa with adults emerging in autumn.

The photos of the *lappella* larva below (bottom left), show an individual located in late August at Carrington Moss, VC58. At such an early date, this may not be the final instar. The prothoracic plate seems more distinctive than in larvae collected in winter.

# Apodia bifractella

| | |
|---|---|
| Gelechiidae | 35.060 *Apodia bifractella* (Duponchel, [1843]) |
| Foodplant | Common fleabane (*Pulicaria dysenterica*), |
| | Ploughman's spikenard (*Inula conyza*), or sea aster (*Aster tripolium*). |
| Life cycle | Larva: October to April. Adult: July to August. |
| Distribution | Widespread in Wales, NW & S England. Absent from Scotland and Ireland. |
| | Local in VC58, 59, 60. |
| Photo details | Larva in cocoon from Rixton, Warrington VC59; 20.01.15 (BS). |
| | Bottom left: larval hibernaculum on fleabane (Jenny Seawright). |

The larvae of this species leave little external visual sign of their habitation. When looking for the species around January, there may be dried remnants of the flower attached to the portion of the flower-head where the cocoon has been spun, as these can be attached to the silk. Gently compressing the dried flower-head may reveal a hard case within, containing the maggot-like larva of *bifractella*. The species is found in a variety of habitats as long as foodplants are present.

Earlier, in the autumn, the larva feeds on the seeds from within the head. When feeding is complete, a cocoon is spun within the receptacle of the flower, comprised of silk, frass, seeds and fragments of seeds. The larva spends the winter within, pupating in April or May.

One may find the adult moth on the flower heads of the foodplants in the late afternoon. A simpler way to detect the species is to collect some of the flower-heads during the winter. Give these chance to dry out (to avoid mould formation), then pop them in a jar and you are likely to be rewarded with some newly emerged adults in early summer. Check the container carefully. The adults may rest on the side of the container, but equally may be motionless on the debris within.

# Coleophora alticolella

| | |
|---|---|
| Coleophoridae | 37.073 *Coleophora alticolella* Zeller, 1849 |
| Foodplant | On the seeds of rushes (*Juncus* spp.). |
| Life cycle | Larva: July to May. Adult: Late May to mid-July. |
| Distribution | Widespread and common throughout British Isles, wherever rushes occur. Common in VC58, 59, 60. |
| Photo details | Larval case from Chorlton, Manchester VC59; 14.01.15 (BS). Larva (Ian Smith). |

The whitish cases of this species can be found throughout the year, throughout the country, wherever rushes are present. Their feeding leaves holes in the seeds. Larvae feed from July but only create a case from the end of the third instar. This is initially small and flimsy but is enlarged by the addition of more silken material as the larva continues to feed. By October the case will be fully-formed. Cases overwinter on the head of the plant, or in leaf litter.

Unfortunately unless the adults are reared and dissected it is almost impossible to separate this species from *C. glaucicolella* as the cases and adults are indistinguishable according to external characteristics. There are some minor differences in the larval appearances of the two species. However to see these requires removal of the larva from its case. The larva of *Coleophora alticolella* usually has a black spot on the dorsal side of the 9th abdominal segment (which is absent in *glaucicolella*), and lacks dorsal sclerites on the third thoracic segment. These features are well illustrated on Ian Smith's larval photo below. More of his larval photos can be seen on the relevant species' web pages at ukmoths.org.uk. If the larva is not examined in this way (or the adult not dissected) then the findings will need to be recorded as *C. alticolella/glaucicolella* agg.

A9 spot

# Adaina microdactyla

| | |
|---|---|
| Pterophoridae | 45.043 *Adaina microdactyla* (Hübner, [1813]) |
| Foodplant | Hemp-agrimony (*Eupatorium cannabinum*). |
| Life cycle | Larva: July to April. Adult: May to June and July to August. |
| Distribution | Common in southern England. Local elsewhere in British Isles. Common in VC58, 59, 60. |
| Photo details | Feeding signs from Rixton, Warrington VC59; 20.01.15 (BS). |

*Adaina microdactyla* is Britain's smallest plume moth. The larva, following an initial mining phase, feeds within the stem of hemp-agrimony, a plant often found in damp habitats. It is a creamy-yellow colour, with a pale brown head, and a dark brown band along the length of the dorsal surface. The species can be recorded by looking at tall stems of the foodplant and checking for a hole in the upper section of the stem created by the larva of this moth. This hole is approximately 1.5mm wide and close to a leaf-node. In narrower stems, a gall may be present in the form of a swelling, further giving a clue as to the larval presence. Frass may also be noted around the hole when the larva is actively feeding. The hole permits the adult to leave on emergence. Whereas some larvae feed up rapidly with adults emerging in July and August, the majority of larvae are fully fed by late summer and overwinter within the stem of the foodplant. They may leave the feeding site for a hibernation chamber higher up the stem.

If collecting stems over the winter to rear the adults, then cut the stems 10cm above and below the hole and, in the spring, place them in damp sand to await emergence of the moths (Hart, 2011). The adults themselves are very variable in size. They may range from 12-20mm wingspan. Hart suggests that the smaller adults may result from eggs that were laid on very thin stems.

# Epinotia immundana

| | |
|---|---|
| Tortricidae | 49.240 *Epinotia immundana* (Fischer von Röslerstamm, 1839) |
| Foodplant | Alder (*Alnus glutinosa*) and birch (*Betula* spp.). |
| Life cycle | Larva: September to March, July. Adult: April-June, August-September. |
| Distribution | Common throughout British Isles. |
| | Common in VC58, 59, 60. |
| Photo details | Feeding signs from Chorlton, Manchester VC59; 07.01.17 (BS). |

The larva of this species can be found feeding inside alder and birch catkins during winter. Its presence may be detected by looking for catkins with holes in the side, as in the photo below. Reddish frass may also be present. The catkin itself will feel softer than untenanted ones, as it is gradually being hollowed out. If you carefully open the catkin by pulling it at both ends, you will hopefully see the larva. It may move from one catkin to the next through the side of the catkin.

The moth is fairly easy to rear in a pot (eg.7x7cm) indoors. Open the pot and remove frass every other day. You will need to add fresh catkin every 4 or 5 days, and remove vacated old catkins.

Be aware that other species can also be found within alder catkins: *Argyresthia brockeella* and *A. goedartella*, *Epinotia demarniana*, and *E. tenerana*. *E. immundana* larvae are likely to be more advanced than these other species and are normally fully developed by February. The prothoracic plate of the larva is fairly distinctive, with a dark band running across the plate posteriorly.

A second generation of *immundana* larvae feed within rolled leaves of the foodplants in July. Check the appearance of the larva to confirm that larvae within rolled alder leaves are *immundana* and not *Caloptilia elongella* (p.172). The larva of the latter species is pale green with no dark markings. Larvae of this second generation of *immundana* seem highly prone to parasitisation.

# Pammene regiana

| | |
|---|---|
| Tortricidae | 49.375 *Pammene regiana* (Zeller, 1849) |
| Foodplant | Sycamore (*Acer pseudoplatanus*). |
| Life cycle | Larva: August to April. Adult: May to mid-August. |
| Distribution | Common throughout Great Britain. Scarce in Ireland. Common in VC58, 59, 60. |
| Photo details | Cocoons from Chorlton, Manchester VC59; 04.01.15 (BS). |

The early stages of this moth can be found throughout the winter by looking under the flaky bark on the lower trunk of sycamore trees. There you may commonly find silken cocoons coated in reddish-brown frass. These may be found singly, or communally (as in the photo below, left). The larva overwinters within this cocoon.

Earlier in its development, the larva feeds on the seeds in August and September. Once feeding is complete, the larva descends on a silken thread to the lower part of the trunk where it goes on to form the cocoon.

Larvae can also be found on norway maple (*Acer platanoides*), and probably field maple (*Acer campestre*).

The larvae can be reared quite easily, by keeping the infested bark in a small pot covered with netting and perhaps containing some dry vegetation, free from other potential predators. Keep the cocoons outside until late April when the larva will likely have entered the pupal stage. Bringing them inside at this period will likely be shortly followed by the emergence of this beautifully marked tortricid. The adult is very distinctive and may also be found in the wild, resting on a leaf of its foodplant following emergence.

# A selection of overwintering larvae

35.017 *Neofaculta ericetella* - heather 9-2.
41.003 *Blastobasis lacticolella* - seeds, fruit, etc. 6-4.
49.029 *Lozotaenia forsterana* - ivy, privet, etc. 9-5.
49.188 *Endothenia marginana* - betony, teasel, 9-6.
49.341 *Cydia splendana* - acorns, etc. 8-5.

49.351 *Grapholita lunulana* - vetch pods 6-4.
62.001 Bee Moth *Aphomia sociella* - bee nests 8-4.
62.059 *Phycitodes saxicola* - ragwort, etc. 7, 9-4.
63.025 Small Magpie *Anania hortulata* - nettles 8-5.
63.080 *Chrysoteuchia culmella* - grasses 9-4.

 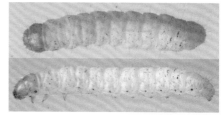

 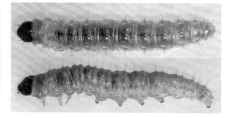

# FEBRUARY FIELD TIPS

February can be a bleak month with snow, frost or persistent rain. Whilst there may be the odd mild day in February, and sheltered locations may see the first butterflies and bees on the wing, one has to look hard for the first signs of new growth and the lepidopterous larvae that may be feeding upon it. Whilst fresh leaves are absent, sallows, willows, alders, hazels and birches will be bearing fresh catkins. Many will contain larvae. Pine trees are worth searching for some of the first miners of the year. Success can also be had in searching the trunks of trees for Psychid larvae, and other species which will have formed cocoons on the trunks or under flakes of bark. Dried stems from last year's plants are a good hiding place for many larvae.

26. *Narycia duplicella*
27. *Triaxomera parasitella*
28. *Psychoides filicivora*
29. *Phyllonorycter leucographella*
30. *Cedestis subfasciella*
31. *Ocnerostoma piniariella*
32. *Glyphipterix simpliciella*
33. *Limnaecia phragmitella*
34. *Metzneria metzneriella*
35. *Spuleria flavicaput*
36. *Blastobasis adustella*
37. *Myelois circumvoluta*

*Freshfield, Merseyside, 15 February 2016*

# *Narycia duplicella*

| | |
|---|---|
| Psychidae | 11.002 *Narycia duplicella* (Goeze, 1783) |
| Foodplant | Algae and lichens on tree trunks and other surfaces. |
| Life cycle | Larva: August to May. Adult: June to July. |
| Distribution | Widespread in England, Wales and S Scotland. Unrecorded in Ireland. Local in VC58. Common in VC59, 60. |
| Photo details | Cases from Chorlton, Manchester VC59; 22.03.15 (BS). |

This species is most reliably recorded by looking for the larval cases on algae and lichen encrusted tree trunks. Those bearing a good coating of the blue-grey to green lichen *Lepraria incana* can be particularly productive for finding the cases of this psychid. Actively feeding larvae may be found from the first mild days of February onwards. Vacated cases may also be found attached to the trunks at any time of year.

As can be seen from the photos below, the larva is a pale grey colour, sometimes with a yellowish or greenish tinge. The head and prothoracic plates are blackish. There is also a large dark sclerotic plate on the second dorsal segment, as well as lateral dark sclerotic segments on the first three dorsal segments. The thoracic legs are also dark; in some cases black.

The case itself is roughly triangular in cross-section, and tapered towards the ends. It usually reaches 5-6mm in length. It is formed with silk and coated with sand and fragments of the algae and the lichen found on its host plant, presumably to help it evade detection. Careful examination of the tree trunk is therefore required! The case may occasionally contain unusual material. The example photographed below bore what appeared to be a spider's leg on the dorsal aspect, perhaps from a spider web on the surface of the trunk.

# Triaxomera parasitella

| | |
|---|---|
| Tineidae | 12.012 *Triaxomera parasitella* (Hübner, 1796) |
| Foodplant | Bracket fungi and dead wood. |
| Life cycle | Larva: September to April. Adult: May to July. |
| Distribution | Widely distributed in S England. Absent from Ireland. Local elsewhere. Local in VC58, 59, 60. |
| Photo details | Larva on unidentified fungus, Dunham Massey VC58; 07.01.07 (BS). |

The larva of this moth can be found during winter feeding on a variety of bracket fungi, often related to dead tree stumps, and sometimes on the dead wood itself. *Coriolus versicolor* has been cited as one of the fungi favoured by this species (Emmet, 1988). Evidence of larval presence is sometimes hard to identify, but look for frass and silk on the underside of the fungus.

The larva below was found in early January as an early instar feeding within a fungus attached to a fallen section of rotten oak. There was little change in the larval appearance as it changed instar and grew in size, with the dark pinaculae and black prothoracic plate being present throughout its development.

Pupation takes place within the feeding place, with moths emerging in late spring.

The adult moth itself is well-marked with a distinctive orange head. Fresh individuals are unlikely to be mistaken for any other species.

There are only a few recent records for this species within Cheshire and in VC60, and the moth was not recorded in VC59 until 2015.

Moths may be found flying at dusk in habitats containing suitable food materials.

# Psychoides filicivora

| | |
|---|---|
| Tineidae | 12.048 *Psychoides filicivora* (Meyrick, 1937) |
| Foodplant | Various ferns. |
| Life cycle | Larvae found in all months of the year; Adult: April to December. |
| Distribution | Local in British Isles, with a western and coastal bias. |
| | Local in VC58, 59, 60. |
| Photo details | Leaf-mine on Polypodium from Formby, Lancs. VC59; 01.02.15 (BS). |

This species was first recorded in Ireland in 1909 and in England in 1940 (Bournemouth). Initially regarded as a coastal species of the south-west, *Psychoides filicivora* has made inroads north and inland in the last twenty years, and is now found frequently throughout Lancashire and Cheshire.

Larval presence can be noted on a variety of ferns at all times of year. Species utilised include male-fern (*Dryopteris filix-mas*), hart's-tongue fern (*Asplenium scolopendrium*) and common polypody (*Polypodium vulgare*). The larva feeds from within an untidy mass of sporangia, feeding on the sporangia, and will also mine leaves. The larva shown mining *Polypodium* has created a frass-coated spinning to retreat into.

The larva can be differentiated from the similar *Psychoides verhuella* (p.43) by virtue of its pale brown head, prothoracic and anal plates. In the latter species, these are black. *P. verhuella* larvae also feed under a somewhat neater mass of sporangia than *filicivora*.

The adult moths can be differentiated as *filicivora* has a violet sheen and a white tornal spot.

One should also beware of mistaking the larval workings of polyphagous species such as *Blastobasis adustella* (p.36) for the *Psychoides* species, so it is always important to check the larval appearance.

# *Phyllonorycter leucographella*

Gracillariidae     15.053 *Phyllonorycter leucographella* (Zeller, 1850)
Foodplant     Firethorn (*Pyracantha*), beech (*Fagus sylvatica*), rosaceous trees.
Life cycle     Larva: October to April, July. Adult: May to June, August to September.
Distribution     Common in England, Wales and S Scotland. Local in Ireland.
    Common in VC58, 59, 60.
Photo details     Leaf-mine from St Helens, Lancs. VC59; 14.01.17 (BS).

Another relatively recent arrival to these shores, *Phyllonorycter leucographella*, was first noted in Essex 1989 and has quickly spread north. The first Cheshire record was in 1998, with the first Lancashire record in VC59 the following year (and 2001 in VC60). The moth is now common throughout north-west England, and indeed most of the country.

The larvae form whitish papery mines on the upperside of the leaves of many trees and shrubs with hawthorn, pear, apple and whitebeam being common hosts in summer and autumn. However as *Pyracantha* keeps its leaves all year, mines can still be found in winter, usually tenanted by early instar larvae with black heads and dark abdominal markings. As they feed, the oval-shaped mine extends across much of the upper side of the leaf. If the leaf is held up to the light it should be possible to make out the larva. The dark abdominal markings are largely faded on the later instar larva, as it moves from the sap-feeding to the tissue-feeding phase (see comparison larval photos below). There is more information on these two phases on p.194.

The adult can be differentiated from most of the genus by virtue of the fine white striae and the bar of dark scales close to the apex of the wing. *P. corylifoliella* is similar but with fewer white markings and more black scales. The mines are also similar (see p.120 to compare the two).

# Cedestis subfasciella

| | |
|---|---|
| Yponomeutidae | 16.022 *Cedestis subfasciella* (Stephens, 1834) |
| Foodplant | Pine (*Pinus* spp.). |
| Life cycle | Larva: December to April. Adult: March to July (occasionally to October). |
| Distribution | Common throughout Great Britain. Local in southern Ireland. Local in VC58, 59, 60. |
| Photo details | Leaf-mine from Formby, Lancs. VC59; 01.02.15 (BS). |

The green larva of *subfasciella* can be found mining pine needles through the winter months. If collecting to rear, the needles can be kept viable for a few weeks in an air tight container. This will probably be enough if the mines collected are reasonably advanced. The larva will then go on to pupate within a white, silken cocoon, with emergence following a few weeks later.

An oval-shaped egg with a longitudinal ridge is laid at the tip of a pine needle. On emergence, the larva bores into the tip of the needle and mines down towards the base of the needle, leaving its frass packing the needle behind it. The area directly behind and in front of the larva can be clear, meaning white margins can be seen. This can be very conspicuous and very helpful in locating the larva. The mine will usually travel the whole length of the needle before the larva is full-fed. On exiting the needle to pupate elsewhere, an exit hole is created at the base of the needle.

This is not the only species to mine pine needles. The *Ocnerostoma* species feed in the same way as *subfasciella*, but their larva is brownish. *Cedestis gysseleniella* has a green larva, but this species mines the needle from base to tip in April and May. There are also a gelechiid (see *Exoteleia dodecella*) and a few tortricid moths, for example *Clavigesta purdeyi*, that mine pine needles, at least for part of their development.

# Ocnerostoma piniariella

| | |
|---|---|
| Yponomeutidae | 16.023 *Ocnerostoma piniariella* Zeller, 1847 |
| Foodplant | Scots pine (*Pinus sylvestris*). |
| Life cycle | Larva: April to May. Adult: June to July. |
| Distribution | Widespread in England and Scotland. Few records in Wales and Ireland. Local in VC58, 59, 60. |
| Photo details | Cocoon from Formby, Lancs. VC59; 01.02.15 (BS). Larva (Willem Ellis). |

The two *Ocnerostoma* species mine pine needles. The similarities of adults, larvae and feeding signs, mean the phenology and distribution of *piniariella* and *O. friesei* is imperfectly understood.

The oval-shaped egg is laid at the tip of a needle in summer. The egg overwinters with feeding not commencing until the following spring. The yellowish brown larva mines a pine needle from the tip, consuming three-quarters of the needle and filling the mine with reddish-brown frass.

Pupation occurs in May to June in a silken spinning between two pairs of needles. The exuvia remains and can be examined at any time of year to help differentiate between piniariella and *friesei,* although it would be wise to seek confirmation if this method of separating the species is new to you and if it would be a notable record locally. The pupa of *piniariella* has distinctive and isolated bumps at the anal end, whereas the corresponding bumps on friesei are smaller and are joined. The ventral and lateral surfaces of the pupae show the differences well. More information can be found in Patocka and Turcani (2005) and at www.leafmines.co.uk (Edmunds et al).

The adult *piniariella* has whitish grey forewings, with the female slightly paler (photographed below). The male *friesei* is pale grey with the female white. The antennae of *friesei* are grey. They are whitish in female *piniariella* and ringed white and grey in male *piniariella*.

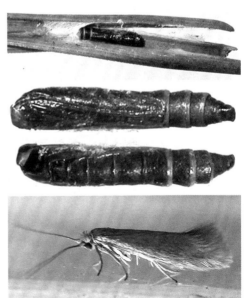

# Glyphipterix simpliciella

| | |
|---|---|
| Glyphipterigidae | 19.007 Cocksfoot Moth *Glyphipterix simpliciella* (Stephens, 1834) |
| Foodplant | Cock's-foot (*Dactylis glomerata*), tall fescue (*Festuca arundinacea*). |
| Life cycle | Larva: July to April. Adult: May to early July. |
| Distribution | Common and widespread throughout British Isles. Common in VC58, 59, 60. |
| Photo details | Feeding signs from Chorlton, Manchester VC59; 02.01.16 (BS). |

This common moth can be recorded throughout winter by looking for the feeding signs on dried stems of cock's-foot grass. The presence of one or more small holes in the stem shows that a stem is tenanted by *G. simpliciella* larvae.

The larva enters the stem of cock's-foot in late summer once full-fed on the flowers of the plant. It makes a hole to enter the stem and then overwinters within a white, papery cocoon inside the stem (see photo: top, right). The larva itself is greenish-white with a dark brown-black head. I think this species can be recorded from the presence of the hole alone but I always have a look inside the stem too, just to be absolutely certain. The holes are usually around one metre or so off the ground and the larvae may be 10-15cm away from the hole. There are often 3-4 larvae in a single stem.

There can be a number of entrance holes in these stems.

Pupation occurs within the cocoon. Collection of the tenanted stems will usually result in successful emergence of a number of adult moths, particularly if the stems are kept outside until closer to the emergence time.

The adult moths emerge in late spring and can be found in large numbers on the heads of flowers such as buttercup (*Ranunculus* spp.).

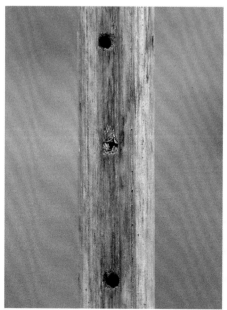

# Limnaecia phragmitella

Cosmopterigidae  34.004 *Limnaecia phragmitella* Stainton, 1851
Foodplant          Bulrush (*Typha* spp.).
Life cycle         Larva: September to May. Adult: late June to August.
Distribution       Locally common throughout British Isles.
                   Common in VC58, 59, 60.
Photo details      Feeding signs from Stretford, Manchester VC59; 24.01.15 (BS).

Signs of tenancy by this small larva can be noted from a good distance away. The larvae live communally in the seed-heads of bulrush plants and produce large amounts of silk within the larval habitation. This means that instead of blowing away, the white downy seeds are held in place by the silken webs, thus remaining attached to the seed-head. Damage to *Typha* seed-heads may also be caused by birds. Therefore to confirm this species it is best to check the larvae, which overwinter inside the seed-head in very large numbers.

To rear, put the whole of the infested seed-head or two in a stocking and tie up outside. Make sure it is tied securely and that there are no holes in the material as these larvae do like to wander once they are disturbed. Alternatively, put a few larvae in an 7cm x 7cm plastic pot with a handful of seeds. Keep the pot in the shed. You should only need to change the seeds every few weeks. Take care, as this larva has amazing powers of escapology. Even in a pot with a very tight fitting lid, one or two managed to squeeze themselves out to freedom!

The larva pupates in an elongated white cocoon amongst the seed-heads in June. Adults emerge in summer and fly around the foodplants at dusk in the usual habitat of fens and marshes. An occasional adult may wander and be trapped at light away from its favoured habitat.

# Metzneria metzneriella

Gelechiidae    35.058 *Metzneria metzneriella* (Stainton, 1851)
Foodplant    Common knapweed (*Centaurea nigra*), saw-wort (*Serratula tinctoria*).
Life cycle    Larva: August to April. Adult: June to early August.
Distribution    Common throughout Great Britain. Local in Ireland.
     Common in VC58, 59, 60.
Photo details    Larval cocoon from St Helens, Lancs. VC59; 25.02.16 (BS).

The species can be recorded by looking for the larva overwintering at the base of the knapweed seed-head in a silken cocoon, or by collecting seed-heads and waiting for the adult to emerge.

The larvae hatch from August onwards from ova laid on knapweed flower-heads. The larva enters and feeds on the seeds within and reaches full growth before overwintering in its feeding place. The top photo on the right shows a larva in its chamber at the base of the seed-head, found on 10.09.16. As with *Metzneria lappella* (p.18), the larva is somewhat slug-like, with vestigial thoracic legs and obsolete prolegs. Occupancy rates vary and may be high as 50% or more on some sites, or as low as 1 in 50, as at the St Helens site where the flower-head, below left, was found.

If opening seed-heads to look for this species do be aware there are a number of dipteran larvae that may also be found within knapweed heads. There is a tephritid fly that overwinters in a hard woody cocoon within the seed-head. If the tephritid cocoon is opened (with great difficulty) it reveals a white larva of similar size to *metzneriella*, but with a dark flat disc at the posterior end, and the absence of a typical lepidopteran head capsule.

The adult moths emerge from late spring onwards. The forewings are yellowish ochreous with darker markings, and a noticeably more contrasting appearance than *Metzneria lappella*.

# Spuleria flavicaput

| | |
|---|---|
| Parametriotidae | 39.003 *Spuleria flavicaput* (Haworth, 1828) |
| Foodplant | Hawthorn (*Crataegus* spp.). |
| Life cycle | Larva: August to October. Adult: May to June. |
| Distribution | Fairly common throughout British Isles except northern Scotland. Local in VC58, 59, 60. |
| Photo details | Larval / pupal signs from Chorlton, Manchester VC59; 07.02.15 (BS). |

The larval stages of this moth are virtually impossible to find as no sign is given of its presence until just before the larva is ready to commence pupation in late autumn.

The adult lays its eggs on a small twig of hawthorn at the base of a small side-shoot. On hatching, the larva enters the twig and feeds inside the side-shoot twig away from the bifurcation. As it feeds, the larva forms a tunnel in the centre of the hawthorn twig which is blackened in colour.

Prior to pupating overwinter, the larva creates an elongate exit-hole on the underside of the twig, about 3cm from the fork. The larva then returns towards the fork and pupates, with the adult moth leaving through the exit-hole on emergence in late spring. Typically, the larvae utilise small twigs, although the twig in the photos (below, left) is an unusually slender one, at only 3mm wide. To find the pupa look at such twigs emanating from a fork. Look underneath for an elongate hole approximately 3mm x 0.5mm. The hole may be partially covered by a thin layer of bark, making its detection even more difficult! Search in small hawthorn trees at the edge of woodland.

The adult moth is rarely seen at light. It will be more likely to be encountered flying around hawthorn in the morning. It is a distinctive moth, with a bright yellow head and dark grey forewings, each bearing a pair of raised scale-tufts.

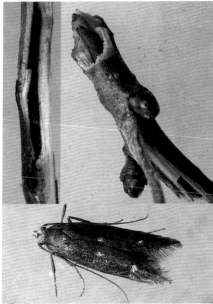

# Blastobasis adustella

| | |
|---|---|
| Blastobasidae | 41.002 *Blastobasis adustella* Walsingham, 1894 |
| Foodplant | A wide variety of vegetable matter (see text below). |
| Life cycle | Larva: September to June. Adult: late June to mid-September. |
| Distribution | Widespread and common throughout British Isles. Common in VC58, 59, 60. |
| Photo details | Spinning on pine from Dunham Massey, Altrincham VC58; 17.02.17 (BS). |

Moths of the *Blastobasis* genus in the UK are adventive species, meaning that they are non-native and have arrived on these shores in recent times, largely or wholly with the assistance of man and our importation of plants and foodstuffs. The larvae of the genus are polyphagous so it is essential to consider the possibility that this species may be present in almost any spinning found in late winter and early spring. I have found spun pine needles and looked for an *Ocnerostoma* pupa within, opened an untidy mass of sporangia on the underside of hart's-tongue expecting to see *Psychoides filicivora*, searched through hogweed seeds for the larva of *Pammene aurana* and opened teasel heads looking for *Endothenia* larvae. In each case the larva of *Blastobasis adustella* has been present instead. It also seems to have a taste for yew, being the only larva I have found feeding on the needles (see photo - bottom, left).

The larva is similar to its close relative *B. lacticolella*; the main difference being that in adustella the prothoracic plate is much darker than the head. In *lacticolella* the colour is the same as the head, or occasionally slightly lighter (p.24). *B. lacticolella* is also polyphagous and I have found it inside dried gorse seedpods, feeding on rosehips and amongst bird-seed in the garden.

The adult *adustella* varies from cream to dark brown. The closed forewings display the letter X.

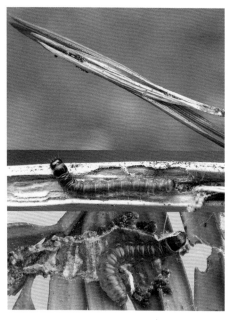

# Myelois circumvoluta

Pyralidae        62.042 Thistle Ermine *Myelois circumvoluta* (Fourcroy, 1785)
Foodplant        Thistles (*Cirsium, Carduus, Onopordum*), greater burdock (*Arctium lappa*).
Life cycle       Larva: August to April. Adult: May to September.
Distribution     Common in England and Wales. Local in Scotland and Ireland.
                 Common in VC58, 59, 60.
Photo details    Feeding signs from Chorlton, Manchester VC59; 11.02.08 (BS).

Larvae feed in late summer in thistle and burdock heads. In autumn they enter the stem of the host plant and create extensive tunnels in the pith of the stem. The larvae overwinter in this environment. There are often several larvae in a single stem. The greyish larva has a number of longitudinal pale brown stripes, tiny black pinaculae, a dark brown head and a blackish brown prothoracic plate. There is sometimes a slightly pink tinge to the larva.

In February or March an exit-hole is cut into the stem. Pupation occurs shortly afterwards close to the hole and within the stem.

The dried stems of the foodplants can be collected throughout the winter. I have found spear thistle (*Cirsium vulgare*) to be frequently used by the larvae. Keep the stems outside, bringing them inside in April. Alternatively, the stems can be opened and examined in early May, by which time the pupa should be present in a net-like cocoon of white threads.

The adult emerges in late spring and is really quite unmistakeable in appearance, due to its size at approximately 15mm in length. The various small ermine moths (*Yponomeuta* spp.) have similar markings but are considerably smaller at approximately 10mm in length.

The moth is common in southern England and Wales, although less so as one moves further north.

# A selection of spring larval cases

11.001 *Diplodoma laichartingella* - lichens, etc. 9-5.
37.005 *Coleophora lutipennella* - oak 10-5.
37.007 *Coleophora flavipennella* - oak 10-5.
37.015 *Coleophora serratella* - birch, alder, etc. 9-5.
37.022 *Coleophora lusciniaepennella* - willows 9-5.

37.032 *Coleophora albitarsella* - marjoram, etc. 9-5.
37.044 *Coleophora discordella* - bird's-foot trefoil 9-5.
37.050 *Coleophora albidella* - sallows 9-5.
37.053 *Coleophora betulella* - birch 9-5.
37.066 *Coleophora laricella* - larch 7-5.

 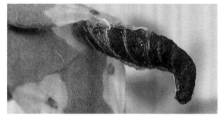

# MARCH FIELD TIPS

As daylight hours lengthen, and conditions start to warm up, March can be an exciting month for the field microlepidopterist.

The winter species are still around and collecting these at this time of year will probably give you a better chance in terms of successful rearing than earlier in winter.

There is also the gradual appearance of a number of early spring species using buds and the first leaves and flowers for their feeding. A few leaf-miners start to appear, such as *Bucculatrix nigricomella* on the tiny, early leaf growth of ox-eye daisies.

Psychids, such as *Narycia duplicella, Luffia ferchaultella,* and with luck some of the rarer species too, will start to appear in greater numbers, climbing walls and tree-trunks.

40. *Trifurcula immundella*
41. *Lampronia fuscatella*
42. *Luffia ferchaultella*
43. *Psychoides verhuella*
44. *Bucculatrix nigricomella*
45. *Phyllonorycter harrisella*
46. *Phyllonorycter trifasciella*
47. *Argyresthia goedartella*
48. *Glyphipterix fuscoviridella*
49. *Agonopterix assimilella*
50. *Scrobipalpa instabilella*
51. *Caryocolum tricolorella*
52. *Cochylis roseana*
53. *Endothenia gentianaeana*
54. *Epinotia ramella*
55. *Cataclysta lemnata*

*Rixton Claypits, Warrington, 18th March 2016*

# Trifurcula immundella

| | |
|---|---|
| Nepticulidae | 4.068 *Trifurcula immundella* (Zeller, 1839) |
| Foodplant | Broom (*Cytisus scoparius*). |
| Life cycle | Larva: October to May. Adult: mid-June to August. |
| Distribution | Widespread and locally abundant throughout Great Britain. Local in VC58, 59, 60. |
| Photo details | Mines from Burton Mere, Cheshire VC58; 17.2.15. Adult (Tymo Muus). |

Although local within Lancashire and Cheshire, the feeding signs of this species are worth looking for wherever the foodplant occurs. The blackened linear discolouration of fresh broom growth represents feeding by one of two broom miners: this species or *Leucoptera spartifoliella*. The mines themselves are very difficult to differentiate. However if you can spot a shiny circular black disc at the start of the mine, then this is the egg of *T. immundella*. The egg can be seen on the top left photo towards the right-hand aspect of the mine. In the middle photo, the egg is central. The egg obviously marks the start of the mine. The larva will usually mine downwards initially, later changing direction a number of times. In mines tenanted by *L. spartifoliella*, the egg falls off shortly after larval hatching.

In both species, the larvae leave their mines to pupate. The larva of *immundella* is yellow with a pale, brown head. This can be contrasted with the *spartifoliella* larva (p.103).

The *immundella* larva forms a brown, oval cocoon (see below), whereas the larva of *spartifoliella* forms a white, silken cocoon attached to a stem of the foodplant.

There is a third broom miner, *Phyllonorycter scopariella*, which creates short grey mines.

Another way to record *immundella* is to beat broom over a collecting tray during its flight period.

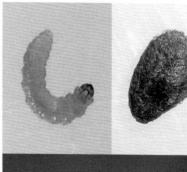

# Lampronia fuscatella

| | |
|---|---|
| Prodoxidae | 9.006 *Lampronia fuscatella* (Tengström, 1848) |
| Foodplant | Birch (*Betula* spp.). |
| Life cycle | Larva: October to April. Adult: May to June. |
| Distribution | Scattered locally throughout Great Britain. |
| | Few records in VC 58, 59, 60. |
| Photo details | Feeding signs from Astley Moss, Wigan VC59; 31.03.07 (BS). |

The feeding signs of this species become apparent from autumn onwards, when a gall forms as a spherical swelling on a birch twig. The gall is usually formed at a node. The twigs used are generally about 1cm in diameter and may be found 1 to 1.5 metres from the ground. The larva feeds within the gall and should be fully developed by the end of the year. It is white with a black head and a small brown prothoracic plate. In early spring the larva creates an exit hole in the gall capped off with red frass, allowing the moth to escape following emergence in late spring. Those larvae that are parasitized do not produce this exit-hole, as in the example below. The presence of the gall however still reveals the location of this species. Pupation occurs inside a thick, white cocoon within the gall. One can find the pupal exuvia protruding from the exit-hole after emergence of the adult.

The moth should be looked for in areas where young birches are common. The adult may be seen flying in afternoon sunshine in late spring. Eggs are then laid on the twigs, usually at a node.

The adult can be separated from most of the *Lampronia* genus by virtue of its plain forewings and orange or yellow head. The exception is *L. pubicornis*, a smaller, paler moth, with a pale yellow head that is probably absent from this region. Its larvae feed on Burnet Rose.

# Luffia ferchaultella

| | |
|---|---|
| Psychidae | 11.009 Luffia ferchaultella (Stephens, 1850) |
| Foodplant | Lichens. |
| Life cycle | Larva: August to May. Adult: June to July. |
| Distribution | Locally common in S Eng, Wales, eastern Ireland. Unrecorded in Scotland. Local in VC58, 59. Unrecorded in VC60. |
| Photo details | Larval case from Chorlton, Manchester VC59; 5.03.16 (BS). |

This Psychid can only be found by looking for its larval case as the whole of its unusual life cycle takes place within the case. The species is parthenogenetic, meaning viable eggs are laid without the need for fertilisation, and only the (wingless) female exists. Certainly in this region this is the case. However there is another species, *Luffia lapidella*, found in Cornwall and on the continent, which does have a winged male as well as the apterous female. DNA tests however have shown no difference between the two species, suggesting *ferchaultella* may be a form of *lapidella*.

On emergence, the *ferchaultella* female lays its eggs within the old case. The small larvae start feeding in late summer. They create their own case, coating it with sand and fragments of lichen and algae. These are sometimes arranged in bands, giving the case a ringed appearance. Even when the bands are not obvious, the shape of the case is diagnostic. It is a slightly curved conical shape about 6mm long in the final instar. If tenanted one can also look at the larva to rule out any possible confusion with *Narycia duplicella* (p.26). *L. ferchaultella* larvae are darker (particularly in final instars, with a triangle-shaped gap in the centre of the prothoracic plate, as below.

Larvae lie dormant over winter, feeding again in spring. They can form large colonies, presumably because of the difficulties of dispersal associated with the lifecycle.

# Psychoides verhuella

| | |
|---|---|
| Tineidae | 12.047 *Psychoides verhuella* Bruand, 1853 |
| Foodplant | Hart's-tongue fern (*Asplenium scolopendrium*), spleenwort (*Asplenium* spp.) and rustyback (*Asplenium ceterach*). |
| Life cycle | Larva: August to April. Adult: May to September. |
| Distribution | Local in Great Britain. Most numerous in western counties. Local in VC58, 59, 60. |
| Photo details | Feeding signs from Martin Mere, Lancashire VC59; 13.03.16 (BS). |

Like its close relative *Psychoides filicivora* (p.28), this tineid is a fern-feeder. It has a particular liking for hart's-tongue fern, and may be looked for in the larval stage in early spring.

Initial feeding takes place in whitish blotch mines, with the dark-headed larva usually visible. It then goes on to feed on the spores below from within a sorus. The sori are the brown collections of spores arranged in transverse stripes on the underside of hart's-tongue fern.

The larva later creates a portable case from empty sporangia. This is a lot neater than the case created by *filicivora*, and resembles a misplaced sorus. The larval identity was confirmed as *verhuella* in the cases photographed below. Pupation occurs within a cocoon also on the underside of the fern, often against a midrib. The pupal ccocoon has a distinct ridge running down its length.

The easiest way to separate the two *Psychoides* species in the early stages is by looking for the larval case and looking within at the larva. In the present species, the larva has a black head with black prothoracic and anal plates. These are all pale brown in *filicivora*.

The adult moth is dark fuscous, with a less obvious violet sheen than *filicivora*. It also lacks the white tornal spot of the latter species.

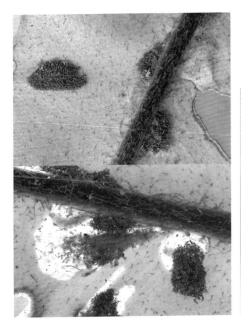

# Bucculatrix nigricomella

| | |
|---|---|
| Bucculatricidae | 14.002 *Bucculatrix nigricomella* (Zeller, 1839) |
| Foodplant | Oxeye daisy (*Leucanthemum vulgare*). |
| Life cycle | Larva: March to April, July. Adult: May to June, August. |
| Distribution | Widely distributed over British Isles. |
| | Local in VC58, 59, 60. |
| Photo details | Leaf-mine from St Helens, Lancashire VC59; 13.03.09 (BS). |

One of the first leaf-miners of the year to look for is the first generation of this species in the young leaves of oxeye daisies. As the young plant develops, there may be little more than a rosette of leaves at ground level, and it is in these that one should look for evidence of mining by the slender, yellow larva of *Bucculatrix nigricomella*. The mine looks a little like a fly mine with untidy black frass present. It spends its first few instars feeding in this mine. The mine is usually on the upper surface of the leaf, but occasionally is on the lower surface, and in some cases may switch between the two. Larvae may also switch from one leaf to another to continue mining. As the larva becomes larger, the mines become full-depth.

After the larva leaves the mine to commence external feeding, further instar changes take place within a moulting cocoonet as on the photo top right. The larva can be seen curled up beneath a white spinning on the underside of a leaf.

When feeding is complete, a long, white cocoon with longitudinal ridges is carefully spun. In captivity this is usually on the sides of the rearing container. In the wild this may occur on a stem of the foodplant, or neighbouring vegetation. Pupation occurs within this.

The species favours waste ground, embankments and grassy meadows where the foodplant occurs.

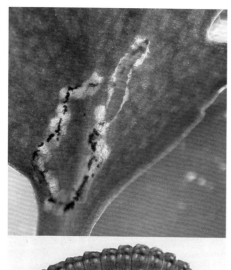

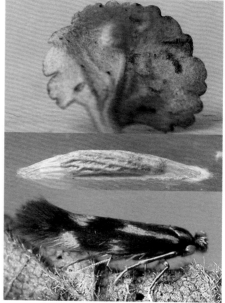

# *Phyllonorycter harrisella*

| | |
|---|---|
| Gracillariidae | 15.034 *Phyllonorycter harrisella* (Linnaeus, 1761) |
| Foodplant | Oak (*Quercus* spp.). |
| Life cycle | Larva: July, August-November. Adult: May-June, August-September. |
| Distribution | Common in Britain, less so in Ireland. |
| | Common in VC58, 59, 60. |
| Photo details | Leaf-mine from Formby, Lancashire VC59; 15.02.16 (BS). |

March is a good time to go into an oak wood and examine fallen leaves from the previous autumn. One can usually find a reasonable number of tenanted mines, and keeping these in a container should usually result in the emergence of a selection of a number of Phyllonorycter species within weeks. The oak miners are worth targeting as it is very difficult to id most of these from the mines alone. On the other hand, the adults are generally reasonably easy to differentiate. Two of the commoner species on oak are *P. harrisella* (top right), and *P. quercifoliella* (centre right).

Some of the rarer oak *Phyllonorycters* feed on leaves in the upper reaches of the trees, so collecting the fallen leaves is an appropriate method of trying to record these. One of the rarer species is *Phyllonorycter muelleriella* (bottom right). This moth has only once been recorded in Cheshire (1916) and never in Lancashire. However collecting leaves, particularly in ancient oak woodland, and awaiting emergence may, with a lot of luck, result in success. The moth photographed was reared in this way from leaves collected in March in Worcestershire.

The other *Phyllonorycter* oak species are *roboris*, *heegeriella* (p.206), *kuhlweiniella*, *messaniella*, *distentella* and *lautella* (p.212) There are no Lancashire or Cheshire records for *kuhlweiniella* or *distentella*.

# Phyllonorycter trifasciella

| | |
|---|---|
| Gracillariidae | 15.083 *Phyllonorycter trifasciella* (Haworth, 1828) |
| Foodplant | Honeysuckle (*Lonicera periclymenum*), snowberry (*Symphoricarpos* albus) and himalayan honeysuckle (*Leycesteria formosa*). |
| Life cycle | Larva: March-April, July-August, October. Adult: May, August, Nov. |
| Distribution | Common in England and Wales, less so in Scotland and Ireland. Common in VC58, 59, 60. |
| Photo details | Leaf-mine from Formby, Lancashire VC59; 31.03.15 (BS). |

This is one of the first *Phyllonorycter* mines to appear in most years. The larvae mine honeysuckle leaves, causing them to become twisted and distorted. A number of long creases can be seen on the underside of the mine. The larva is yellowish-green with pale brown mouthparts.

There is nothing else that the leaf-mine can be mistaken for at this time of year. The only other species of this genus on honeysuckle, *Phyllonorycter emberizaepenella*, does not produce its mines until July. The mines of *emberizaepenella* also differ in being much larger and in not causing such distortion of the leaf shape (p.212). Opening an *emberizaepenella* mine, following feeding, will reveal the large brown, rugby ball-shaped pupal cocoon. In contrast, the *trifasciella* pupa lies in the leaf without an obvious cocoon.

*P. trifasciella* may have at least three generations a year, the timing of which is incompletely known. It is also uncertain in what stage the species overwinters. In mild winters leaf-mines can be found on new honeysuckle growth as early as mid-February.

Well developed mines will quickly give rise to adults if kept in an air-tight container. The adult moth is very well marked and unlike other related species with orange and dark brown forewings.

# Argyresthia goedartella

| | |
|---|---|
| Argyresthiidae | 20.012 *Argyresthia goedartella* (Linnaeus, 1758) |
| Foodplant | Birch (*Betula* spp.) and alder (*Alnus glutinosa*). |
| Life cycle | Larva: November to April. Adult: mid-June to late September. |
| Distribution | Common throughout British Isles. |
| | Common in VC58, 59, 60. |
| Photo details | Feeding signs from Chorlton, Manchester VC59; 27.03.15 (BS). |

The larvae of this beautifully marked moth overwinter within the male catkins of birch and alder. Their presence can be confirmed by the detection of a hole in the side of the catkin to facilitate the expulsion of frass. One may see the yellow frass around the exit hole.

Of course larvae of other species will also utilise these catkins in a similar way. One is the close relative, *Argyresthia brockeella*. A number of tortricid moths of the *Epinotia* genus may also be found feeding in this way. However a close look at the larva should be enough to determine whether this is an Argyresthia or an *Epinotia* (see entries for *E. immundana* (p.22), and *E. ramella* (p.54)). The two *Argyresthia* larvae are approximately 1cm long when full fed. They both have a pinkish colour, often with a greenish tinge, a dark brown head and a black-edged prothoracic plate. According to Emmet (ed.) (1996), catkins tenanted by *A. brockeella* have a hole at the tip, rather than at the side, to enable frass ejection.

I have not found enough *brockeella* larvae to fully confirm this finding and so prefer to rear through to confirm identity. The quality of the fresh adult justifies doing so in any case.

The adult moth is quite variable. The typical form is white with golden markings as below, but there is a form with brassy forewings and barely discernible markings.

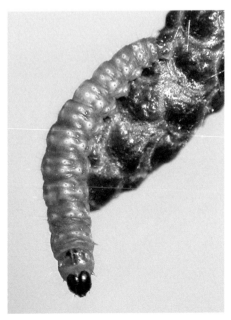 

# Glyphipterix fuscoviridella

Glyphipterigidae   19.003 *Glyphipterix fuscoviridella* (Haworth, 1828)
Foodplant          Field wood-rush (*Luzula campestris*).
Life cycle         Larva: February to April. Adult: May to June.
Distribution       Common in England, Wales and southern Scotland. Absent elsewhere.
                   Common in VC58, 59, 60.
Photo details      Feeding signs from Chorlton, Manchester VC59; 27.2.16 (BS).

*Glyphipterix fuscoviridella* is a common species of unimproved grassland. The larvae can be found in early spring feeding in the stems of field wood-rush, and mining down to the roots. Tenanted plants are difficult to identify, but may show browning of young leaves, In the plant photographed below, some of these leaves were brownish and some showed obvious external feeding damage, where the upper epidermis of the leaf had been nibbled away. Larvae are present within the stem of the foodplant until pupation in April, within a pale brown open network cocoon. This is reportedly found among the roots of the foodplant (Heath and Emmet, 1985). The cocoon photographed, below left, was found attached to the base of a neighbouring moss species.

The larva is pale ochreous with darker pinkish markings on the dorsum, a light brown head and pale brown thoracic legs.

It is really a day-flying moth, so it is unlikely to turn up in a moth trap. However the adult moth can be seen in some numbers flying in sunshine in grassland where the foodplant is prevalent.

In dull light, the forewings appear plain brown. In sunlight, they can be seen to have a brassy metallic sheen. The lack of markings distinguishes this from other *Glyphipterix* species. Markings may also be faint in *G. thrasonella*, but there is a definite indentation of the termen in *thrasonella*.

# Agonopterix assimilella

| | |
|---|---|
| Depressariidae | 32.024 *Agonopterix assimilella* (Treitschke, 1832) |
| Foodplant | Broom (*Cytisus scoparius*). |
| Life cycle | Larva: October to April. Adult: April to September. |
| Distribution | Common in England, Wales and Scotland, less so in Ireland. Local in VC58, 59, 60. |
| Photo details | Feeding signs from Burton, Cheshire VC58; 17.02.15 (BS). |

After hatching in the autumn, the larva enters a stem of the foodplant to overwinter. The hole is protected by a silken covering. From late January onwards, the larva leaves the stem to feed externally in a silken spinning between a few stems of broom. The species is most easily detected at this stage.

For purposes of identification, it is unfortunate that *Epiphyas postvittana* larvae also have a particular liking for broom stems as they also form similar spinnings. In general these tend to be larger than *assimilella* spinnings, covering a greater number of stems and containing a greater amount of silk. However to be definite about the identification, make sure you get a look at the larva. The typical *assimilella* larva is dark brown in its early stages with a black head and prothoracic plate. Later instars may vary from black, brown, grey or green, but the black-marked brown head, black prothoracic plate with brown markings anteriorly (at the end adjoining the head), and black pinaculae (spots) are all constant. These features all help to differentiate *assimilella* from the green larva of *Epiphyas postvittana* (p.211).

The moth flies at night throughout spring and summer and is attracted to light. It is widely distributed in all habitats where its foodplant occurs.

49

# Scrobipalpa instabilella

| | |
|---|---|
| Gelechiidae | 35.114 *Scrobipalpa instabilella* (Douglas, 1846) |
| Foodplant | Sea-purslane (*Atriplex portulacoides*). |
| Life cycle | Larva: March to May. Adult: June to August. |
| Distribution | Widely distributed in coastal habitats throughout the British Isles. Local in VC58, 59, 60. |
| Photo details | Larvae from Burrows Marsh VC60; 30.03.16 (BS); Adult (Chris Manley). |

This species can be locally common but is restricted to those coastal sites where its foodplant occurs. Salt-marshes, mudflats and tidal riverbanks are the usual habitats for sea-purslane growth. The larvae seem quite able to survive the intermittent submerging of the vegetation associated with such sites. *S. instabilella* larvae have also been recorded on other salt-marsh plants such as sea aster, grass-leaved orache, etc., although if correct these are probably accidental.

The grey larva has prominent pinaculae and brown dorsal and dorsolateral stripes.

In summer the adult can easily be disturbed from the foodplant. However it is very similar to other salt-marsh *Scrobipalpa* moths and dissection is required to be certain of identification unless it has been bred from the larval stage.

The larva feeds within a leaf of sea-purslane causing it to swell up slightly. A hole is made to allow expulsion of frass. The leaf below right shows the hole in the upper left, and the larva within the clean mine at the lower centre of the leaf. Other larvae feed externally in spinnings between leaves and into the shoots as in the photo below left.

The full-fed larva forms its mud-covered cocoon on the ground or in its spinnings. It remains in the larval stage for weeks before pupation.

# *Caryocolum tricolorella*

| | |
|---|---|
| Gelechiidae | 35.137 *Caryocolum tricolorella* (Haworth, 1812) |
| Foodplant | Greater stitchwort (*Stellaria holostea*). |
| Life cycle | Larva: December to April. Adult: late June to early September. |
| Distribution | Local in England, Wales and Ireland. Unrecorded in Scotland. Local in VC58, 59, 60. |
| Photo details | Feeding signs from Scorton, Lancashire VC60; 30.03.16 (BS). |

The larvae of this gelechiid moth are found at best locally within the region. The species is most readily located in early spring by looking for spun tips of the young growth of greater stitchwort. This is caused by the later instar larva which spins the upper leaves shut and feeds within. As the plant grows the upper shoots can become conspicuously distorted. Tenanted plants are most likely to be found in sheltered, shaded banks and in woodland edges. Early instars produce gallery-like mines in a leaf (Emmet and Langmaid (ed.), 2002).

The larva itself is quite distinctive with its red dorsal stripe as well as subdorsal and lateral markings. It has a black head and prothoracic plate and a pale brown anal plate.

The related species *Caryocolum blandella* and *kroesmanniella* also feed on *Stellaria holostea*, but in each case the larva lacks the pink markings of *tricolorella*. *C. blandella* larvae are yellowish green with a black head and prothoracic plate. They feed in spun shoots which become wrinkled and whitened, or in a seed capsule which turns grey. Records of *kroesmanniella* locally are unconfirmed as no specimen has been found.

The adult is one of the more colourful of the genus, and is separable with care from the other *Caryocolum* species because of the black triangle on each forewing.

51

# *Cochylis roseana*

| | |
|---|---|
| Tortricidae | 49.134 *Cochylis roseana* (Haworth, 1811) |
| Foodplant | Teasel (*Dipsacus fullonum*) |
| Life cycle | Larva: August to May. Adult: May to August |
| Distribution | Widely distributed in S England, Wales. Unrecorded in Scotland, Ireland. Scarce in VC58, 59. Unrecorded in VC60. |
| Photo details | Feeding signs from Irlam, Salford VC59; 12.03.05 (BS). |

Unlike *Endothenia marginana* and *gentianaeana*, the larva never enters the central cavity of the teasel seed-head. Instead it burrows through the seeds, forming a tough silken tunnel, and leaving tell-tale holes in many of the seeds. The larva is greenish white, with a green prothoracic plate and brown head. Other larvae found in teasel heads include the two *Endothenia* species, *Blastobasis adustella* (p.36), *B. lacticolella*, and *Epiphyas postvittana* (p.211). I have found the latter tunnelling through teasel seeds in a similar method to *roseana*, although producing more silk.

The larva of *Cochylis roseana* is best looked for in rough grassland and waysides wherever the foodplant grows plentifully. There are very few records locally. There are a couple of historical VC 58 records, and also a few from a single site in VC 59, first noted by Kevin McCabe. The likelihood is that there will be other sites where *roseana* occurs within the region, and that these are most likely to be detected by opening teasel heads and looking for the larva and feeding signs.

To rear through to the adult stage it is best to leave the teasel heads outside until nearer the time of emergence. Any that have been opened and found to contain larvae should be closed back up again, secured with cotton, and enclosing in fine netting, such as stocking material.

The adult will rest on the teasel head following emergence, but is surprisingly well camouflaged.

# Endothenia gentianaeana

| | |
|---|---|
| Tortricidae | 49.186 *Endothenia gentianaeana* (Hübner, [1799]) |
| Foodplant | Teasel (*Dipsacus fullonum*) |
| Life cycle | Larva: September to May. Adult: late May to July. |
| Distribution | Common in S Eng, Wales. Local in N England. Not in Scotland or Ireland. Local in VC58, 59. Unrecorded in VC60. |
| Photo details | Feeding signs from Chorlton, Manchester VC59; 15.02.15 (BS). |

This is one of two *Endothenia* larvae found in teasel and is generally much the more likely encountered as its larvae feed on teasel alone, whereas the second species, *Endothenia marginana* (p.24), also feed on betony, hemp-nettle, yellow rattle and lousewort.

The *Endothenia* larvae feed on the pith in the central section of the teasel seed-head. There is only ever one larva within a seed-head. The larva is fully fed by winter and its presence is obvious on opening the seed-head, due to the large quantities of frass and silk within.

Separation of the two larvae is possible although tricky. Differences between the two are as follows. *E. gentianaeana* typically has a brown head and anal plate, whereas *E. marginana* has a black head, and anal plate. The latter larva tends to have a pinkish hue and also seems more thickset in comparison to *gentianaeana*. Thoracic legs of *marginana* are also black, whereas in *gentianaeana*, these are golden brown. Not easy to see, but *marginana* also has an anal comb (two to six prongs) beneath the anal plate, best viewed from underneath with a hand-lens after placing the larva in a clear container. This structure is absent in *gentianaeana*.

Keep occupied seed-heads outside in netting, before bringing them in to emerge. Ideally identify the larva first, as the adults are harder to identify, and would usually require dissection for id.

# Epinotia ramella

| | |
|---|---|
| Tortricidae | 49.249 *Epinotia ramella* (Linnaeus, 1758) |
| Foodplant | Birch (*Betula* spp.). |
| Life cycle | Larva: April to May. Adult: mid-July to early October. |
| Distribution | Common throughout British Isles. |
| | Common in VC58, 59, 60. |
| Photo details | Feeding signs from Chorlton, Manchester VC59; 19.04.15 (BS). |

This is one of a number of tortricid larvae that may be found in male birch catkins in early spring. The shape of the catkin will frequently be distorted and frass may be seen exuding from it. There may also be a spinning including the adjacent bud or young leaves as in the photo below.

This species may be found in woodland and heaths where birch is common.

The adult moth can be reared by keeping the inhabited catkin within a container. One that allows a little air to circulate is preferable to prevent the catkin from quickly going mouldy. If using an airtight pot, mould can be prevented by only including a small amount of catkin, frequently changing it and by removing all frass. Either way, when adding fresh catkins, be careful to open them up first to avoid inadvertently introducing other larvae which may confound the results of the rearing.

Other birch catkin feeding tortricid larvae include *Epinotia immundana* (p.22), *E. bilunana*, *E. demarniana*, *Pammene obscurana* and *Cochylis nana* (the latter two in late summer to autumn). Of these, *demarniana* has a very pale brown head and prothoracic plate (and is very local in VC 58/59, and unrecorded in VC 60), whereas *bilunana* has a blackish head and prothoracic plate. The other two species that utilise this pabulum are *Argyresthia brockeella* and *A. goedartella*.

# Cataclysta lemnata

| | |
|---|---|
| Crambidae | 63.116 Small China-mark *Cataclysta lemnata* (Linnaeus, 1758) |
| Foodplant | Duckweed (*Lemna* spp.). |
| Life cycle | Larva: October to April. Adult: late May to mid-September. |
| Distribution | Widespread throughout Great Britain, but rare in Scotland. Common in VC58, 59, 60. |
| Photo details | Feeding signs from Rixton, WarringtonVC59; 31.03.09 (BS). |

In common with the other China-mark moths, this species is closely associated with various freshwater habitats. This is because the larva makes its home in the ponds and ditches where duckweed is present. It feeds on the duckweed and makes a case from leaves of the food plant. The case may be found attached to structures or plants at the water surface. As the larva grows, it creates a larger case, again out of duckweed leaves and filled with air.

To rear, keep the larva in an aquatic environment at least until pupation, with some duckweed for it to feed upon. A small and cheap 'starter' tank, sold in most pet shops is a good container for this. Make sure there is also some vegetation emerging from the water as the larva will want to attach itself to something of this nature, prior to pupation. The water and the foodplant will need to be changed regularly to keep it fresh.

The pupa forms in a duckweed coated cocoon just below the waterline.

The other three China-mark moths feed in a variety of ways. The Beautiful China-mark (*Nymphula nitidulata*) larva spins bur-reed leaves and other aquatic plants. Ringed China-mark (*Parapoynx stratiotata*) larvae are truly aquatic, bearing gills and feeding on a variety of plants including *Potamogeton*. Details of the Brown China-mark can be found in the April section (p.73).

# A selection of April larvae

12.010 *Morophaga choragella* - fungi 8-5.
20.022 *Argyresthia bonnetella* - hawthorn 4-5.
20.023 *Argyresthia albistria* - blackthorn 4-5.
49.004 *Ditula angustiorana* - polyphagous 8-5.
49.028 *Syndemis musculana* - birch, oak, etc. 7-4.

49.156 *Hedya nubiferana* – hawthorn, etc. 8-5.
49.285 *Epiblema scutulana* - thistle stems 8-4.
63.074 *Eudonia mercurella* - mosses 9-4.
63.086 *Crambus lathoniellus* - grasses 7-4.
63.093 *Agriphila straminella* - grasses 9-6.

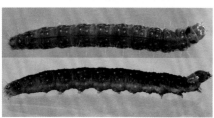
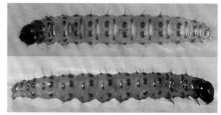

# APRIL FIELD TIPS

As buds, flowers and leaves appear on most of our deciduous trees during this month, one may start to see the first larval spinnings appearing on these.

Low-growing plants such as thistles, knapweeds, plantains and coltsfoot can also be a good source of microlepidoptera larvae.

April is also an ideal month to look for the aquatic larvae of the China-mark group of Crambids.

Although it can be like looking for a needle in a haystack, this month is a good time to search grasses, rushes and sedges for the mines of the various *Elachista* species. To rear, try and keep the plant intact, or keep the leaf blade in a sealed plastic bag to stop drying out. Include some plant material as substrate for pupation.

58. *Nemapogon clematella*
59. *Bucculatrix maritima*
60. *Aspilapteryx tringipennella*
61. *Glyphipterix haworthana*
62. *Argyresthia dilectella*
63. *Argyresthia cupressella*
64. *Helcystogramma rufescens*
65. *Caryocolum viscariella*
66. *Teleiodes vulgella*
67. *Exoteleia dodecella*
68. *Coleophora juncicolella*
69. *Coleophora paripennella*
70. *Elachista maculicerusella*
71. *Elachista cinereopunctella*
72. *Platyptilia gonodactyla*
73. *Elophila nymphaeata*

*Warton Crag, Lancashire, 2nd April 2017*

# Nemapogon clematella

| | |
|---|---|
| Tineidae | 12.021 *Nemapogon clematella* (Fabricius, 1781) |
| Foodplant | Fungi (*Hypoxylon fuscum, Fomes fomentarius*). |
| Life cycle | Larva: August to April. Adult: May to July. |
| Distribution | Local in England and Wales. A few records in Ireland and S. Scotland. Local in VC60. Records from 19th Century in VC58, 59. |
| Photo details | Feeding signs from Gait Barrows, Lancashire VC60; 10.04.16 (BS). |

The larvae of this tineid feed on the small fungal growths found on the branches and stems of hazel, alder and birch in woodland. This fungus is hazel woodwart (*Hypoxylon fuscum*). Like other *Hypoxylon* species, the fungus has small, round, and dark brown fruiting bodies. The fungus favours partially rotten wood and so affected branches may fall to the ground or will easily come away from the rest of the plant. Searching for larval signs amongst hazel rods of approximately 3-5 cm in diameter growing from coppiced plants is most likely to be successful.

Larval presence is evidenced by the development of frass-covered tubes between the fungal growths. The frass contains distinct dark and pale brown patches, presumably related to the colour of the fungus and that of the wood itself. Further investigation may reveal tunnels into the wood itself. Carefully opening up one of the surface tubes may reveal a larva. The *clematella* larva is greyish white with a pale brown head. If frass is present, but not obviously in tubular structures, then beetle larvae are more likely to be responsible.

Pupation takes place within the feeding site. Just prior to emergence, the pupa pushes to the surface of the wood. After emergence the pupal exuvia is left partially exposed and visible.

The adult moth is white with distinctive blackish brown markings.

# Bucculatrix maritima

| | |
|---|---|
| Bucculatricidae | 14.003 *Bucculatrix maritima* Stainton, 1851 |
| Foodplant | Sea aster (*Aster tripolium*). |
| Life cycle | Larva: April to May and July to August. Adult: June and August. |
| Distribution | Found in salt-marshes throughout British Isles. |
| | Local in VC58, 59, 60. |
| Photo details | Leaf-mines from Southport, Lancashire VC59; 05.05.15 (BS). |

The first generation of this bivoltine species can be found mining in April and early May. Like the foodplant it is a species found in coastal habitats particularly on salt-marshes.

The early instars make small mines on the upper or lower surface of the leaf. A large number may be found on one leaf. The later instar yellow larva makes a full-thickness gallery mine, sometimes making a series of such mines, and sometimes leaving the mine and feeding externally on the underside of the leaf creating feeding 'windows'.

On completion of feeding the larva leaves the mine (if it hasn't already done so) and selects a spot to form its cocoon which may be on the foodplant, other nearby plants or on the debris beneath the plant. The cocoon formed is a white, ribbed cocoon typical of the Bucculatricidae

There is a second larval generation of this species in July and early August, with adult emergence occurring in late summer.

The adult is somewhat similar to one of the paler *Phyllonorycter* species with a sandy brown ground coloured forewing and variably distinct white oblique streaks. It rarely travels a long way from the foodplant and may be found flying low down in its habitat on warm evenings.

The pinkish larva of *Scrobipalpa salicorniae* also mines sea aster in April and May.

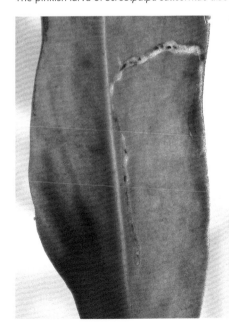
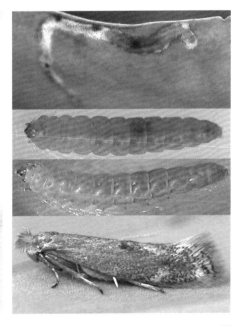

# Aspilapteryx tringipennella

| | |
|---|---|
| Gracillariidae | 15.015 *Aspilapteryx tringipennella* (Zeller, 1839) |
| Foodplant | Ribwort plantain (*Plantago lanceolata*). |
| Life cycle | Larva: June to July, October to April. Adult: May and mid-July to August. |
| Distribution | Widespread in British Isles. |
| | Common in VC58, 59, 60. |
| Photo details | Leaf-mine from Formby, Lancashire VC59; 18.04.15 (BS). |

The early stages of this common species can be recorded through much of the year by looking for the leaf-mines on ribwort plantain. The initial mine is a silvery gallery mine in the lower epidermis. When it reaches the later sap-feeding instars, changing its mouthparts to do so (Heath and Emmet ed., 1980), the larva chews through the tissue to the upper surface. This results in the development of a large pale brown blotch across the midrib on the upper surface of the leaf. As feeding continues, the leaf contracts over the mine almost concealing it, as in the photo below. The larvae found at this time of year are able to complete their feeding in a fresh leaf, as the overwintering leaf may dry out and be unsuitable for prolonged feeding.

The full grown larva is greyish green with a black or brown head, a divided dark prothoracic plate, dark thoracic legs, and a small brown anal plate.

The adult moth has a shape and posture typical of the closely related *Caloptilia* genus. The forewings are long and narrow with a pale brown ground colour and a white costal streak and with small black spots. The moth rests with the long legs holding the head upright, with the abdomen and forewings held at an approximate 45 degree angle to the resting surface. Where present they can be very common and one may see 'swarms' of males surrounding a newly emerged female.

# Glyphipterix haworthana

| | |
|---|---|
| Glyphipterigidae | 19.005 *Glyphipterix haworthana* (Stephens, 1834) |
| Foodplant | Cottongrass (*Eriophorum* spp.). |
| Life cycle | Larva: July to April. Adult: mid-April to May. |
| Distribution | Widely distributed in British Isles. |
| | Local in VC58, 59, 60. |
| Photo details | Spinning from Astley Moss, Lancashire VC59; 22.03.15 (BS). |

*Glyphipterix haworthana* is the largest and most clearly marked member of this genus. It has a wingspan of 11-15mm, approximately twice as large as the much more widespread and familiar Cocksfoot Moth (*Glyphipterix simpliciella*). The moth has dark brown forewings with a lighter brown patch at the tornus and prominent silvery white fascia.

The species is a specialist of boggy habitats and will only be found where cotton-grass is present.

The early instar larvae start feeding on the seeds of the foodplant as early as July. Over winter the larva remains within the cottony seed-head of the foodplant and spins it on to surrounding vegetation, meaning the individual seeds do not get blown away and the greyish mass can be easily spotted in early spring with the full-fed larva still present.

The larva is white with a dark brown head and thoracic legs. It has a finely divided lighter brown prothoracic plate as well as light brown plates on the final three abdominal segments.

In early April, the larva pupates after forming a tough silken cocoon coated in the hairs of the cotton-grass. This cocoon remains within the spinning and so spinnings collected at this time of year are very likely to give rise to the adult moths. One may also find the adults in the day, flying close to their foodplant, or easily disturbed from surrounding vegetation.

# Argyresthia dilectella

Argyresthiidae      20.006 *Argyresthia dilectella* Zeller, 1847
Foodplant           Juniper (*Juniperus*), cypress (*Chamaecyparis*).
Life cycle          Larva: Autumn to May. Adult: mid-June to mid-August.
Distribution        Widely distributed in British Isles.
                    Common in VC58, VC 59, 60.
Photo details       Feeding signs from Gait Barrows, Lancashire VC60; 01.04.16 (BS).

This is one of a number of many *Argyresthia* species that feed on juniper. Whilst the larva over-winters in an early instar, its presence becomes apparent in early spring as the larvae feed within the juniper shoots. Frass is expelled through small holes at the nodes. The feeding causes the end portion of the shoot to become brown as in the photo below (top left).

Although feeding signs were apparent I found it difficult to actually find the larva, so resorted to potting a couple of shoots and waiting for the larva to vacate the feeding habitation, which it did two weeks later. It then wandered around the pot, presumably looking for a pupation site.

The full-fed larva is pale green with pink rings on the first part of each segment. It has a light brown head with darker brown prothoracic and anal plates, and dark thoracic legs.

Pupation occurs amongst detritus on the ground. The adult below emerged approximately five weeks after completion of the feeding phase.

Other *Argyresthia* species mining juniper shoots include *arceuthina*, *cupressella* and *trifasciata*. *Argyresthia praecocella* feeds in green juniper berries in August, with a hole demonstrating the larval presence. *A. aurulentella* and *abdominalis* mine the juniper leaves in May. There are no confirmed records for the latter three species in Lancashire or Cheshire.

# *Argyresthia cupressella*

| | |
|---|---|
| Argyresthiidae | 20.007 Cypress Tip Moth *Argyresthia cupressella* Walsingham, 1890 |
| Foodplant | Cypresses (*Leylandii, Chamaecyparis lawsoniana*), juniper (*Juniperus*). |
| Life cycle | Larva: April to May. Adult: mid-May to July. |
| Distribution | Widespread in S. England. Scarce in Wales and Ireland. Local in VC58. 59, 60. |
| Photo details | Cocoons from Little Woolden Moss. Salford VC59; 21.04.16 (BS). |

*Argyresthia cupressella* is an adventive species, accidentally introduced on the foodplant at the end of the twentieth century. It was first recorded in Suffolk in 1997. It has since spread north and west to much of England, and where present larvae can be extremely plentiful on *Leylandii* cypresses. Those below were taken from the cypresses at the entrance to Little Woolden Moss.

I initially detected these by beating (eight larvae dropped into the upturned umbrella). Mines were then noted to be incredibly common, probably numbering into the thousands - on just six trees!

The hollowed out section of the leaves shows as white, compared to the older brown mines of the last winter's *Argyresthia trifasciata* (p.208). Each mine has a hole to facilitate expulsion of frass. The first photo shows a tenanted mine and the larva can just about be made out in the darker upper section of the mine. Larvae were also noted to re-enter fresh leaves, and recommence feeding. I also found a few larvae dangling from silken threads, probably looking for pupation sites.

The larva is light green and differs from that of *Argyresthia trifasciata* in that it has an amber coloured head, whereas that of *trifasciata* is dark brown to black.

Papery white cocoons were also noted between the leaves, as in the middle photo on the right. The adult emerged about four weeks after formation of the cocoon.

# Helcystogramma rufescens

| | |
|---|---|
| Gelechiidae | 35.031 *Helcystogramma rufescens* (Haworth, 1828) |
| Foodplant | Grasses (Poa spp., *Arrhenatherum elatius, Brachypodium* spp. etc.). |
| Life cycle | Larva: late March to June. Adult: mid-June to early September. |
| Distribution | Common in England and Wales. Local in Ireland and Scotland. Common in VC 58, 59, 60. |
| Photo details | Feeding signs from Chorlton, Manchester VC59; 29.03.15 (BS). |

The adult of this moth is quite nondescript with plain ochreous forewings. The larva however is quite a different matter, and cannot be confused with any other larva found in NW England.

The larva feeds within a tube spun from grass blades, and can be encountered on grasslands throughout the region from late March onwards. The grass blade is somewhat twisted within the spinning. The larva consumes the inner surface of the grass from within the tube, causing blanching of the affected section. It will move between a variety of leaves, creating a succession of rolls until feeding is complete. Watch out for the common *Aphelia paleana* larva, an equally distinctive larva (black with large white pinaculae; see p.95) which forms successive rolls on grass blades, although these are less twisted than those formed by *rufescens*.

The head of the *rufescens* larva is black as is the prothoracic plate, the thorax (although with intersegmental white lines) and the first two abdominal segments. The rest of the abdomen has a white dorsal line between a pair of black subdorsal lines, and alternate black and white diagonal lines along the abdomen. The only similar Gelechiid larva is *Helcystogramma lutatella*, a rare species in Britain only known from the south coast. The large sclerotised plate on the dorsal surface of the second abdominal section is dark olive in *rufescens* and reddish brown in *lutatella*.

# Caryocolum viscariella

| | |
|---|---|
| Gelechiidae | 35.129 *Caryocolum viscariella* (Stainton, 1855) |
| Foodplant | Red campion (*Silene dioica*), white campion (*S. latifolia*), sticky catchfly (*Lychnis viscaria*). |
| Life cycle | Larva: April to May. Adult: late June to August. |
| Distribution | Widespread in England. Local in Scotland, Wales and Ireland. Local in VC 58, 59, 60. |
| Photo details | Feeding signs from St Helens, Lancashire VC59; 23.04.15 (BS). |

Representatives of the *Caryocolum* genus are rarely encountered at light, and when they are, the very similar adults are likely to require dissection for accurate identification. The adult moth of this species is particularly similar to *Caryocolum fraternella*.

Recording the presence of the genus is therefore best attempted by looking for the early stages, and this is one of the commoner members of the genus with quite noticeable feeding signs. It is best looked for in hedgerows, open woods and open grassland. The larva feeds in a campion shoot, spinning the upper leaves together, leading to distorted growth. Opening up this spinning reveals a large quantity of frass and hopefully the larva will be present. If not immediately apparent it may be enclosed within the developing bud or have bored into the central stem. The larva is pale greyish green, occasionally with a pinkish tinge, most apparent in the prothoracic segment. The head, prothoracic plate and thoracic legs are all black. It is important to check the larva to ensure the spinning is not made by a polyphage such as *Celypha lacunana* (p.96).

It can be reared in an 7cm x 7cm pot, removing frass and adding fresh foodplant every few days. It may be easier to keep on a netted fresh plant. Pupation is on detritus in May and June.

# Teleiodes vulgella

Gelechiidae     35.141 *Teleiodes vulgella* ([Denis & Schiffermüller], 1775)
Foodplant     Hawthorn (*Crataegus* spp.), blackthorn (*Prunus spinosa*),
rowan (*Sorbus aucuparia*), Cotoneaster.
Life cycle     Larva: April to May. Adult: June to mid-August.
Distribution     Common in England and Wales Local in Ireland. Unrecorded in Scotland.
Common in VC 58, 59, 60.
Photo details     Feeding signs from Chorlton, Manchester VC59; 18.04.15 (BS).

The larva of this very common species is known to feed on hawthorn and blackthorn. Personally I have only ever found it on rowan (in Manchester). In other districts its food preferences may be different. The larvae spin two leaves flatly together and graze beneath, creating holes in the lower leaf and causing a browning of the upper surface of the top leaf.

The larva is green with small black pinaculae, a black prothoracic plate and an orange brown head. The shape is typical of the the *Teleiodes/Carpatolechia* group with obvious tapering towards the head and anal ends of the larva.

*T. vulgella* has been thought likely to overwinter in the egg form (Emmet and Langmaid (ed.), 2002), although I wonder if it may sometimes (always) overwinter as a small larva. I have found a very similar larva (below left), approximately 5mm long, feeding between two hawthorn leaves in October on a few occasions. Unfortunately as yet I have been unable to successfully get the larva through the winter, although I am at a loss to know what else it might be.

Other *Teleiodes* species in the region are *sequax* (p.85) on rock-rose and *luculella*. Larvae of the latter feed in spun oak leaves in autumn. The larva is whitish green with black pinaculae.

# Exoteleia dodecella

| | |
|---|---|
| Gelechiidae | 35.159 *Exoteleia dodecella* (Linnaeus, 1758) |
| Foodplant | Scots pine (*Pinus sylvestris*), larch (*Larix decidua*). |
| Life cycle | Larva: September to May. Adult: June to mid-August. |
| Distribution | Widespread in British Isles. |
| | Local in VC58, 59, 60. |
| Photo details | Leaf-mine from Formby, Lancashire VC59; 03.04.15 (BS). |

*Exoteleia dodecella* larvae mine pine needles over winter and into the spring. It may occasionally also be found on larch. It is common within conifer plantations and may sometimes cause severe damage.

Feeding begins in autumn when the larva feeds inside the tip of needle. It feeds from within a larval chamber at the base of the mined portion of the needle. One or two holes are created on the side of the needle to facilitate the expulsion of most of the frass. Unlike the *Cedestis* and *Ocnerostoma* species that also mine pine needles, there is no egg visible at the start of the mine.

The larva continues to feed in the spring, extending the mine away from the tip before leaving to feed from within a spinning at the base of the needles. This spinning can be seen in the top right hand photo below.

The larva is reddish brown with a black head and black prothoracic and anal plates.

The adult moth can be beaten from the foodplant and may also be attracted to the light trap, where worn individuals may present an identification challenge. The grey adult is not particularly distinctive although the two poorly defined dark bands at one-third and two-thirds and the presence of dark scale tufts can help.

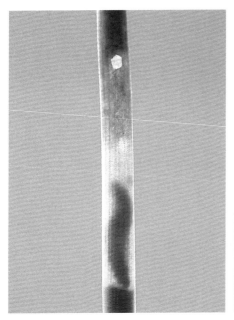 

# Coleophora juncicolella

Coleophoridae     37.028 *Coleophora juncicolella* Stainton, 1851
Foodplant     Ling (*Calluna vulgaris*), bell heather (*Erica cinerea*).
Life cycle     Larva: September to May. Adult: June to July.
Distribution     Common in Great Britain. Local in Ireland.
    Local in VC58, 59, 60.
Photo details     Cocoons from Lindow Moss, Wilmslow VC58; 15.04.15 (BS).
    Adult (Oliver Wadsworth).

This, our smallest Coleophorid with a wingspan of only 6-8mm, makes a beautifully detailed and well disguised case. With a case of only 4mm in length, the only real likelihood of detecting it is to beat or sweep some heather (*Calluna* or *Erica*). This should dislodge lots of small leaves. The cases photographed below were obtained by carefully beating heather into an upturned umbrella. After a minute or two of careful observation, what appeared to be a dry piece of the heather started to walk about! An alternative method is to place the contents of the sweeping or beating into a clear container and wait for the *Coleophora* larvae to walk up the side of the container.

The case is constructed from a number of leaves from the foodplant arranged in a neat pattern as shown below. Initial feeding is within a single leaf as the parenchyma is hollowed out. This then becomes the initial case as the larva mines adjacent leaves from within the security of the case. Other mined leaves are gradually attached to the case, leading to a final case composed of seven or nine leaves (Emmet ed., 1996). The larvae are full-fed by the end of March and rest high up on the heather in the sunshine prior to pupation in late May and June. To rear it is essential to keep the cases exposed to the elements, so keeping on a netted plant is ideal.

# Coleophora paripennella

| | |
|---|---|
| Coleophoridae | 37.106 *Coleophora paripennella* Zeller, 1839 |
| Foodplant | Common knapweed (*Centaurea nigra*), creeping thistle (*Cirsium arvense*). |
| Life cycle | Larva: September to May. Adult: June to August. |
| Distribution | Common in British Isles, although less so in northern Scotland. Local in VC58, 59, 60. |
| Photo details | Feeding signs from Rixton, Warrington VC59; 20.04.15 (BS). |

The larva of this moth leaves these distinctive feeding signs on the leaves of knapweed in spring. If you look on the underside of the affected leaf you will hopefully find the razor-shell shaped case of this species. The larva mines the leaf creating these white blotches. Each blotch has a puncture hole in the centre. Beware of confusion with the feeding signs of larval and adult Thistle Tortoise Beetles (*Cassida rubiginosa*), which make numerous partial and full thickness holes in the leaf blades of knapweed and thistle. The partial holes created by *Cassida* lack the central puncture of those created by *paripennella*.

*C. paripennella* larvae may also be found on creeping thistle, although rarely so in spring.

The larvae overwinter in small black-brown cases of a similar shape to the final cases. These are extended further in spring as feeding continues until the case is approximately 8mm in length. When full-fed the larva attaches the case to a stem of knapweed or other vegetation prior to pupation. If rearing in captivity it is best to keep the larva outside at this point, ideally on some netted foodplant.

The only other *Coleophora* that feeds on knapweed, *C. conspicuella*, is confined to the south-east of England. It feeds in a much larger (15mm long), black, sabre-shaped case.

# Elachista maculicerusella

| | |
|---|---|
| Elachistidae | 38.039 *Elachista maculicerusella* (Bruand, 1859) |
| Foodplant | Reed canary-grass (*Phalaris arundinacea*), common reed (*Phragmites*). |
| Life cycle | Larva: March to April, June to July. Adult: May to June, July to August. |
| Distribution | Widespread throughout British Isles. |
| | Common in VC 58, 59, 60. |
| Photo details | Leaf-mine from Astley Moss, Lancashire VC59; 01.04.07 (BS). |

Members of the *Elachista* genus mine the leaves of various grasses, sedges and rushes, and are often at fairly low densities making their mines a challenge to locate and correctly identify.

One of the easiest is *Elachista maculicerusella*. Its large and conspicuous whitish green blotch mines can be found on reed canary-grass as soon as new growth appears in the spring. The leaf-mines progress downwards from the tip of the leaf and are quite common wherever the foodplant occurs. If the mined leaf blade is held up to the light, then the larva can be observed in-situ with irregular patterns of greenish frass.

The pale yellow larva is deeply segmented with a green gut line (whilst still feeding), a pale brown head and a pale brown and divided prothoracic plate. Like other *Elachista* larvae, the head of *maculicerusella* is extremely flattened aiding its ability to mine its chosen leaf blade. The larva may change leaf to continue feeding. It can also change leaf in captivity

The only likely confusion species is with the *Diptera* (fly) larvae that also mine reed canary-grass. The fly larvae are shorter with no obvious head capsule. *Cosmopterix orichalcea* also mines reed and reed canary-grass but this is a moth of southern England, Wales and Ireland and creates a much longer and narrower mine than that of *maculicerusella*, with most of the frass ejected.

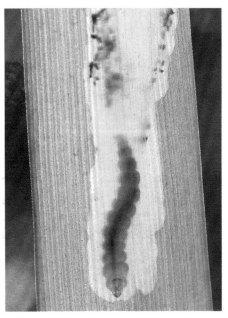 

# *Elachista cinereopunctella*

| | |
|---|---|
| Elachistidae | 38.041 *Elachista cinereopunctella* (Haworth, 1828) |
| Foodplant | Glaucous sedge (*Carex flacca*). |
| Life cycle | Larva: October to April. Adult: May to June. |
| Distribution | Local throughout British Isles. |
| | Local in VC58 and VC60. No recent records in VC59. |
| Photo details | Leaf-mine from Gait Barrows, Lancashire VC60; 10.04.16 (BS). |

This is a quite a scarce, although in the larval stage very distinctive, leaf-mining *Elachista species*. The larvae feed on various sedges, primarily glaucous sedge, although there are also records of the species using tufted hair-grass and (on the continent) blue moor-grass.

Larval feeding commences in autumn as the early instar larval mine descends from the tip of the leaf. The mine is extended, filling in an area between the leaf edge and the midrib. Brown frass remains within the mine and is deposited in a trail behind the larva as it heads down the plant.

The larva overwinters in its mine, but unlike most other *Elachista* species does not change its leaf with the arrival of spring. Instead the mine is extended further, sometimes filling the leaf width.

The larva itself is very well-marked and its distinctive colouration can be seen whilst it is within the leaf-mine. It is yellowish white with red spots on each segment coalescing to form a pair of subdorsal red lines, enclosing a broad white dorsal line. The head and divided prothoracic plate are dark brown.

On leaving the mine, the larva first secures itself to the upper surface of a leaf by means of a silken thread looped around the abdomen. Immediately following pupation, the pupal colouration is similar to the final instar larva. As it develops, a more reddish-brown hue is attained.

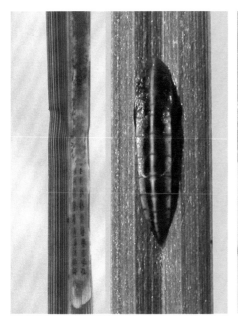

# Platyptilia gonodactyla

| | |
|---|---|
| Pterophoridae | 45.004 *Platyptilia gonodactyla* ([Denis & Schiffermüller], 1775) |
| Foodplant | Coltsfoot (*Tussilago farfara*). |
| Life cycle | Larva: July-August, September-May. Adult: May-June, August-September. |
| Distribution | Common throughout most of British Isles. |
| | Common in VC 58, 59, 60. |
| Photo details | Pupa from Chorlton, Manchester VC59; 14.05.04 (BS). |

The young larva of this plume moth can be found inside coltsfoot stems from February onwards as it moves up from its overwintering site at the base of the plant. As there is no external sign of their presence at this stage, the early larva can only be detected by opening up randomly selected stems.

The late instar larva inhabits the upper section of the stem and goes on to consume buds, flowers and seeds. Frass is plentiful The larva makes a hole at the base of the flower-head to facilitate access to the seeds. Whilst feeding it can move between stems. The yellowish larva has pink dorsal, sub-dorsal and lateral lines, a black head and black prothoracic and anal plates.

When full-fed the larva spins a group of seeds together and pupates within, meaning that section of seed-head remains when all others have been blown away. Another clue to the presence of the species is that the seed-head will tend to droop as the contents of the upper stem have been consumed. If one very gently squeezes the affected seed-head then it is possible to detect the firm presence of a pupa within. The pupa is quite colourful with a red and green hue.

There is also a second generation feeding in summer, initially in a leaf-mine and later externally on a leaf, going on to pupate in a spun cocoon on the underside of a leaf.

The adult moth has a conspicuous brown triangle 2/3rds down the length of the forewing.

# *Elophila nymphaeata*

| | |
|---|---|
| Crambidae | 63.114 Brown China-mark *Elophila nymphaeata* (Linnaeus, 1758) |
| Foodplant | Pondweed (*Potamogeton* spp.), other aquatic plants – see below. |
| Life cycle | Larva: throughout the year. Adult: June to late September. |
| Distribution | Widespread and common in British Isles. |
| | Common in VC 58, 59, 60. |
| Photo details | Cases from Lindow Common, Wilmslow VC58; 15.04.15 (BS). |

*Elophila nymphaeata*, in common with the other china-mark moths, has an aquatic larval stage. In this case the larva can be primarily found feeding on pondweed on ponds, lakes and slow-moving rivers. May also be found using water lilies, frogbit and bur-reed.

The early instar larva mines the foodplant (see top right photo). Later instars feed in a case from two roughly oval leaf cuttings spun flatly together. The resultant shape of the leaves with the distinctively shaped areas cut out is a definite indicator for the presence of the species. The small larva overwinters within a gelatinous mass within its case often attached to the underneath of a leaf of the foodplant. The larva cuts out a fresh case in spring and continues to feed within. The case contains a large air bubble and the larva's head is kept within this. Oxygen is obtained from air spaces within the plant. When full-fed the larva secures a silken cocoon covered with pieces of leaf to nearby vegetation just below the water surface and pupates within.

The yellow larva has a brown head and a black-lined prothoracic plate, with a blackish blotch in the centre of the plate. Earlier instars may lack the dark colouring of head and prothoracic plate.

The adult moth is quite variable with some individuals being particularly dark brown, whereas others are paler with distinct white patterning.

# Leaf-mines and larvae of the birch-feeding Eriocraniidae.

2.003 *Eriocrania unimaculella*. Larva has appearance of 2 brown spots just behind dark brown head. 4-5.
2.004 *Eriocrania sparrmannella*. Linear mine becomes blotch in centre of leaf in late June-July. Reddish. 6-8.
2.005 *Eriocrania salopiella*. Linear mine becomes blotch in centre of leaf in May. Extends to leaf edge. 5-6
2.006 *Eriocrania cicatricella*. Greenish blotch with 2-4 larvae. Larva has swollen thoracic segments. 5.
2.007 *Eriocrania semipurpurella*. Larva mines large blotch. Early instar has dark head/prothoracic plate. 4-5.

# MAY FIELD TIPS

Larval spinnings abound in May as fresh leaves appear on all our deciduous trees. Microlepidoptera larvae are easy to find, rolling and spinning these leaves in gardens and woodland. Particularly widespread are Tortricidae larvae on oak, sallow, poplar, birch, hawthorn and apple. Their spinnings alone are diagnostic in some cases. In others, combining the spinning with the larval appearance is enough to secure identification. If not, then rearing through will usually do the trick, and many of the larvae found at this time of year will quickly feed up and emerge after a couple of weeks as pupae.

Leaf-mining larvae are also common on birch and oak in the form of the Eriocraniidae and the case –bearing larvae of the Coleophoridae.

76. *Eriocrania sangii*
77. *Ypsolopha dentella*
78. *Argyresthia pygmaeella*
79. *Argyresthia retinella*
80. *Prays fraxinella*
81. *Scythropia crataegella*
82. *Agonopterix angelicella*
83. *Depressaria daucella*
84. *Anacampsis populella*
85. *Teleiodes sequax*
86. *Mompha conturbatella*
87. *Anthophila fabriciana*
88. *Eudemis profundana*
89. *Epinotia sordidana*
90. *Epinotia brunnichana*
91. *Gypsonoma aceriana*
92. *Lathronympha strigana*
93. *Pleuroptya ruralis*

*Healey Dell, Rochdale, Greater Manchester, 7th May 2016*

# *Eriocrania sangii*

| | |
|---|---|
| Eriocraniidae | 2.008 *Eriocrania sangii* (Wood, 1891) |
| Foodplant | Birch (*Betula* spp.). |
| Life cycle | Larva: April to May. Adult: March to April. |
| Distribution | Local in British Isles. |
| | Local in VC58, VC 59, 60. |
| Photo details | Leaf-mine from Astley Moss, Lancashire VC59; 06.05.08 (BS). |

Eriocraniidae is a relatively small family of leaf-miners with eight UK representatives. Of these, *Dyseriocrania subpurpurella* is an extremely common oak miner. *Paracrania chrysolepidella* is a miner of hazel, only found in the Morecambe Bay area of VC60 within the Lancs and Cheshire region. The other six Eriocraniidae species are birch miners (see p.74). With the exception of *Eriocrania sparrmannella* (late June-July), all can be found locally as leaf-mines in May.

All are identifiable from a combination of larval appearance and leaf-mine form, although the simplest to identify is *E. sangii*. The leaf-mine starts at the leaf edge with the developing blotch filling most of the leaf. The mine contains spaghetti-like black frass (as with all Eriocraniidae). The distinctive feature of this species is the grey larva. All other Eriocraniidae have white larvae. The shed skins of previous instars are also quite conspicuous within the mine of *sangii*.

If in any doubt as to identity, collect the leaf and keep it in an air-tight pot. Once feeding is complete the larva will leave the leaf and can be examined. To rear, transfer the larva into a small netted flowerpot half-filled with soil and some leaf litter. Leave it in a sheltered part of the garden and check daily from the following March and with luck the adult will emerge.

Identification of most trapped or netted birch *Eriocrania* is not possible without dissection.

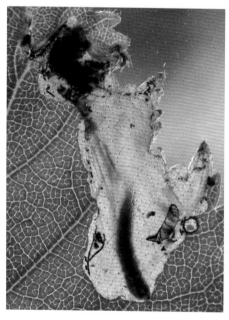

# *Ypsolopha dentella*

| | |
|---|---|
| Ypsolophidae | 17.003 Honeysuckle Moth *Ypsolopha dentella* (Fabricius, 1775) |
| Foodplant | Honeysuckle (*Lonicera periclymenum*). |
| Life cycle | Larva: May to June. Adult: July to mid-September |
| Distribution | Common throughout British Isles. |
| | Common in VC58, 59, 60. |
| Photo details | Feeding signs from Chorlton, Manchester VC59; 22.05.16 (BS). |

*Ypsolopha dentella* larvae can be found on wild-growing honeysuckle as well as garden varieties.

The larva makes a fairly inconspicuous spinning between two leaves at the tip of a honeysuckle stem and consumes the new leaf growth within. Small amounts of silk and fragments of frass will help to notify the presence of a larval tenant. Try to rule out the presence of polyphagous larvae such as *Epiphyas postvittana* (p.211), or the yellowish brown larva of *Ditula angustiorana* (p.56).

The early instar larva of *Ypsolopha dentella* is pale brown but with a narrow white dorsal stripe running down the middle of a darker dorsal band. The final instar larva is unmistakeable. It has a light brown head and a pale green abdomen with a broad red dorsal stripe. It also has a shape typical of *Ypsolopha* larvae, being wide in the middle of the abdomen and tapering in width towards the head and anal ends.

When full-fed the larva leaves the spinning and creates a buff coloured pupal cocoon shaped a little like an upturned boat. The cocoon may be found on adjacent vegetation or leaf litter.

This is one of a number of spring honeysuckle feeders. Others include the brown larva of *Ypsolopha nemorella*, distinguished by the presence of three dark patches along the length of the body, and *Athrips mouffetella*, whose larva is black with a few white markings (p.95).

# Argyresthia pygmaeella

| | |
|---|---|
| Argyresthiidae | 20.013 *Argyresthia pygmaeella* ([Denis & Schiffermüller], 1775) |
| Foodplant | Sallows and willows (*Salix* spp.). |
| Life cycle | Larva: April to May. Adult: June to August. |
| Distribution | Common throughout British Isles. |
| | Common in VC58, 59, 60. |
| Photo details | Feeding signs from Irlam Moss, Salford VC59; 12.05.16 (BS). |

This species may be easier to locate by searching for the larval signs than looking for the adults. After overwintering as an early instar in a leaf-bud, the larva makes a spinning at the terminal shoot of sallow twigs. The shoot may be noted to droop slightly. The larva produces copious amounts of silk which is combined with the downy tissue from the developing leaves to make quite a dense, white mass. This may need to be carefully and fully opened up before the larva is revealed.

The larva is pale green, tapering towards the tip of the abdomen. It has a black head, black prothoracic plate and black thoracic legs.

When full-fed the larva leaves its spinning to pupate on the ground or occasionally within the spinning itself. Pupation is within an intricate double netted cocoon as in the photo below. The construction of this is quite impressive and must take some doing to make sure the larva ends up on the inside where it can safely pupate.

The species can be successfully reared in an air-tight 7cm x 7cm pot (or similar). Remove frass and old plant material every couple of days, adding in the occasional young sallow shoot as required. My experience is that the adult will emerge 13-15 days after pupation.

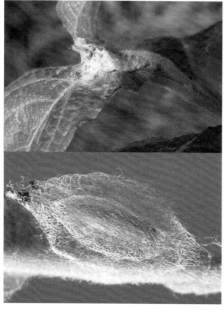

# *Argyresthia retinella*

| | |
|---|---|
| Argyresthiidae | 20.016 *Argyresthia retinella* Zeller, 1839. |
| Foodplant | Birch (*Betula* spp.). |
| Life cycle | Larva: October to May. Adult: June to early August. |
| Distribution | Common throughout British Isles. |
| | Common in VC58, 59, 60. |
| Photo details | Feeding signs from Irlam Moss, Salford VC59; 12.05.16 (BS). |

The larva feeds within the developing shoots of birch trees. Late April-May is the best time to look for this species. Signs of its tenancy are quite easy to detect, as one will see wilted shoots. A closer look shows small darkened leaves with buds not fully opened and frass evident at the base of the shoot. Carefully opening up the shoot will reveal a small amber-coloured larva with a pale, brown head, feeding within. Pupation occurs in late May-June with the metamorphosis taking place within a cocoon, usually on the trunk of the host tree.

If trying to rear this species they do need quite a lot of attention. If not kept in an air-tight container the shoots will quickly dry out. Unfortunately the buds become very sticky and prone to mould development if left in such a container. The best option is to put in a small amount of plant material at a time, and to go for fully opened leaves. The larvae will eat these and they are less likely than shoots to become mouldy. Remove all frass. Add tissue and dry soil for pupation.

Another way to look for the presence of this moth is to gently beat birch twigs over a beating tray or umbrella in June or July. This will usually result in a number of the adults descending to the tray or umbrella. They will stay still for a few seconds allowing you to pot up one or two to facilitate a closer look and confirmation of identity, before they fly back up to the tree.

# *Prays fraxinella*

| | |
|---|---|
| Praydidae | 22.002 Ash Bud Moth *Prays fraxinella* (Bjerkander, 1784). |
| Foodplant | Ash (*Fraxinus excelsior*). |
| Life cycle | Larva: October to May. Adult: June to July. |
| Distribution | Common throughout British Isles. |
| | Common in VC58, 59, 60. |
| Photo details | Feeding signs from Chorlton, Manchester VC59; 30.05.15 (BS). |

Early May is the best time to look for the feeding signs of this species, as small saplings of ash may contain noticeably wilted shoots. If one looks carefully at these, frass may be seen emanating from the base of the shoot. If you carefully break off the shoot, you will see a hole beneath which links to the main twig and neighbouring shoots, as in the top right photo below. The larva can be seen within, along with a quantity of frass.

The small larva initially mines the leaves of ash in October, moving on to mine the bark of a twig. Frass may be seen beside the buds. The larva overwinters in this stage, before moving on to a shoot in the spring, causing the leaves to droop. Pupation occurs within a netted cocoon, either within the feeding place or elsewhere on the tree. The larva, in captivity, will feed on fresh ash shoots.

There is a certain amount of debate about the taxonomy of this species. *Prays fraxinella* (f. *rustica*) has dark wings, although the usual markings can just be made out, and has a white or buff head. It seems there is also a similar species, *Prays ruficeps*, which tends to be smaller and emerges later in the year. This has dark wings with no evidence of the black costal triangle of *fraxinella*, and a reddish brown head. *P. ruficeps* was accepted onto the British list in 2013.

# Scythropia crataegella

Scythropiidae    25.001 Hawthorn Moth *Scythropia crataegella* (Linnaeus, 1767)
Foodplant    Hawthorn (*Crataegus* spp.), blackthorn (*Prunus spinosa*), *Cotoneaster* spp.
Life cycle    Larva: Sept.-June. Adult: June-July. Possible occasional 2nd generation.
Distribution    Common in southern England, Wales. Unrecorded in Ireland and Scotland.
   Common in VC58, 59. Unrecorded in VC60.
Photo details    Larval spinning from Chorlton, Manchester VC59; 01.05.16 (BS).

One can find larval webs of this gregarious species on hawthorn and blackthorn branches in May. These may be conspicuous with silk, frass, dead leaves and partially eaten fresh leaves all caught in the web along with the reddish brown larvae. The hairy larva has a black head, black thoracic legs and a pale dorsal stripe.

Pupation occurs within the web with no cocoon being spun.

The adults emerge in summer and in my experience do not seem to venture far from the original web so that eggs are laid close to the same branches as the previous generation.

Larvae hatch in September and immediately begin mining, with many found in a single leaf (below left). The larvae then leave the mine to feed in a small web before re-entering a fresh leaf. The tenanted leaves, along with partially eaten and previously mined leaves, are spun on to the branch making the presence of the colony quite apparent even in the depths of winter.

Avoid confusion with the web made on hawthorn (and pear) by the sawfly *Neurotoma saltuum*. The larvae are bright orange with a black head and a pair of black spots just behind the head. They keep closely together in a mass within the web, waving their heads if disturbed.

*Yponomeuta padella* (grey larvae with large black spots) also form hawthorn and blackthorn webs.

# Agonopterix angelicella

| | |
|---|---|
| Depressariidae | 32.032 *Agonopterix angelicella* (Hübner, [1813]) |
| Foodplant | Angelica (*Angelica sylvestris*), hogweed (*Heracleum sphondylium*). |
| Life cycle | Larva: May to June. Adult: July to September. |
| Distribution | Locally common in British Isles. Local in VC58, 59, 60. |
| Photo details | Larval spinning from Burton Mere, Wirral VC58; 31.05.16 (BS). |

The larvae of this depressariid feed communally within a very obvious and untidy spinning of leaves and shoots, usually on wild angelica, but occasionally on hogweed or milk parsley. The spinning contains large amounts of frass and silk as well as numerous dull green larvae covered in black pinaculae. The larva has a light brown head with greenish thoracic legs, prothoracic plate and anal plate. The usual habitat is damp areas such as riversides and marshes where the preferred foodplant is common.

On completion of feeding, the larvae leave the web and pupate amongst the detritus below, a stage lasting two to three weeks. The pupa is reddish brown.

Adults emerge from July onwards, although this may be a little earlier amongst reared individuals. The adult has a buff head and pinkish brown forewings with a dark blotch containing a black spot in the middle of each forewing.

The other *Agonopterix* larvae found on angelica are *A. ciliella* and *A. heracliana* (p.104). These do not make a large communal spinning, but feed individually on leaves spun into a tube. They are much brighter green than *angelicella* larvae, with darker green dorsal and dorsolateral lines. The black on the head and prothoracic plate is also quite extensive in the *A.ciliella* larva.

# Depressaria daucella

| | |
|---|---|
| Depressariidae | 32.039 *Depressaria daucella* ([Denis & Schiffermüller], 1775) |
| Foodplant | Hemlock water-dropwort (*Oenanthe crocata*), *Oenanthe* spp. |
| Life cycle | Larva: May to July. Adult: August to April. |
| Distribution | Locally common in British Isles. |
| | Common in VC58, 59, 60. |
| Photo details | Larval spinning from Burton Mere, Wirral VC58; 31.05.16 (BS). |

The first spinnings of the species on hemlock water-dropwort and other closely related umbellifers can be found from late May onwards. These spinnings are very conspicuous as the flowers and upper leaves are pulled together with large quantities of frass sticking to the silken threads at the base of the flower-head. The larvae feed communally within the spinning. At this time of year the larvae are likely to be in a stage prior to the final instar and will have a dark greyish green abdomen with a black head, prothoracic plate and anal plate. Large black pinaculae are edged with a slight grey ring.

As the larva enters its final instar its appearance becomes very distinctive. The large pinaculae are now edged with white rings. It has a bright orange or yellow stripe along the lateral aspect of the body and an orange mark in the centre of the otherwise black prothoracic plate. The prolegs are yellow. The thoracic legs are black. When full-fed the larva pupates within the stem of the foodplant. The adult is relatively plain with brown forewings bearing a few black dashes.

Other *Depressaria* species found within this region include *radiella*, *ultimella*, *pulcherrimella* and *sordidatella* on various umbellifers, and *badiella*, whose early instar larvae spin leaves of cat's-ear, perennial sow-thistle and dandelion in May, later feeding on the tap-root from a silken tube.

# *Anacampsis populella*

| | |
|---|---|
| Gelechiidae | 35.011 *Anacampsis populella* (Clerck, 1759) |
| Foodplant | Poplars and aspen (*Populus* spp.), sallows and willows (*Salix* spp.). |
| Life cycle | Larva: May to June. Adult: July to August. |
| Distribution | Common in England and Wales. Local in Scotland and Ireland. Common in VC58, 59. Local in VC60. |
| Photo details | Spinning on sallow from Chorlton, Manchester VC59; 15.5.16 (BS). |

The feeding signs of this Gelechiid are quite easy to detect, although the species is much more local north of the River Ribble. The larva spins the leaves of poplars and sallows longitudinally along the midrib with a few silken threads keeping the leaf rolled into a tube. The larva feeds within this rolled leaf, switching to a fresh leaf as required.

The greyish green larva has black pinaculae, a black head and black anal and prothoracic plates.

A possible confusion species in the larval stage is the tortricid *Epinotia maculana* which also feeds from within rolled leaves on aspen. *E. maculana*, however is very rare within this region. The larva of *maculana* is superficially similar to *A. populella*, but it has grey pinaculae and a white edged prothoracic plate.

Two other *Anacampsis* species are also found within the region. *Anacampsis blattariella* makes a similar spinning on birch and occasionally alder (p.10). The larva of the nationally rare *A. temerella* feeds within a tube constructed from the terminal leaves of a shoot of creeping willow.

*A. populella* adults tend to be much plainer than the typically contrasting black and white markings on the forewings of *blattariella*. However this is not 100% reliable and dissection is the only way to be certain of the identity of unreared *populella* and *blattariella*.

# Teleiodes sequax

| | |
|---|---|
| Gelechiidae | 35.145 *Teleiodes sequax* (Haworth, 1828) |
| Foodplant | Rock-rose (*Helianthemum* spp.). |
| Life cycle | Larva: May to June. Adult: mid-June to mid-August. |
| Distribution | Local in Great Britain. Unrecorded in Ireland. |
| | Local in VC60. Unrecorded in VC58, 59. |
| Photo details | Larval spinning from Warton Crag, Lancashire VC60; 17.05.15 (BS). |

Limited by the local nature of its foodplant, *Teleiodes sequax* is only known from VC60 within our region, where it is restricted to the limestone habitats of Morecambe Bay where common rock-rose grows.

The larva hatches in spring and feeds within spun leaves at the tip of the foodplant. As feeding progresses the spinning becomes more conspicuous with a tight, ball shaped appearance where the pale undersides of the leaves are exposed. The larva can move from one shoot to another if the initial spinning loses nutritional value.

The larva is greyish white, sometimes with a greenish tinge. The head is light brown with the prothoracic plate similarly or lighter coloured. The pinaculae are small and grey. It is important to check the larva to confirm identity as polyphagous species such as *Epiphyas postvittana*, (p.211) may make similar spinnings on rock-rose.

Other microlepidoptera that specialise on *Helianthemum* are the leaf-miners *Coleophora ochrea* and *Mompha miscella* (p.114), and the *Scythris* species *fallacella* and *crassiuscula*, both of which feed on the leaves from a silken web on the stems. Of these species only *fallacella* and *miscella* have been found in VC60.

# Mompha conturbatella

| Momphidae | 40.001 Mompha conturbatella (Hübner, [1819]) |
| Foodplant | Rosebay willowherb (*Chamerion angustifolium*). |
| Life cycle | Larva: May to June. Adult: mid-June to August. |
| Distribution | Common in Great Britain. Unrecorded in Ireland. Local in VC58, 59, 60. |
| Photo details | Larval spinning from Chorlton, Manchester VC59; 16.05.15 (BS). |

This large (wingspan 17mm) member of the Momphidae family is one of a number of the group that feed on rosebay willowherb, but is the only one that feeds within the crown. The larva of *Mompha conturbatella* tightly spins the top leaves of rosebay willowherb and feeds within. The spun leaves point upwards in line with the plant stem. There is lots of silk and frass present at the top of the spinning with the larva below. The larva may be clearly visible or may have bored downwards into the stem of the plant. The larva is light brown with a black head and black divided prothoracic plate.

One needs to be careful to rule out confusion species that may utilise spinnings on the same foodplant, and this is best done by checking larval appearance. *Celypha lacunana* is a very commonly found species, with a blackish brown larva with a large black anal plate (p.96). The spinning of *lacunana* tends to protrude at an angle from the stem rather than the vertical spinning of *conturbatella*. The green polyphagous larva of *E. postvittana* also needs to be excluded.

The adult moth can be separated from similar momphids, such as *Mompha propinquella* and *Mompha lacteella*, by virtue of its larger size, darker colouration and the ochreous-grey blotch at the base of the forewing.

# Anthophila fabriciana

| | |
|---|---|
| Choreutidae | 48.001 Nettle-tap *Anthophila fabriciana* (Linnaeus, 1767) |
| Foodplant | Nettle (*Urtica* spp.). |
| Life cycle | Larva: August to May, June to July. Adult: May to October. |
| Distribution | Common in British Isles. |
| | Common in VC58, 59, 60. |
| Photo details | Larval spinning from Gait Barrows, Lancashire VC60; 21.05.16 (BS). |

*Anthophila fabriciana* larvae feed on nettle in two or sometimes three overlapping generations. One may find feeding larvae and flying adults in the same location at the same time. Consequently feeding signs can be found in most months outside winter. Certainly larval searches in May are likely to be successful for this common species.

The species overwinters as an early instar larva before recommencing feeding in April and May. The larva feeds under a web on the upperside of a nettle leaf with the edges folded up and over to partially cover the web. Lots of frass and silk are immediately obvious. Beneath the web should be the larva of *fabriciana*, unless it has already moved on. They can switch leaves particularly if disturbed. If opening a spinning to examine the larva, do note that when disturbed the larva will move rapidly backwards wriggling from side to side as it retreats, so if opening the spinning it is wise to have a container beneath the leaf.

The larva is greyish green with large black pinaculae, black thoracic legs and plates. The prothoracic plate is clearly divided by a pale line.

The spinning should be reasonably easy to differentiate from *Pleuroptya ruralis*, which rolls the leaf around the midrib (p.93). Larval appearance should confirm identification.

# *Eudemis profundana*

Tortricidae | 49.144 *Eudemis profundana* ([Denis & Schiffermüller], 1775)
Foodplant | Oak (*Quercus* spp.).
Life cycle | Larva: May to June. Adult: July to August.
Distribution | Local in England, Wales and Ireland. Unrecorded in Scotland. Local in VC58, 59, 60.
Photo details | Larval spinning from Chorlton, Manchester VC59; 30.05.15 (BS).

In oak woodland the larva of this tortricid can be found by looking for spinnings along the midrib of fresh oak leaves in late May and early June. The edges of the leaf are rolled so as to construct quite a tight tube with the larva feeding within. Opening up the tube should reveal frass and the dull green larva. The larva has a pale brown head, a greenish prothoracic plate and small pinaculae just a little darker than the abdomen.

The greenish brown pupa is formed within the spinning or amongst the leaf litter, and in captivity was noted to remain in this stage for approximately four weeks.

The adult emerges from July onwards. It is quite an attractive moth with intricate markings. The ground colour varies from reddish brown to dark brown and is crossed by greyish fascia.

The larva of a similar species, *Eudemis porphyrana*, the only other British representative of this genus, can be found in longitudinally rolled leaves of apple, and possibly oak also. The larva is similar to *profundana* but with a black anal plate and much more conspicuous black pinaculae.

*E. porphyrana* is a moth of southern England and thus unrecorded from Lancashire and Cheshire.

Other tortricid larvae spinning oak leaves in May include *Archips podana* (p.95), *Tortricodes alternella* (p.95), *Tortrix viridana* (p.96), *Aleimma loeflingiana* and *Zeiraphera isertana*.

# Epinotia sordidana

| | |
|---|---|
| Tortricidae | 49.228 *Epinotia sordidana* (Hübner, 1824) |
| Foodplant | Alder (*Alnus glutinosa*). |
| Life cycle | Larva: May to June. Adult: August to October. |
| Distribution | Widespread and locally common in British Isles. Local in VC58, 59, 60. |
| Photo details | Larval spinning from Chorlton, Manchester VC59; 25.05.15 (BS). |

The larvae of this alder-feeding species seem to have a preference for saplings. My experience of looking for larvae of this species is that *E. sordidana* may be somewhat more common in the region than the relatively few records of adults recorded at light may suggest. This may be related to the fact that sordidana adults, unless reared, cannot be reliably identified. They are classified as Category 4 on the Micro-moth Grading Guidelines, meaning dissection is required for accurate identification (Langmaid et al, 2016). Of course dissection is not required for reared adults, known to have emerged from alder-feeding larvae. The adult moth has brown forewings with paler speckling and a poorly defined dorsal blotch.

Larval feeding begins in mid-May as small larvae feed under folds of alder leaves. As the larva develops it forms a pod by folding an alder leaf in half, sealing the edges and feeding within. Holes start to appear in this leaf as it is consumed from the inside. If required, the larva can switch to a fresh leaf.

The larva is bluish grey with dark grey pinaculae and a black head. The prothoracic plate is black also but with a fine white medial line. The anal plate and thoracic legs are also black. The larval appearance does not significantly change from mid- to late instar.

# Epinotia brunnichana

| | |
|---|---|
| Tortricidae | 40.231 *Epinotia brunnichana* (Linnaeus, 1767) |
| Foodplant | Birch (*Betula* spp.). |
| Life cycle | Larva: May to June. Adult: July to August. |
| Distribution | Widely distributed in British Isles. |
| | Common in VC58, 59, 60. |
| Photo details | Larval spinning from Chorlton, Manchester VC59; 23.05.15 (BS). |

As with *Epinotia sordidana* (p.89) this is a difficult moth to safely identify from external appearance in the adult stage, but it can be identified based on a combination of the larval feeding signs and larval appearance.

The larvae of *E. brunnichana* feed on birch leaves and make a distinctive spinning. The leaf is rolled from tip to base with the sides sealed shut as the larva feeds within.

The larva has a greyish green abdomen with dark grey pinaculae. The head is dark brown with black markings. The brown prothoracic plate is marked with black on the posterior edge.

When feeding is complete the larva leaves the habitation to pupate within a silken cocoon in the soil. The pupa is reddish brown and, like other tortricid pupae, has prominent rows of dorsal spines on most of the segments.

There are two other microlepidoptera larvae making similar spinnings on birch. However in the case of *Epinotia solandriana* and the Gelechiid *Anacampsis blattariella* (p.94), the leaf is spun into a tube from side to side along the length of the midrib. The larva of *E. solandriana* (p.96) is similar to that of *brunnichana*, but with a light brown head and prothoracic plate, and generally with less dark markings on the head and plate.

# Gypsonoma aceriana

| | |
|---|---|
| Tortricidae | 49.283 *Gypsonoma aceriana* (Duponchel, [1843]) |
| Foodplant | Black poplar (*Populus nigra*), *Populus* spp. |
| Life cycle | Larva: May to June. Adult: July to August. |
| Distribution | Locally common in England and Wales. Rare in Scotland and Ireland. Local in VC58, 59, 60. |
| Photo details | Larval spinning from Chorlton, Manchester VC59; 25.05.15 (BS). |

Quite a local species in Lancashire and Cheshire, one may with persistence and good fortune, find the feeding signs of this species on poplar, with black poplar being the likeliest host.

The larva feeds inside a poplar shoot hollowing out the centre as in the top right photo below, later, moving into one of the leaf stalks. Brown frass is expelled from the shoot into a silk-lined frass tube protruding outwards from the shoot at the base of the leaf stalk. In the shoot below, I found a 7mm dark pink mid-instar larva feeding within on 25th May. This seemed likely to be *aceriana* on the basis of foodplant, timing, larval colour and feeding signs, but was able to confirm identity as the adult emerged on July 1st.

To rear I placed a few tenanted shoots in a sealed plastic bag. A small sandwich or freezer bag is ideal for this purpose. I also added a few leaves from the foodplant, and some tissue paper to help absorb any excess moisture. In captivity the larva seemed happy enough to feed in a spinning between the leaves once the shoot had become inedible. The bag was opened every couple of days to allow air to circulate and to remove any frass, rotten plant material or early signs of mould. Occasionally a fresh leaf or two was added. By 14th of June the now pale pinkish brown larva was full-fed, and shortly after pupated amongst the spinning, with the adult emerging two weeks later.

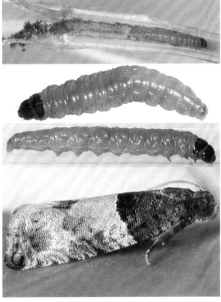

# Lathronympha strigana

| | |
|---|---|
| Tortricidae | 49.345 *Lathronympha strigana* (Fabricius, 1775) |
| Foodplant | St John's-wort (*Hypericum* spp.). |
| Life cycle | Larva: April to May, July. Adult: late May to June, August to September. |
| Distribution | Common in British Isles. |
| | Common in VC58, 59, 60. |
| Photo details | Larval spinning from Rixton, Warrington VC59; 1.05.15 (BS). |

The moth can be found wherever St John's-wort occurs, with typical habitats being woodland edges, meadows and gardens. Signs of larval habitation are very conspicuous as the larva makes a tight but untidy spinning in the upper leaves of a stem of the foodplant. The larva will eat the contents of this spinning, leading to frass becoming visible around the spinning. The shoot may also start to droop and become discoloured. The example photographed below is quite a fresh spinning and lacks this discolouration.

The larva within is pale greyish brown, sometimes appearing darker with a visible gut line. The head is orange brown and the prothoracic plate is black. The anal plate is yellow and edged with black. The orange adult emerges from the end of May onwards. In favourable seasons there can be a second generation (Bland (ed.), 2015), although in recent years this has been the norm.

A similar, but less tight, spinning on St John's-wort is made by *Agonopterix liturosa* in May and June. The larva of *liturosa* is greyish green with black pinaculae, and greenish prothoracic and anal plates. *A. liturosa* is unrecorded in VC59, with very few VC58 and VC60 records.

The other possibility to consider when examining *Hypericum* spinnings is the usual polyphagous culprit, the green larva of *Epiphyas postvittana* (p.211).

# Pleuroptya ruralis

| | |
|---|---|
| Crambidae | 63.038 Mother of Pearl *Pleuroptya ruralis* (Scopoli, 1763) |
| Foodplant | Common nettle (*Urtica dioica*). |
| Life cycle | Larva: September to June. Adult: July to early September. |
| Distribution | Common in British Isles. |
| | Common in VC58, 59, 60. |
| Photo details | Larval spinning from Chorlton, Manchester VC59; 01.06.15 (BS). |

This large (wingspan 30-40mm) member of the Crambidae family is one of the microlepidoptera least deserving of the term, being much larger than many macro-moths.

The larva feeds in spinnings on nettle, rolling the leaf around the midrib. The species overwinters as a small larva and can be found during spring wherever nettle patches occur. The spinning differs from that of *Anthophila fabriciana* where the leaf is rolled upwards enclosing a web. *Anania hortulata* larvae also spin nettle but appear later in the season (p.24).

Hop, meadowsweet and *Atriplex* spp. are rarer alternative larval foodplants for *ruralis*.

The two larval photos on the left were of the same larva on 17th May and 31st May (bottom photo).

The dark head and dark pinaculae present on the first of these images disappear by the emergence of the penultimate instar. The two larval images on the right are of the final instar photographed on 6th June. By this stage it is green all over with just a few small black markings on the head. The larva then pupates in a chamber lined with silk between the nettle leaves.

Adults emerge in July. When fresh there can be a lovely pink sheen to the wings, hence the vernacular name. There is evidence of an occasional second generation, presumably when conditions are optimum, particularly in southern England.

# A selection of larvae from May and June

16.004 *Yponomeuta cagnagella* - spindle ?9-6.
16.020 *Paraswammerdamia nebulella* - hawthorn 9-6.
17.005 *Ypsolopha scabrella* - hawthorn, apple 5-6.
17.010 *Ypsolopha parenthesella* - oak, hazel, etc. 5-6.
32.007 *Agonopterix ocellana* - willows 6-7.

32.011 *Agonopterix scopariella* - broom 6-7.
32.013 *Agonopterix carduella* - knapweed, etc. 5-7.
32.026 *Agonopterix kaekeritziana* - knapweed 5-6.
32.030 *Agonopterix nervosa* - broom, gorse, etc. 5-6.
35.012 *Anacampsis blattariella* - birch 5-6.

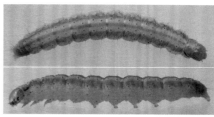

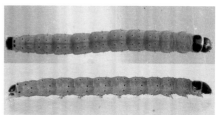

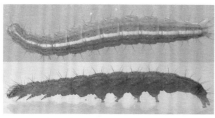

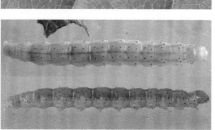

35.018 *Hypatima rhomboidella* - hazel, birch 5-6.
35.020 *Anarsia spartiella* - broom, gorse, etc. 5-6.
35.085 *Athrips mouffetella* - honeysuckle, etc. 5-6.
35.132 *Caryocolum fraternella* - stitchworts, etc. 4-5.
35.149 *Carpatolechia alburnella* - birch 5-6.

48.007 *Choreutis pariana* - apple, hawthorn, etc. 5-6,8
49.013 *Archips podana* - apple, cherry, oak, etc. 7-5.
49.022 *Ptycholoma lecheana* - sallow, lime, etc. 8-5.
49.031 *Aphelia paleana* - grasses, etc. 8-6.
49.044 *Tortricodes alternella* - oak, hornbeam, etc. 5-6

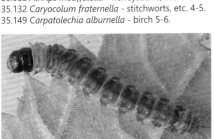
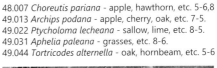

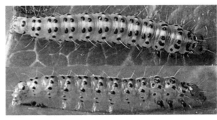

# A selection of larvae from May and June

49.050 *Cnephasia stephensiana* – dock, etc. 5-6.
49.051 *Cnephasia asseclana* - herbaceous plants 9-6.
49.059 Green Oak Tortrix *Tortrix viridana* - oak 4-6.
49.070 *Acleris rhombana* - cherry, hawthorn, etc. 4-6.
49.149 *Apotomis turbidana* - birch 5.

49.166 *Celypha lacunana* - herbaceous plants 8-6.
49.233 *Epinotia solandriana* - birch, hazel 5-6.
62.035 *Acrobasis advenella* - hawthorn, rowan 9-6.
63.033 *Udea lutealis* - thistle, knapweed, etc. 9-6.
63.057 *Evergestis forficalis* – crucifers 6-7, 9-5.

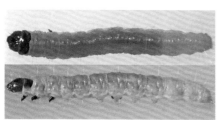

# JUNE FIELD TIPS

Whilst there are still plenty of larval spinnings to be found, they seem progressively harder to find as the month comes to an end. One exception is the conspicuous spinnings of *Acleris schalleriana*, scarce in the region, but occurring on *Viburnum* in the Morecambe Bay area of VC60 during this month.

One can also find some of the early nepticulid mines, particularly towards the second half of the month, such as *Stigmella hybnerella* on hawthorn, *S. lapponica* on birch, and *S. sorbi* on rowan. The early mines of *Incurvaria pectinea* may also be found on hazel, birch etc, usually numerous where they occur.

Look for *Coleophora* cases on uppersides of leaves, as pupation may have already occurred and adult emergence may be imminent.

| | |
|---|---|
| 98. | *Bohemannia pulverosella* |
| 99. | *Heliozela resplendella* |
| 100. | *Acrocercops brongniardella* |
| 101. | *Yponomeuta evonymella* |
| 102. | *Yponomeuta plumbella* |
| 103. | *Leucoptera spartifoliella* |
| 104. | *Agonopterix heracliana* |
| 105. | *Coleophora peribenanderi* |
| 106. | *Mompha epilobiella* |
| 107. | *Mompha langiella* |
| 108. | *Alucita hexadactyla* |
| 109. | *Oidaematophorus lithodactyla* |
| 110. | *Epermenia chaerophyllella* |
| 111. | *Rhopobota naevana* |
| 112. | *Acrobasis consociella* |
| 113. | *Anania crocealis* |

*Fletcher Moss Gardens, Didsbury, Manchester, 2nd June 2015*

# *Bohemannia pulverosella*

| | |
|---|---|
| Nepticulidae | 4.071 *Bohemannia pulverosella* (Stainton, 1849) |
| Foodplant | Apple (*Malus* spp.). |
| Life cycle | Larva: June to July. Adult: May. |
| Distribution | Common and widespread in British Isles. |
| | Common in VC58, 59, 60. |
| Photo details | Leaf-mine on apple from Flixton, Manchester VC59; 20.07.15 (BS). |

This apple leaf-miner is a representative of the Nepticulidae family. This is a large global family of tiny moths, most of which mine leaves during their larval stage. Research has recently been published with a new classification of the family based on their DNA which recognises almost 900 species worldwide, whilst noting there are probably many more species still undiscovered. A number of species only known from the occurrence of leaf-mines in fossilised leaves from around 100 million years ago were also identified (Nieukerken, EJ van ed. 2016).

As with most nepticulids, the adult moth of *B. pulverosella* is rarely encountered. It lacks any particularly distinctive markings, but its combination of orange yellow head, speckled forewings with pale cilia and lack of any transverse fascia separate it from most of the Nepticulidae. If one can identify the patch of dark scales at the apex of the underside of the forewing, then one can also rule out the similar *Trifurcula* species.

The egg is laid on either side of an apple leaf, although more commonly on the underside and usually at the leaf edge. The yellow larva initially mines a gallery, leading to a large blotch containing irregularly deposited frass. The larva then exits the leaf via the underside of the leaf, unlike *Ectoedemia atricollis* which forms a similar mine on apple but exits via the upper surface.

# Heliozela resplendella

| | |
|---|---|
| Heliozelidae | 6.004 *Heliozela resplendella* (Stainton, 1851) |
| Foodplant | Alder (*Alnus* spp.). |
| Life cycle | Larva: June to September. Adult: May to June, and occasionally July. |
| Distribution | Widespread and locally common in Great Britain. Very local in Ireland. Local in VC58, 59. Unrecorded in VC60. |
| Photo details | Leaf-mine from Chorlton, Manchester VC59; 16.06.07 (BS). |

The leaf-mines of this alder feeder can be found from June onwards. The larva mines up the midrib and down one of the veins. It then cuts across the leaf to re-enter an adjacent vein to return to the midrib. A blotch is later mined in the blade of the leaf. The larva then cuts out an oval-shaped 5mm long case, within which it falls to the ground and pupates.

One may often find aborted mines where the full mine has not been completed and the blotch and cut-out are missing. However the progress of the mine down the midrib and between two veins is still enough to allow diagnosis of this as the work of *Heliozela resplendella*. Affected leaves may also display a slight twist.

The other two *Heliozela* species can also be found locally and both are reasonably common. The larva of *Heliozela sericiella* makes a similar cut-out at the base of an oak leaf in June-July (p.114). A more obvious cut-out is formed on birch by the larva of *Heliozela hammoniella* in July-August (p.130). All the *Heliozela* species overwinter in the pupal stage with adults flying in afternoon sunshine the following spring. However a second generation of *resplendella* can occur in good years. The adult moth below emerged from its case on 8th July, just over three weeks after being located in the larval stage on 16th June (top, left).

# *Acrocercops brongniardella*

| Gracillariidae | 15.019 *Acrocercops brongniardella* (Fabricius, 1798) |
|---|---|
| Foodplant | Oak (*Quercus* spp.). |
| Life cycle | Larva: June to July, occasionally August. Adult: July to early-May. |
| Distribution | Local in England, Wales, Ireland. Absent from Scotland. |
| | Local in VC58, 59. Unrecorded from VC60. |
| Photo details | Leaf-mine from Lindow Common, Wilmslow VC58; 16.06.15 (BS). |

One of the more obvious leaf-mines is that of *Acrocercops brongniardella*. The fully developed mine is a large silvery blotch taking up much of the oak leaf. The only species to make a similar mine is the sawfly *Profenusa pygmaea*. The two can be separated by looking for the initial narrow, serpentine galleries of *brongniardella*. These are absent from the sawfly mine.

The *brongniardella* mine will usually contain a number of larvae whose initial mines fuse to form the large blotch. By holding the mine up to the light these can be seen clearly. For instance, the photo below left shows a mine tenanted by four larvae. This also shows the feeding pattern on the upperside of the leaf and the granular frass around the edge of the mine. During most of the feeding phase the larvae are pale green. However just prior to leaving the mine and up to pupation, the larvae possess vivid pink stripes.

Pupation is relatively short at 10-14 days. The adult that emerges has quite a ferocious look about it with its bright red eyes and curved, upturned palps. Its normal resting position is with the head and thorax raised up on its forelegs, as with the *Caloptilia*. However it was very difficult to photograph it in this position. I've reared quite a few of this species and I would say that when it comes to being a photographic subject, they are just about the least co-operative micro-moth!

# *Yponomeuta evonymella*

| | |
|---|---|
| Yponomeutidae | 16.001 Bird-cherry Ermine *Yponomeuta evonymella* (Linnaeus, 1758) |
| Foodplant | Bird cherry (*Prunus padus*). |
| Life cycle | Larva: Autumn to June. Adult: July to August. |
| Distribution | Widespread in British Isles. Common where the foodplant occurs. Common in VC58, 59, 60. |
| Photo details | Larval web from Chorlton, Manchester VC59; 01.06.15 (BS). |

The feeding signs of this species can be quite extreme as larval webs can occasionally engulf a whole bird cherry tree, leading to the consumption of all foliage. One example in Manchester in 2012 saw a roadside bird cherry wholly encased in silk from the tips of the branches down to ground level. The silken web extended along the kerb and onto the tyres of nearby parked cars. The tree recovered and now annually hosts *evonymella* webs of a more manageable size.

The eggs are laid in batches onto a branch in summer, with the larvae hatching and overwintering as early instars. Initial feeding is within a shoot, causing it to droop, before the larvae begin to feed gregariously in a web. The grey webs are very obvious, containing much frass, many larvae and become extended to involve more leaves.

The larvae are similar to *Y. padella* on blackthorn, hawthorn etc., *malinellus* on apple, *rorrella* on willow and *cagnagella* on spindle (p.94), all of which have a black or dark brown head. The clearest difference is that the lateral black spot on each abdominal segment is divided into two in evony-mella, but remains whole in the other four. All species feed in communal webs.

When full-fed the larvae form white, silken cocoons gregariously in the web, and pupate within.

*Y. evonymella* adults are separable from others of the genus by the large number of smaller spots.

# Yponomeuta plumbella

| | |
|---|---|
| Yponomeutidae | 16.007 *Yponomeuta plumbella* ([Denis & Schiffermüller], 1775) |
| Foodplant | Spindle (*Euonymus europaeus*). |
| Life cycle | Larva: Autumn to June. Adult: July to August. |
| Distribution | Local in England, Wales and Ireland. Absent from Scotland and N. Ireland. Local in VC59, 60. Unrecorded in VC58. |
| Photo details | Feeding signs from Gait Barrows, Lancashire VC60; 21.05.16 (BS). |

Eggs are laid on the twigs of spindle in summer and the species overwinters as a small larva below the covering of the egg. In spring each larva burrows into a developing shoot causing it to droop as in the photo below, left. The larva at this stage is only 3-4mm in length. Careful examination should reveal a small hole in the side of the shoot to allow expulsion of frass.

The larva later forms a web covering a few spindle leaves and continues to feed within for the rest of its development. The species is much less gregarious in the larval stage than others of the *Yponomeuta* genus although there may be a few larvae in each web.

The larva is quite different to the typical larvae of the genus, such as the more commonly found *Yponomeuta cagnagella* (p.94). *Y. plumbella* larvae are yellowish grey with the yellow tone being particularly intense in the thorax and in the last abdominal segments. The head is yellowish brown and the full grown larva (2nd and 3rd photos below, right) show a divided black prothoracic plate.

*Y. cagnagella* is also a spindle feeder but feeds in much larger, conspicuous webs containing large numbers of larvae and is more likely to be encountered within this region than *plumbella*.

*Y. plumbella* moths can be separated from other members of the *Yponomeuta* genus by the large black spot roughly in the middle of each forewing and the black patch at the apex of the forewing.

# Leucoptera spartifoliella

| | |
|---|---|
| Lyonetiidae | 21.005 *Leucoptera spartifoliella* (Hübner, [1813]) |
| Foodplant | Broom (*Cytisus scoparius*). |
| Life cycle | Larva: September to May. Adult: June to July. |
| Distribution | Common in Great Britain. Local in Ireland. |
| | Local in VC58, 59, 60. |
| Photo details | Pupal cocoon from Burton Mere, Wirral VC58; 31.05.16 (BS). |

The simplest way to record this species is to look on broom stems for the distinctive silken white pupal cocoon in May and June. There is more chance of successful rearing by cutting and keeping the twig bearing the cocoon. Trying to lift the cocoon from the twig risks damaging the pupa.

The life cycle of this species begins with the oviposition of oval-shaped eggs on young twigs of broom. The larva begins feeding in October by mining the broom, forming a narrow brown mine, usually progressing upwards. As the larva develops the mine becomes greyish and fills the width of the broom twig although remaining relatively superficial.

Separating this species from the virtually identical mine of *Trifurcula immundella* (p.40) can be done by looking for the black egg of *immundella* at the start of the mine. If careful examination of the mine definitely reveals no egg then *spartifoliella* is probable, as the egg falls off the twig shortly after hatching, whereas that of *immundella* stays attached. Examination of the larva is advised to confirm identification. The larval images below show the dark head and the dark markings on the prothoracic plate. The lower larval photo shows the ventral chain of dark spots.

Other *Leucoptera* found locally are *laburnella*, mining laburnum in June & Sept (p.186), and *malifoliella* on hawthorn and apple (p.176).

# Agonopterix heracliana

Depressariidae       32.018 *Agonopterix heracliana* (Linnaeus, 1758)
Foodplant            Cow parsley (*Anthriscus sylvestris*) and many other umbellifers.
Life cycle           Larva: May to early August. Adult: late July to May.
Distribution         Common throughout the British Isles.
                     Common in VC58, 59, 60.
Photo details        Feeding signs from Chorlton, Manchester VC59; 03.06.15 (BS).

The larvae of this Depressariid will feed on many species of Apiaceae, such as hogweed, angelica, pignut and wild carrot, but most commonly found in spinnings on cow parsley.

One may find a number of larvae on the same leaf, with each tenanting an individual leaflet, rolling it into a tube and venturing out to feed on the leaflet. The larva will form a number of similar tubes during the course of its development.

The larva is green throughout its instars although it takes on a pinkish hue in the pre-pupal stage. It has a yellowish green head with a small black dot on both sides, and small black pinaculae. The body has a dark green dorsal line, either side of which is a dark green dorso-lateral line. These lines are faded by the time the larva reaches the final instar. This is an easy species to rear and will pupate in dry soil or within spun leaves.

The larva is similar to *A. ciliella*, which also feeds on a wide range of Apiaceae. Unlike *heracliana*, the *ciliella* larval head is black or brown with extensive black markings laterally on the prothoracic plate. The adults are very similar and may require dissection to separate. Generally *ciliella* is pinkish underneath and the hindwing bears five distinct ciliary lines, whereas there may be only two or three indistinct lines in *heracliana* (Emmet and Langmaid, ed., 2002).

# Coleophora peribenanderi

| | |
|---|---|
| Coleophoridae | 37.093 *Coleophora peribenanderi* Toll, 1943 |
| Foodplant | Thistles (*Carduus* and *Cirsium* spp.) and burdock (*Arctium* spp.). |
| Life cycle | Larva: August to June. Adult: mid-June to mid-August. |
| Distribution | Common in England and Wales. Rare in Scotland and Ireland. Common in VC58, 59, 60. |
| Photo details | Larval case from Chorlton, Manchester VC59; 20.06.09 (BS). |

The case-bearing larvae of *Coleophora peribenanderi* can be encountered by looking for the whitish blotches on thistle and knapweed leaves resulting from larval leaf-mining activity. Look on the underside for the cases, and compare any cases found to this species and the black cases of *Coleophora paripennella* (p.69). As with most of the genus, successful rearing is more likely if the larva can be kept outside on some potted foodplant covered with fine netting.

After hatching in August, the larva mines a blotch, constructing the case from this section of the leaf. As the larva feeds, the ochreous case is extended lengthways and later widthways.

Larval development varies, and cases of differing size may be found on the same plant. Some larvae are full-fed before winter whereas others continue to feed until June, and if so should certainly be in their final instar at this time of year. The case on the left was found as late as 20th June, whereas the larva on the right was photographed on 14th June 2015.

The larva is whitish green (although sometimes with a yellowish tinge as with the individual photographed below), with a brown head and a large, black, medially divided prothoracic plate. There are four dorsal, black sclerites on the 2nd thoracic segment, and two small dorsal sclerites on the 3rd segment. The pale brown thoracic legs are black-banded.

# Mompha epilobiella

| | |
|---|---|
| Momphidae | 40.010 *Mompha epilobiella* ([Denis & Schiffermüller], 1775) |
| Foodplant | Great willowherb (*Epilobium hirsutum*). |
| Life cycle | Larva: mid-May-June, July-early August. Adult: July-August, Sept.-June. |
| Distribution | Common in England and Wales. Local in Scotland and Ireland. Common in VC58, 59, 60. |
| Photo details | Feeding signs from Chorlton, Manchester VC59; 03.07.16 (BS). |

The easiest way to record this species is to look for the frass-filled spinnings in the shoots of great willowherb plants. These can be very common, particularly in damp habitats. Just to be certain of the identity it is best to open the spinning and look for the black-headed creamy yellow larva. Towards the end of June one may find that instead of the larva, one discovers the black pupa within a white, silken cocoon hidden in the spun shoot. Potting the pupa should result in the emergence of an adult *epilobiella* within a couple of weeks.

*Mompha epilobiella* larvae have also been recorded on evening primrose, broad-leaved willowherb and marsh willowherb.

The adult moths are easily disturbed from vegetation during the day, and may be found flying around the foodplants. The adults are also attracted to light.

The species is bivoltine with adults in summer and again in autumn. The second generation over-winter and may occasionally be found indoors during the winter months.

The other momphids feeding on *Epilobium hirsutum* are *langiella* (p.107), *bradleyi* (p.139), *ochra-ceella* and *propinquella*. The latter two mine the lower leaves of the foodplant in spring. The *ochra-ceella* larva is yellowish white, whereas the *propinquella* larva is brown with a black head.

# Mompha langiella

| | |
|---|---|
| Momphidae | 40.011 *Mompha langiella* (Hübner, 1796) |
| Foodplant | Enchanter's-nightshade (*Circaea lutetiana*), great willowherb (*Epilobium hirsutum*). Occasionally on other willowherbs. |
| Life cycle | Larva: June to July. Adult: August to April. |
| Distribution | Local in England and Wales. Scarce in Scotland and Ireland. Local in VC58, 59, 60. |
| Photo details | Leaf-mine from Didsbury, Manchester VC59; 14.06.15 (BS). |

In the last century this momphid was unrecorded in Lancashire and Cheshire other than a single 1984 VC59 record. Since the first VC58 record at Petty Pool, Cheshire in 2007, the moth has been spreading through the region. 2015 saw the first record of this species from VC60 at Torrisholme.

By looking for the leaf-mines, I have found the species to be common in south Manchester on enchanter's-nightshade and on great willowherb, particularly in damp, shady habitats.

Initial feeding is in a small blotch or gallery, later making large pale blotches with widely dispersed frass. The larva is pale yellow with a green gut line, and has a dark prothoracic plate and head. Mines may merge with larvae feeding gregariously, as in the photo below.

The only other lepidopterous leaf-miner of enchanter's-nightshade is *Mompha terminella* (p.140). The initial convoluted mines of *terminella* are followed by clear mines with the frass deposited in a line and containing a larva with a pale brown head and prothoracic plate.

When full-fed, the *langiella* larva may leave its mine and re-enter a leaf, pupating within. More usually the white pupal cocoon is spun on detritus. The adult is relatively plain although the white markings may be more extensive than shown. It is easily disturbed during the day.

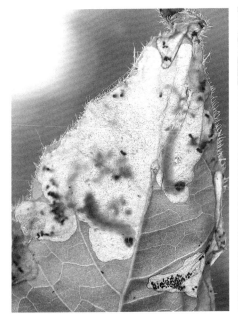

# Alucita hexadactyla

| | |
|---|---|
| Alucitidae | 44.001 Twenty-plume Moth *Alucita hexadactyla* Linnaeus, 1758 |
| Foodplant | Honeysuckle (*Lonicera periclymenum*). |
| Life cycle | Larva: June to July. Adult: July to early June. |
| Distribution | Common throughout Great Britain. |
| | Common in VC58, 59, 60. |
| Photo details | Feeding signs from Chorlton, Manchester VC59; 21.06.15 (BS). |

The early stages of this species, the sole British representative of the Alucitidae, are best looked for by searching for the discoloured buds of honeysuckle flowers. These buds contain small round holes made as the larva moves around, consuming a number of such buds during its development. The greyish discolouration is the result of frass being deposited within the buds. The larva is more likely to still be present if one examines an unopened bud containing a small amount of frass.

Earlier in the life cycle, eggs are laid at the base of the flowers in May. These are initially white, but quickly turn yellow and then become orange prior to hatching (Hart, 2011).

The larva is greyish-white with no obvious markings. The head and prothoracic plate are pale brown. Thoracic legs and prolegs are concolourous with the abdomen. The larva becomes pink prior to pupation, which is within a light brown netted silken cocoon.

The moth is unique amongst our lepidopterous fauna in its appearance with each wing divided into six plumes, giving it a feathered appearance. One may potentially be fooled when encountering a moth with its wings closed, superficially giving it the appearance of one of the *Scoparia* or *Eudonia* moths of the Crambidae family.

The moth overwinters and can be found indoors, sometimes flying on mild winter days.

# *Oidaematophorus lithodactyla*

| | |
|---|---|
| Pterophoridae | 45.037 *Oidaematophorus lithodactyla* (Linnaeus, 1758) |
| Foodplant | Fleabane (*Pulicaria dysenterica*), ploughman's spikenard (*Inula conyza*). |
| Life cycle | Larva: mid-April to mid-July. Adult: July and August. |
| Distribution | Widely distributed in England. Local in Wales and Ireland. Local in VC58, 59, 60. |
| Photo details | Larval feeding from Rixton, Warrington VC59; 10.06.15 (BS). |

The feeding signs of this plume larva are quite easy to spot as it feeds on the upperside of a leaf of fleabane, the normal foodplant of the species in its northern range. Typical habitat is in damp woodland and along riverbanks where the plant may be found.

The larva makes numerous holes in the leaf, generally avoiding the edges, the midrib and the larger veins, giving the leaves a distinctive lace-like appearance.

The early instar larva is pale green. As it enters its final instar the larva becomes purplish red dorsally. The larva is covered with long setae at all stages.

The pupa shares similar colouration to the larva, as can be seen from the photos below right, and is also covered in long setae (rigid hair-like structures). Hart (2011) noted that pupal colouration varied according to pupation site, so that a pupa tends to be green when found on fresh leaves, and brownish if found on dead leaves of the foodplant.

The species is quite easy to rear, especially from the final instar. Just keep the larva in an air-tight container, removing frass and dead leaves every couple of days. Add the occasional fresh leaf. Pupation is relatively brief at 2-3 weeks before the adult emerges. The adult is greyish brown with a diagonal line crossing the relatively broad forewings from the dark mark on the costa.

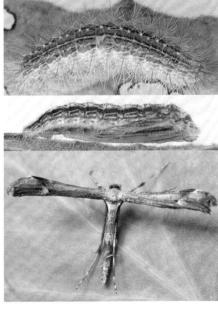

# Epermenia chaerophyllella

| | |
|---|---|
| Epermeniidae | 47.005 *Epermenia chaerophyllella* (Goeze, 1783) |
| Foodplant | Hogweed (*Heracleum sphondylium*), angelica (*Angelica sylvestris*), etc. |
| Life cycle | Larva: mid-May to September. Adult: October to May, July to August. |
| Distribution | Widespread throughout the British Isles. Common in VC58 59, 60. |
| Photo details | Feeding signs from Chorlton, Manchester VC59; 30.06.15 (BS). |

This species has 2 or 3 generations, and is found in gardens, woods, meadows and hedgerows.

The early stages of *Epermenia chaerophyllella* can be recorded by looking for feeding signs on hogweed, angelica and other umbellifers. Initially the larvae feed as leaf-miners, later feeding externally and gregariously on the underside of the leaf in a slight web. This results in brown patches appearing on the upperside of the affected leaves, making the larval presence obvious.

The larvae feeding externally are yellowish white with large dark pinaculae, a pale brown head and black thoracic legs. It also has quite a glossy appearance.

When full-fed the larvae pupate in a netted cocoon. This can be on detritus or on the underside of the umbellifer leaf close to the midrib, as in the photo below left. These two pupae were found in the wild beneath the hogweed leaf pictured below left.

The resultant adult is quite distinctive, especially in Lancashire and Cheshire where it is the only member of the genus *Epermenia* to have been recorded. The other British *Epermenia* are *E. insecurella* (feeding on bastard-toadflax), *E. aequidentellus* (feeding on wild carrot and burnet-saxifrage) and *E. falciformis* (feeding on wild angelica and ground-elder). All are species of southern England, although the latter is also found in the Midlands and in Wales.

# *Rhopobota naevana*

| | |
|---|---|
| Tortricidae | 49.223 Holly Tortrix *Rhopobota naevana* (Hübner, [1817]) |
| Foodplant | Holly (*Ilex aquifolium*), bilberry (*Vaccinium myrtillus*), etc. |
| Life cycle | Larva: May to June. Adult: late June to early September. |
| Distribution | Common throughout the British Isles. |
| | Common in VC58, 59, 60. |
| Photo details | Feeding signs from Lindow Common, Wilmslow VC58; 13.06.16 (BS). |

The larval stage of this tortricid can be found within spinnings on holly as it tightly draws together the terminal shoots in May and June. Silk and frass can be obvious, as in the photos below. Rowan, blackthorn, hawthorn, apple, pear, bilberry and heather are all alternative foodplants for *naevana*, although their spinnings may be a little harder to detect. The larvae may be found in gardens, hedgerows, woodland and moorland with foodplants varying depending on habitat. (Bland (ed.), 2015) state that the feeding of *Rhopobota naevana* larvae on heather can cause sufficient damage to be troublesome on grouse moors, citing Dunn's report on a County Durham epidemic (1991).

The larva varies from greenish to yellow brown. The head and prothoracic plate are black. The anal plate in the final instar is concolourous with the abdomen (2nd and 3rd photos, right). Earlier instars are similarly coloured but with a dark anal plate, as in the penultimate instar larva below (top, right). Pupation is either within the spinning or in a cocoon amongst the leaf litter.

The adult has very variable markings but usually with a greyish band across the forewings. It also has quite a distinctive shape when at rest. The forewing is extended to form a lobe at the apex, with a notch below at the termen. There is also an obvious crease in the wing from the apex.

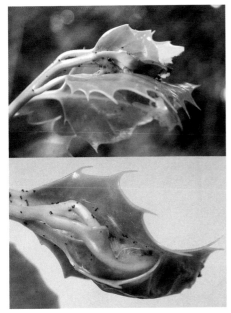

# Acrobasis consociella

| | |
|---|---|
| Pyralidae | 62.038 *Acrobasis consociella* (Hübner, [1813]) |
| Foodplant | Oak (*Quercus* spp.). |
| Life cycle | Larva: September to June. Adult: July and August. |
| Distribution | Locally common in England, Wales, Ireland. No recent Scottish records. Local in VC58, 59, 60. |
| Photo details | Spinning on oak from Lindow Common, Wilmslow VC58; 16.06.15 (BS). |

The larvae of this pyralid can best be detected by looking for bunches of oak leaves spun together with lots of silk in May and June. The species has a preference for the leaves of saplings.

However the first signs of larval presence can be found in autumn when the young larvae feed gregariously upon a single oak leaf as in the photos below left. The upperside of the leaf becomes discoloured due to the many larvae feeding on the lower epidermis. Examination of the underside of the leaf reveals masses of frass covered silken tubes, each belonging to a larva and serving as protection. As the larvae develop a few leaves are spun together and overwintering is within the feeding tubes in this spinning.

As the new leaves appear in spring a larger spinning is made encompassing a mass of leaves. Pale patches on the leaves are evidence of larval feeding.

The larvae on the right show, from the top, an overwintered larva in early April, then one from the end of April. The two larval photos below that show a final instar larva from the large spinning on 16.6.15. The final instar is greyish with dorsal, sub-dorsal and lateral brown stripes, an orange brown head, anal plate and prothoracic plate. The plates are speckled with black spots.

The moth is greyish, although sometimes has a purple tinge, particularly when newly emerged.

# Anania crocealis

| | |
|---|---|
| Crambidae | 63.022 *Anania crocealis* (Hübner, 1796) |
| Foodplant | Fleabane (*Pulicaria dysenterica*), ploughman's-spikenard (*Inula conyza*). |
| Life cycle | Larva: October to June. Adult: mid-June to mid-August. |
| Distribution | Common in southern England. Local in the rest of the British Isles. Local in VC58, 59, 60. |
| Photo details | Larval feeding from Rixton, Warrington VC59; 08.06.15 (BS). |

The same patches of fleabane that hold populations of *Oidaematophorus lithodactyla* (p.109) can also be productive places to look for the larva of *Anania crocealis*. The larva is yellowish green with a dark green dorsal stripe and black pinaculae. Thoracic legs are pale brown. The anal plate is greenish white and speckled with small black spots. The head is black, and the green prothoracic plate is extensively marked laterally with black.

The larva can be found in the shoots of fresh fleabane growth in late spring feeding in the heart of the plant. The affected plant is clearly twisted and deformed and further examination will show silk, frass and partially eaten leaves. Opening up the shoot should reveal the distinctive larva.

The dark brown pupa is formed in a cocoon amongst the leaves. The adult below emerged after a fourteen day pupation period. The adult is yellowish ochreous with two distinctively shaped crosslines, and greyish white hindwings. It can be disturbed from the foodplant during the day.

Recent taxonomic changes have moved this species from *Ebulea* to *Anania*, which is now a genus of ten species. The other species found locally are *A. fuscalis* on yellow rattle, *A. perlucidalis* on thistle, *A. terrealis* and *A. funebris* on goldenrod, and the Small Magpie *A. hortulata* (p.24) on nettle, bindweed and woundwort. *Anania coronata*, feeding on elder, is discussed on p.166.

# A selection of leaf-mines from June and July

2.001 *Dyseriocrania subpurpurella* - oak 5-7.
4.023 *Stigmella crataegella* - hawthorn 6-8.
4.041 *Stigmella sorbi* - rowan 6-7.
4.042 *Stigmella plagicolella* - blackthorn, etc. 7, 9-10.
4.056 *Stigmella speciosa* - sycamore 7-8, 9-10.

6.003 *Heliozela sericiella* - oak 6-7.
8.001 *Incurvaria pectinea* - hazel etc 6-9. (R.Edmunds)
15.089 *Cameraria ohridella* - horse chestnut 6-11.
35.035 *Chrysoesthia drurella* - orache, etc. 7-8, 9-5.
40.012 *Mompha miscella* - rock-rose 7, 10-4.

 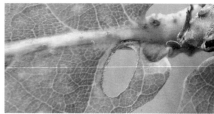

 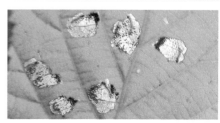

 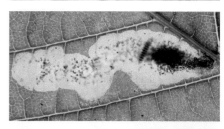

 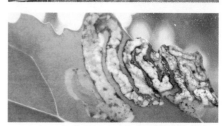

# JULY FIELD TIPS

Whilst July is a month when adult moths are in abundance, the early stages can be harder to find than in the spring months.

Larvae feeding within spinnings are particularly difficult to track down, although leaf-mines start to appear in number, particularly of the *Phyllonorycter* species and the bivoltine nept-iculids. These may not be quite as numerous as the autumn generation, but they do have the advantage of being relatively quick and easy to rear through.

As *Phyllonorycter* species pupate within the mine, collecting a few of these leaves often results in the appearance of a nice, fresh adult within a day or two. The nepticulid mines will need to be collected when the larva is present and so will take longer for adult emergence.

116. *Stigmella nylandriella*
117. *Ectoedemia louisella*
118. *Caloptilia cuculipennella*
119. *Callisto denticulella*
120. *Phyllonorycter corylifoliella*
121. *Phyllocnistis unipunctella*
122. *Lyonetia clerkella*
123. *Diurnea fagella*
124. *Coleophora striatipennella*
125. *Mompha subbistrigella*
126. *Mompha raschkiella*
127. *Stenoptilia zophodactylus*
128. *Prochoreutis myllerana*
129. *Acleris sparsana*

*Dunham Massey, Altrincham, Cheshire, 28 July 2016*

# Stigmella nylandriella

| Nepticulidae | 4.025 *Stigmella nylandriella* (Tengström, 1848) |
| --- | --- |
| Foodplant | Rowan (*Sorbus aucuparia*). |
| Life cycle | Larva: July to August. Adult: May to June. |
| Distribution | Widespread throughout British Isles. |
| | Common in VC58, 59, 60. |
| Photo details | Leaf-mine from Chorlton, Manchester VC59; 19.07.15 (BS). |

The bright green larva of this nepticulid makes an attractive gallery mine on rowan in summer. Typically this begins with a fine frass line in a slender mine, progressing from the egg site on the underside towards the leaf edge. The mine then follows the jagged edge of the rowan leaf, with the brown frass laid down in arcs giving quite a wide frass line. As feeding progresses, the gallery widens, sometimes forming a false blotch as the loops of the mine coalesce.

Not all *nylandriella* mines keep to the leaf-edge (below, right), but in these cases the relatively wide gallery and arced frass help to confirm the species is this rather than that of *Stigmella magdalenae* (p.168). The green larva of the latter species also mines rowan, but with a shorter mine containing fine, linear frass, and is far less commonly found.

When full-fed, the *nylandriella* larva leaves the mine, spinning a reddish brown oval-shaped cocoon on the detritus and dead leaves beneath the tree.

To rear, it is preferable to keep the cocoons outside in a netted pot due to the long pupal period.

Green larvae are occasionally found on rowan in September and October. It is at present unclear whether these represent a partial second generation of *nylandriella*, a delayed first generation, or even whether they may possibly be *Stigmella oxyacanthella* (p.150).

# Ectoedemia louisella

| | |
|---|---|
| Nepticulidae | 4.075 *Ectoedemia louisella* (Sircom, 1849) |
| Foodplant | Field maple (*Acer campestre*). |
| Life cycle | Larva: June to October. Adult: April to September. In 3 generations. |
| Distribution | Local in southern England and Wales. Unrecorded in Scotland and Ireland. Local in VC58, 59. Unrecorded in VC60. |
| Photo details | Mines from Chorlton, Manchester VC59; 19.07.15 (BS). |

The feeding signs of this tiny moth can be found on the keys of the field maple. The egg is laid on a wing of the key. After hatching, the larva mines towards the seed leaving a dark brown gallery as in the photos below. On reaching the seed, the larva feeds within, hollowing out the seed. When feeding is complete, the larva of the summer generation leaves the seed to form its orange cocoon, often on the wing of another key, rather than the one on which it fed.

The species has two or three generations. Larvae found in autumn hibernate after feeding, and then climb the trunks in spring to spin a cocoon on the bark.

Two other *Ectoedemia* moths with similar lifecycles can be found on *Acer* species. *Ectoedemia decentella* larvae mine the keys of sycamore (*Acer pseudoplatanus*), whereas the larvae of *Ectoedemia sericopeza* mine the keys of norway maple (*Acer platanoides*). Like *louisella*, these two species are (at least) bivoltine.

The moths do occasionally turn up at light. The easiest of the three to identify is *Ectoedemia decentella*, which is distinctive with its black head, white thorax, and extensive white patches at the base of the forewings. *E. louisella* and *sericopeza* on the other hand are very difficult to separate unless reared and any that turn up at light are not safely identifiable unless dissected.

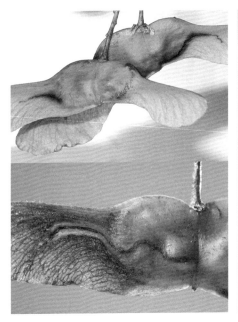 

# *Caloptilia cuculipennella*

| Gracillariidae | 15.002 *Caloptilia cuculipennella* (Hübner, 1796) |
| --- | --- |
| Foodplant | Ash (*Fraxinus excelsior*), wild privet (*Ligustrum vulgare*). |
| Life cycle | Larva: July to August. Adult: September to May. |
| Distribution | Scattered locally throughout Great Britain and Ireland. Local in VC60. Unrecorded in VC58, 59. |
| Photo details | Feeding signs on ash from Gait Barrows, Lancashire VC60; 08.08.16 (BS). |

This is one of two similar species that can be found on ash and privet. The other is *Gracillaria syringella* (p.193) which makes brownish mines on the foodplants, followed by an untidy, discoloured leaf-roll or cone with lots of frass deposited around the rolled leaf.

In contrast, the feeding signs of the scarcer *Caloptilia cuculipennella* are much cleaner, with less frass evident and much less discolouration of the leaf.

The early mine is evidenced by a silvery gallery in the upper epidermis around the perimeter of the leaf, causing the edge to fold up and over itself and obscure the mine, as in the top left photo below.

After leaving the mine, the larva rolls a pair of successive cones in a fresh leaf and feeds within. The leaf is rolled downwards at an angle thus creating the cone seen in the photo below.

When feeding is complete, the larva chews a small hole in the leaf at the base of the cone allowing the pupa to project through this hole just prior to adult emergence. Pupation occurs within the final cone in a distinctive white spindle-shaped cocoon. This cocoon is another feature helping to separate the early stages of this species from *syringella*.

The moth is generally scarce in our region although possibly under recorded.

# Callisto denticulella

| | |
|---|---|
| Gracillariidae | 15.022 *Callisto denticulella* (Thunberg, 1794) |
| Foodplant | Apple (*Malus* spp.). |
| Life cycle | Larva: July to August. Adult: May to June. |
| Distribution | Widespread throughout British Isles. Common in England and Wales. Common in VC58, 59, 60. |
| Photo details | Feeding signs on apple from Chorlton, Manchester VC59; 05.08.15 (BS). |

The first sign of the early stages of this moth is the appearance of a fine upper epidermal gallery with a reddish brown line of frass. As the larva feeds, this initial gallery is developed into an orange blotch with a silvery edge on the upper surface of the leaves of wild or cultivated apple trees. The blotch is a little similar to that produced by the larva of *Phyllonorycter corylifoliella* (p.120), a species that feeds on apple as well as hawthorn and other rosaceous trees. However it lacks the brown speckling of the *corylifoliella* mine.

The larva then vacates the mine to feed within a fold of the leaf, sometimes on the same leaf as the initial mine. The edge of the leaf is folded downwards and the larva feeds on the leaf within, causing browning of the upper epidermis on the upper and lower aspects of the fold. It makes two successive folds before it is full-fed.

The larva is greenish yellow with a dark brown head. There is a pair of fairly obscure brown marks on the prothoracic plate. When feeding is complete, the larva descends to the ground and spins a brown cocoon amongst the leaf litter, pupating within and overwintering in this stage.

When rearing, it is ideal to keep the cocoon outside over winter. Place with some leaves in a small yoghurt pot enclosed in stocking material, secured at both ends, and tied in a sheltered spot.

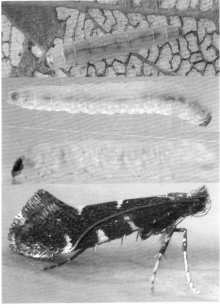

# Phyllonorycter corylifoliella

Gracillariidae  15.052 *Phyllonorycter corylifoliella* (Hübner, 1796)
Foodplant  Hawthorn (*Crataegus* spp.), apple (*Malus* spp.), *Sorbus* spp., etc.
Life cycle  Larva: July and September to October. Adult: May to June and August.
Distribution  Widespread throughout British Isles.
Common in VC58, 59, 60.
Photo details  Leaf-mine on hawthorn from Rixton, Warrington VC59; 08.07.09 (BS).

The feeding signs of this species are somewhat similar to the previous species, *Callisto denticulella*. Both produce a silvery upperside mine with an orange brown tint. The other possible confusion species for the *corylifoliella* mine is *Phyllonorycter leucographella*, a somewhat polyphagous close relative that produces a white papery mine on the upperside of leaves of *Pyracantha* and rosaceous plants (p.29)

The leaf-mine of *P. corylifoliella* is distinguished from both of these by a number of features. The well-developed mine contains brown speckling within, as the frass is laid down in roughly circular patterns. The mine itself is actually a double mine. If one looks at the well-developed mine in the top left photo, one can see the initial mine at the centre. The mine will usually be formed over the midrib or major vein of the leaf, causing the leaf edges to contract upwards. The larva within is yellow with a dark brown head.

The adult photographed emerged on 6th August from a well developed mine found on hawthorn on 25th July. No special care was needed because of the short pupation time, and the larva was simply kept in an airtight pot. If attempting to rear one of the autumn mines, one is more likely to be successful if keeping the leaves in a netted pot over winter in a sheltered location.

# Phyllocnistis unipunctella

| | |
|---|---|
| Gracillariidae | 15.092 *Phyllocnistis unipunctella* (Stephens, 1834) |
| Foodplant | Black poplar (*Populus nigra*), lombardy poplar (*P. nigra* var. *italica*). |
| Life cycle | Larva: April to September. Adult: June to September. In 2-3 generations. |
| Distribution | Widespread throughout British Isles. Common in England and Wales. Common in VC58, 59, 60. |
| Photo details | Feeding signs from Chorlton, Manchester VC59; 14.07.15 (BS). |

Although the adults are superficially similar to the *Phyllonorycter* species, the early stages of the *Phyllocnistis* species are very different. The larva is extremely flattened, lacks thoracic legs and prolegs, and has a long tubular posterior abdominal segment. *Phyllocnistis* larvae are highly specialised with mouthparts adapted for sap-feeding. The first three instars mine the leaf (or stem in some species), creating a silvery serpentine sub-epidermal gallery, similar to a 'snail trail'. The fourth instar larva lacks feeding mouthparts and functions simply to spin a cocoon under a small fold at the leaf-edge within which it pupates.

*Phyllocnistis unipunctella* mines can be extremely common on black poplar, with larvae mining on either side of the leaf although upperside mines are normally the more frequent.

Jordan, Langmaid and Doorenweerd (2016) have described how the phenology of this species seems to have changed, so that larvae have been recorded feeding as early as April, and in three generations rather than the previously recognised two. These findings were made in southern England and in the Netherlands. It was also noted that the dark prothoracic plate found on larvae mining the upperside of the leaf, was colourless in those larvae mining the underside of the leaf. Examples of both are illustrated below from mines found in VC59.

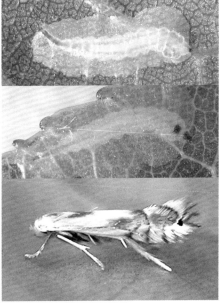

# Lyonetia clerkella

| Lyonetiidae | 21.001 *Lyonetia clerkella* (Linnaeus, 1758) |
| Foodplant | Apple (*Malus* spp.), birch (*Betula* spp.), hawthorn (*Crataegus* spp.), etc. |
| Life cycle | Larva: May, July, September-October. Adult: June, August, October-April. |
| Distribution | Common throughout Great Britain and Ireland. |
| | Common in VC58, 59, 60. |
| Photo details | Leaf-mine on hawthorn from Chorlton, Manchester VC59; 17.07.15 (BS). |

Perhaps the easiest leaf-miner of all to locate, with the possible exception of *Stigmella aurella*, this species can be exceedingly common and can be found on a very wide variety of foodplants. In addition to those listed above, the mines can also be found on cherry, blackthorn, rowan, whitebeam and cotoneaster.

The larva makes a long, narrow gallery curving around the leaf. The frass is laid down in a central line, broken in places. The larva is grey green with clearly marked segments. The thoracic legs are clearly visible in the mine, immediately distinguishing this from any nepticulid leaf-miners. There may be many mines on a single leaf, often including a high number of aborted mines.

The pupal stage takes place in a delicate white silken cocoon, usually suspended below the leaf by silken threads. There will usually be two of these threads at each end of the cocoon.

The adult is commonly attracted to light, and so is familiar to anyone who has tried to identify the micros attracted to a light-trap. The typical form is pictured. There is also a dark form with forewings of dark brown, although the dark spot and the black lines in the terminal cilia remain.

A similar species, *Lyonetia prunifoliella*, may also be found mining rosaceous trees with a gallery leading to a blotch. At present it is restricted to a few sites in southern England.

# Diurnea fagella

Chimabachidae 29.001 *Diurnea fagella* ([Denis & Schiffermüller], 1775)
Foodplant Oak (*Quercus* spp.), beech (*Fagus*), hazel (*Corylus*), sallow (*Salix*) etc.
Life cycle Larva: June to October. Adult: March to early May.
Distribution Common throughout Great Britain.
Common in VC58, 59, 60.
Photo details Feeding signs from Lindow Common, Wilmslow VC58; 21.06.16. (BS).

The larva of this species is quite a slow feeder, and its development may take three months or more. The larva is common on oak, but also utilises many other tree species. It feeds between two leaves, one spun flatly over the other, with larval feeding resulting in bare patches on the surface of the upper leaf. Early instars have a black head and prothoracic plate, giving way to the pale plate and yellowish orange head of the final instar larva.

*Diurnea* larvae on oak can be immediately identified to genus level by the presence of the swollen third pair of thoracic legs, a little like a pair of boxing gloves. The only other British species with these swollen legs is *Dasystoma salicella* (feeding mainly on sallow and bog myrtle), which has a black head with dark plates and thoracic legs. The other *Diurnea* species, *D. lipsiella*, feeds mainly on oak, but occasionally on aspen and lime, from June to early August. The larva can be separated with care from *D. fagella* by its darker brown head, but is very similar in appearance.

The species overwinters as a pupa. Pupation usually occurs within a silken cocoon amongst the leaf-litter, although I have also found a pupa in a folded leaf edge on sweet chestnut in November.

The adult is sexually dimorphic, with the female having very short, pointed wings, and the male being fully winged. Forewing colour varies from pale grey to almost black.

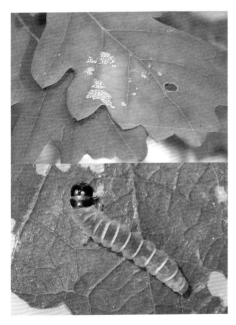
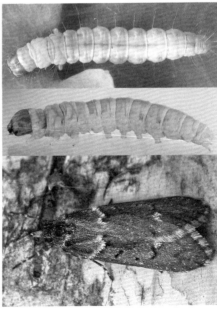

# Coleophora striatipennella

| | |
|---|---|
| Coleophoridae | 37.099 *Coleophora striatipennella* Nylander [1848] |
| Foodplant | Common mouse-ear (*Cerastium fontanum*), lesser stitchwort (*Stellaria graminea*), common chickweed (*S. media*). |
| Life cycle | Larva: July to October. Adult: June to July. |
| Distribution | Widespread throughout British Isles. Common in VC58, 59, 60. |
| Photo details | Feeding signs from Chorlton, Manchester VC59; 15.08.15 (BS). |

Almost all the UK Coleophoridae larvae feed from within a protective silken case, usually constructed, at least partially, with material from their foodplant. The larva moves around the foodplant and later to its pupation site, carrying the case with it. The early instar *Coleophora* larva typically has no case, often feeding on seeds, within a flower or within a leaf-mine.

The early instar larva of *C. striatipennella* feeds on seeds from within the flower capsule, before constructing a silken case decorated with fragments of plant material and frass. The case is cream coloured and can be found protruding from the flower-head of mouse-ear and similar species, as in the photos below. Cases can be found from late July onwards, wherever the foodplants occur.

Many of the *Coleophora* larvae require exposure to the elements to ensure successful emergence. For this reason, it is best to keep them outside over winter with some plant material in a netted pot. The adult of this species was reared by leaving the cases and plant material in a small yoghurt pot, enclosed in stocking material and tied at each end, with one end secured to the lower branch of a thick shrub, providing some protection from the worst of the weather.

The adult is white with buff streaks, and is not identifiable without dissection, unless reared.

# *Mompha subbistrigella*

| | |
|---|---|
| Momphidae | 40.008 *Mompha subbistrigella* (Haworth, 1828) |
| Foodplant | Broad-leaved willowherb (*Epilobium montanum*), other willowherbs. |
| Life cycle | Larva: July to August. Adult: July to June. |
| Distribution | Common in England and Wales. Local in Scotland and Ireland. Common in VC58, 59, 60. |
| Photo details | Feeding signs from Chorlton, Manchester VC59; 05.07.15 (BS). |

The moth is quite a common sight and can often be found indoors in the winter period as, like the majority of *Mompha* species, it hibernates as an adult. (The known exceptions to the overwintering of Momphidae adults are *M. terminella, conturbatella, raschkiella, ochraceella* and *miscella*).

The forewing is dark greyish brown with two bars crossing the wings, roughly separating the forewing into thirds. The wingspan is 7-11mm. A similar but less common species, *Mompha sturnipennella*, is a little larger with wingspan 9-13mm and has white costal streaks in the apical area, although these can be difficult to see at times.

The eggs of *M. subbistrigella* are laid on some of the smaller willowherb species. The larva feeds within the seedpod and eats the developing seeds, replacing them with frass, as in the picture on the top right. The larval presence causes the seedpod to bend, and in extreme cases to curl up, making tenanted pods quite obvious amongst the straight seedpods. Careful examination will also reveal a hole in the side of the pod. The larva is whitish yellow, becoming pink as feeding nears completion. It then leaves the seedpod prior to pupation and forms a white cocoon amongst the leaf litter. Emergence occurs from August onwards after a pupation period of 3-4 weeks.

# Mompha raschkiella

| | |
|---|---|
| Momphidae | 40.015 *Mompha raschkiella* (Zeller, 1839) |
| Foodplant | Rosebay willowherb (*Chamerion angustifolium*). |
| Life cycle | Larva: May to September. Adult: May to October. In two generations. |
| Distribution | Common throughout British Isles. |
| | Common in VC58, 59, 60. |
| Photo details | Feeding signs from Chorlton, Manchester VC59; 04.07.15 (BS). |

The majority of Momphidae larvae feed upon willowherb species, and this moth is no exception as the larvae mine the leaves of rosebay willowherb in two generations.

The leaf-mines are common, distinctive and very obvious, even when the larva has exited, meaning that the species can easily be recorded any time from late May onwards. The initial mine is a gallery filled with frass and often staying close to the midrib. This widens to form a yellowish blotch containing the larva and dispersed frass. The larva is a yellowish orange colour with dark brown head, brown prothoracic plate and legs. Occasionally the larva will leave the initial mine to commence a new one. On completion of the feeding stage, the larva leaves the mine to form a grey cocoon and pupate within. The second generation overwinter in the pupal stage.

The vacated mine turns whitish and remains apparent until the plants are killed off by the onset of winter.

Feeding signs of the other Momphidae found on rosebay willowherb are very different. *Mompha conturbatella* (p.86) spins the terminal leaves together causing them to point straight upwards, and feeds within in May. The larva of *Mompha sturnipennella* feeds in the stem of the foodplant in May, with second generation larvae feeding in seedpods in July and August.

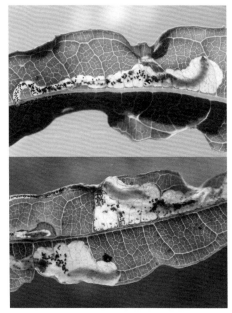

# Stenoptilia zophodactylus

Pterophoridae    45.021 *Stenoptilia zophodactylus* (Duponchel, 1840)
Foodplant    Centaury (*Centaurium erythraea*), yellow-wort (*Blackstonia perfoliata*).
Life cycle    Larva: May to September. Adult: June to October. In 2-3 generations.
Distribution    Widespread throughout British Isles.
   Local in VC58, 59, 60.
Photo details    Feeding signs from Formby, Lancashire VC59; 28.07.14 (BS).

It is quite difficult to spot the larva of this plume moth in the field, although it is always worth looking for wherever one sees a reasonable growth of centaury, particularly where it is growing on dry soil. One can hope for the best and search through the flower-heads looking for the well-camouflaged larva. Alternatively, and very gently so as not to damage the plant, tap the flower-heads into your cupped hand or into a net or similar to try and loosen the larvae from their plant. With luck, you may find one or two curled up in the collecting vessel. The typical larva is a greenish yellow with a darker dorsal line and paler sub-dorsal lines. It feeds in two or three generations within the summer months.

The larva will feed on a few flowers collected from the plant, and if reasonably advanced will pupate in a couple of days. The elongated pupa is a pinkish colour, presumably to camouflage its presence amongst the seed-cases of centaury. The pupal stage appears to be relatively brief with the adult pictured having emerged ten days after pupation.

If caught in the field, it is difficult to differentiate from similarly plain Plume Moths. The most helpful feature to look for is the saddle-shaped structure formed by the third part of the thorax and the first two segments of the abdomen, which is white, unlike that of its close relatives.

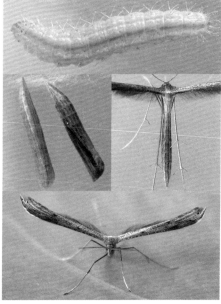

# Prochoreutis myllerana

| | |
|---|---|
| Choreutidae | 48.002 *Prochoreutis myllerana* (Fabricius, 1794) |
| Foodplant | Skullcap (*Scutellaria* spp.). |
| Life cycle | Larva: April to October. Adult: May to September. In 2-3 generations. |
| Distribution | Widespread and locally common throughout British Isles. Local in VC58, 59, 60. |
| Photo details | Feeding signs from Elterwater, Cumbria VC69; 04.08.16 (BS). |

This moth is a close relative of the familiar Nettle-tap (*Anthophila fabriciana*), but is much less frequently seen, presumably at least partially related to the comparative scarcity of its foodplant. The larvae feed on skullcap in the damp areas where the plant may be found.

Signs of larval feeding are easy to spot as the larva spins silk on the underside of the leaf, causing the edges to fold over, forming a tube-like structure. Windows appear on the leaf as the lower epidermis is eaten from within the spinning. Large amounts of frass can also be seen. If one finds leaves in a similar condition to those photographed below, they may be empty as the larva can move on to another leaf. It is therefore worth closely looking at the adjacent leaves where early feeding signs may not be quite so obvious. The larva itself is pale green with concolourous thoracic legs, small blackish pinaculae and a pale brown head. Pupation takes place within a white spindle-shaped cocoon, usually on the underside of a neighbouring leaf. Emergence does not take long. The adult photographed appeared only nine days after I found the full-fed larva.

One of the difficulties with this species is the problem of differentiating it from *P. sehestediana*, whose very similar larvae also feed on skullcap, sometimes at the same site. The adults may be separated with great care, and so expert advice should be sought if one suspects *sehestediana*.

# Acleris sparsana

| | |
|---|---|
| Tortricidae | 49.069 *Acleris sparsana* ([Denis & Schiffermüller], 1775) |
| Foodplant | Beech (*Fagus*), sycamore (*Acer pseudoplatanus*), field maple (*Acer campestre*). |
| Life cycle | Larva: June to August. Adult: August to April. |
| Distribution | Common and widespread throughout British Isles. Common in VC58, 59, 60. |
| Photo details | Feeding signs from Chorlton, Manchester VC59; 17.07.15 (BS). |

The feeding signs of this species can easily be found in gardens and in woodland, on beech and various maples, including sycamore. I find it commonly on field maple as in the example pictured below. The larva feeds between two leaves, one spun flatly over the other. Larval feeding is indicated by a slight fold in the upper leaf and browning of this area as the lower epidermis is consumed. If one lifts the leaves apart, amongst a quantity of frass and silk, one should find a green larva with green legs and a pale brown head.

It may be approximately one month before the larva is full-fed. Following completion of the feeding stage, pupation occurs. Sometimes this is in the larval habitation or in a slight cocoon amongst the leaf litter.

The adult flies in early autumn. When newly emerged, the typical *A. sparsana* has quite delicate reddish markings on a purplish grey ground colour, with a number of white scales on the forewing, as well as a few black scales near the base of the median fold. Moths attracted to the light-trap are usually quite worn in comparison, and may be a more uniform grey colour. The broad forewing remains apparent in all forms of the species, worn and unworn.

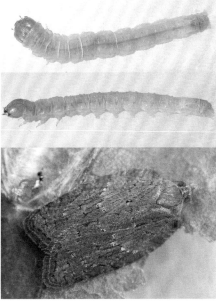

# A selection of summer birch leaf-mines

4.002 *Stigmella lapponica* - green frass at start 6-7.
4.003 *Stigmella confusella* - no green frass 7-8.
4.005 *Stigmella betulicola* - yellow larva 7, 9-11.
4.006 *Stigmella sakhalinella* - coiled frass 7-10.
4.007 *Stigmella luteella* - contorted start 7-11.

4.044 *Stigmella continuella* - frass-filled mine 6-10.
4.100 *Ectoedemia minimella* - blotch mine 7-9.
6.005 *Heliozela hammoniella* - larva cuts case 7-8.
8.005 *Phylloporia bistrigella* - case cut from blotch 7-9
37.009 *Coleophora milvipennis* - larval mine 8-5.

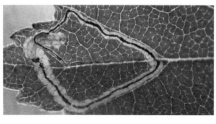

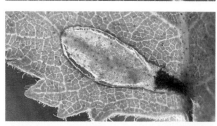

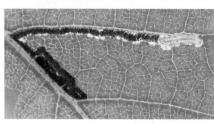

# AUGUST FIELD TIPS

August is not always the most productive time to look for the early stages. Many species are still in the adult stage, or exist as recently laid ova. Larval spinnings are not as abundant as they were a few months earlier. This may be because the approaching of summer's end means many flowering plants are a long way past their best, with the leaves less nutritious than they were in May and June.

There is though the first appearance of some of the fruit feeding larvae and overwintering leaf-miners typical of autumn. There are also the larvae of species present in their second generation, such as *Acleris ferrugana, A. notana* and *A. hastiana,* which will give another emergence of adults before the end of the season.

132. *Caloptilia populetorum*
133. *Parornix betulae*
134. *Bedellia somnulentella*
135. *Agonopterix propinquella*
136. *Chrysoesthia sexguttella*
137. *Coleophora trifolii*
138. *Coleophora deauratella*
139. *Mompha bradleyi*
140. *Mompha terminella*
141. *Amblyptilia acanthadactyla*
142. *Acleris hastiana*
143. *Eucosma cana*
144. *Cydia pomonella*
145. *Pammene aurana*
146. *Phycitodes maritima*
147. *Pyrausta aurata*

*Gait Barrows, Lancashire, 27th August 2015*

# Caloptilia populetorum

| | |
|---|---|
| Gracillariidae | 15.003 *Caloptilia populetorum* (Zeller, 1839) |
| Foodplant | Birch (*Betula* spp.). |
| Life cycle | Larva: July to August. Adult: August to May. Occasionally bivoltine. |
| Distribution | Local in British Isles. |
| | Local in VC58, 59. Unrecorded in VC60. |
| Photo details | Feeding signs from Chorlton, Manchester VC59; 20.08.16 (BS). |

Despite the name (suggesting a poplar feeder), the larvae of this species feed on birch, with saplings usually preferred by ovipositing females. The egg can be laid on either side of the leaf. The larva, in its first instar, makes a gallery mine which can be quite short or may traverse the length of the leaf. This leads to a blotch which is subsequently folded upwards in a tent-like structure, as the larva continues to feed on the parenchyma of the leaf from within. The larva then goes on to form two leaf rolls. The first may be little more than a leaf fold, while the second sees the leaf rolled longitudinally along the midrib, as in the top right photo. *C. betulicola*, which also feeds on birch, rolls the final leaf transversely.

The positioning of the pupa will also vary. The cocoon of *C. populetorum* is formed within a rolled up leaf or beneath the edge of a leaf, whereas *C. betulicola* pupates beneath a silken membranous cocoon on the underside of a leaf.

The larva itself is essentially featureless and offers no help in differentiating between this species and *Caloptilia betulicola*, so it is better to breed through to be certain of the identification.

The first Lancashire and Cheshire records were both in 2013. This moth is said to favour moorland and heathland, although I have found it common in the Mersey Valley in VC59.

 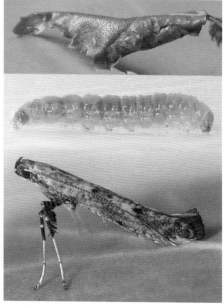

# Parornix betulae

| | |
|---|---|
| Gracillariidae | 15.025 *Parornix betulae* (Stainton, 1854) |
| Foodplant | Birch (*Betula* spp.). |
| Life cycle | Larva: June, August to Oct. Adult: May to mid-June, mid-July to August. |
| Distribution | Common throughout British Isles. |
| | Common in VC58, 59, 60. |
| Photo details | Feeding signs from Rixton, Warrington VC59; 31.08.16 (BS). |

The moth is similar to other species in this genus, the forewings being greyish fuscous with white streaks. As a result, rearing the adult from its larval stage is the best way to see this moth, and to confirm this species without the need for dissection. Those that turn up at moth traps need to be recorded as *Parornix* agg. unless dissected.

The larvae and subsequent mines are most commonly found on young birches in heaths, mosses and open woodland. An initial larval gallery in the epidermis is extended to form a reddish blotch between veins, as in the bottom left photo. As feeding progresses, the lower epidermis contracts and the mine arches upwards. After leaving the mine, the larva feeds beneath a fold at the edge of the leaf. The prothoracic plate's four black spots clearly separate the larva from *Caloptilia* species. Pupation is in a pale brown cocoon under a slightly folded leaf edge (photo bottom centre).

The other *Parornix* species on birch, *P. loganella*, has not been recorded in VC58, 59 or 60 with certainty. Although the mine and larva are not separable from *betulae*, the adult is, with care. It is much darker, with prominent white dorsal spots. Due to the lack of any definite records within the region, any putative *loganella* should be checked out by the relevant county micro-moth recorder. *P. loganella* is a moth of woodlands and hillsides.

# *Bedellia somnulentella*

| | |
|---|---|
| Bedelliidae | 24.001 *Bedellia somnulentella* (Zeller, 1847) |
| Foodplant | Bindweeds (*Convolvulus arvensis, Calystegia sepium*) and morning glory (*Ipomoea purpurea*). |
| Life cycle | Larva: July to August, September. Adult: August, October to May. |
| Distribution | Widespread in southern Britain. Unrecorded in Scotland. Local elsewhere. Local in VC58, 59, 60. |
| Photo details | Leaf-mine from Chorlton, Manchester VC59; 29.08.04 (BS). |

Locally this species seems to be a fairly recent arrival into the region. It was unrecorded in Cheshire and Lancashire until 1998, when a number of records were made here, as well as in neighbouring counties. However it remains quite a difficult species to find as it is quite erratic in its frequency, seeming to disappear for a number of years before becoming quite common again.

It can be locally abundant in coastal regions, although whether this is as a result of migration or due to a preference for milder winter conditions is unclear.

The larva initially makes a gallery mine on bindweed, containing some frass and leading to a clear blotch. Frass is ejected from the mine and tends to collect on silken threads on the underside of the leaf. The larva is capable of changing its mine, and occasionally its leaf.

Two or three larvae may occupy the same single blotch, as in the leaf-mine photo below. There is an early gallery mine at the bottom of the same photo. The larvae are pale green with subdorsal brown spots, although those on the 1st, 4th and 5th abdominal segments have white edging.

When feeding is complete, the larvae leave the mine to pupate on the strands of silk beneath the leaf, without the protection of a cocoon. The second generation of adults overwinter.

# Agonopterix propinquella

| | |
|---|---|
| Depressariidae | 32.016 *Agonopterix propinquella* (Treitschke, 1835) |
| Foodplant | Creeping thistle (*Cirsium arvense*), spear thistle (*C. vulgare*). |
| Life cycle | Larva: July to August. Adult: August to late June. |
| Distribution | Common in England and Wales, less so in Scotland and Ireland. Local in VC58, 59, 60. |
| Photo details | Feeding signs from Chorlton, Manchester VC59; 05.08.15 (BS). |

Whilst the early instars of this depressariid moth feed by mining thistle leaves, the later instar larvae can be found on the underside of thistle leaves in late summer. They feed below a silken membrane along the midrib of the leaf consuming much of the lower epidermis, thus creating obvious windows in the leaf.

The adult, emerging in early autumn, will overwinter in this stage, often reappearing at light on the first mild nights of the new year.

There are other *Agonopterix* species that also feed on thistles, so the larva should be checked to ensure it is this species rather than any of its relatives (or the green polyphagous larva of *Epiphyas postvittana*, p.211).

The following descriptions relate to the final instar larva only. That of *Agonopterix propinquella* is green with a black head and prothoracic plate. *A. subpropinquella* is similarly coloured, but the abdomen bears black pinaculae which are absent from *propinquella*. The head, prothoracic plate, anal plate and pinaculae of the final instar of a scarcer species, *A. carduella*, are all black, while the abdomen is green (p.94). *A. arenella* has a greenish-brown head and prothoracic plate, the latter bearing lateral black spots (p.7).

# Chrysoesthia sexguttella

| | |
|---|---|
| Gelechiidae | 35.036 *Chrysoesthia sexguttella* (Thunberg, 1794) |
| Foodplant | Orache (*Atriplex* spp.), goosefoot (*Chenopodium* spp.). |
| Life cycle | Larva: June, August to October. Adult: May to June, August. |
| Distribution | Locally common throughout British Isles. |
| | Local in VC58, 59, 60. |
| Photo details | Feeding signs from Chorlton, Manchester VC59; 13.08.06 (BS). |

The larva of this gelechiid moth forms a short gallery mine which quickly leads to a large clear blotch as in the first photo below. Most of the frass is expelled from the mine although some typically remains and is usually stacked up to one side. During the feeding stage, the larva is able to change to a new leaf if required.

Although the literature states that the larval stages are in June and September to October, I have only ever found it in August. The two mines below were found in 2006 and 2008 – one produced an adult in September, and one produced an adult the following May – so it is a little unclear to which generation these August larvae belong, or whether perhaps in good years there may be a third generation.

A close relative, *Chrysoesthia drurella*, also feeds on orache and goosefoot at similar times of year. The mine of *drurella* is quite different from the blotch of *sexguttella*. The colourful *drurella* larva (p.148) mines to form a contorted gallery. This contains plenty of frass and is greenish in the early workings (p.114).

Leaf-mines of the two species can often be found on waste-ground, particularly where the land has been recently disturbed, as this tends to facilitate the growth of the foodplants.

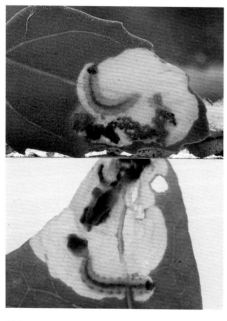
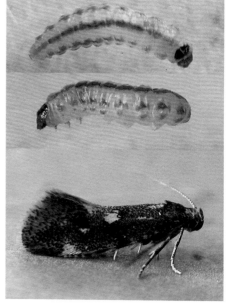

# Coleophora trifolii

| Coleophoridae | 37.033 *Coleophora trifolii* (Curtis, 1832) |
|---|---|
| Foodplant | Ribbed melilot (*Melilotus officinalis*), tall melilot (*Melilotus altissimus*). |
| Life cycle | Larva: from July to spring. Adult: June to July. |
| Distribution | Common in S England. Unrecorded in Scotland. Local elsewhere. Local in VC58, 59, 60. |
| Photo details | Feeding signs from Chorlton, Manchester VC59; 20.08.16 (BS). |

The tall yellow spikes of melilot flowers are quite distinctive in late summer. As the flowers start to wither and seeds appear, quickly turning dark brown, one may find the larval cases of *Coleophora trifolii* amongst them. The larva commences feeding within a single seed. It uses the outer shell of the seed as a case, and later adjoins this to another seed securing it with silk, again feeding within. The case is then enlarged to include the shell of this second seed. Usually a third seed will also be incorporated into the case, and a trivalved anal opening is spun, as can be seen on the case below. The larva then continues to feed from within the safety of the case, latching onto other seeds and feeding on the contents within. This leaves a hole on the side of the affected seed as can be seen in the bottom right of the first photo below, left.

Once feeding is completed in late August to early September, the larva moves down to the lower aspect of the plant and spends the winter in its case amongst the detritus on the ground.

The adult emerges in early summer and is sometimes attracted to light. It is generally larger than its close relatives within the *trifolii* group with a wingspan of 15-20mm. It has metallic golden green forewings and has the upper margin of the eye edged orange-yellow. The dark antennae have white tips, and lack the extensive basal thickening seen in some closely related species.

# Coleophora deauratella

Coleophoridae     37.046 *Coleophora deauratella* Lienig & Zeller, 1846
Foodplant     Red clover (*Trifolium pratense*).
Life cycle     Larva: from August to spring. Adult: June to July.
Distribution     Locally common in S England, Wales and Ireland. Scarce in Scotland. Local in VC58, 59, 60.
Photo details     Larval case from Chorlton, Manchester VC59; 14.08.08 (BS).

Like their close relatives in the *trifolii* group, the adults have metallic looking wings with colouring that appears to vary between golden green and dark fuscous depending on the effect of the light. The adult photos below show the female (upper) and the male.

*Coleophora deauratella* adults can be separated with difficulty from their close relatives by a combination of size (wingspan 10.5-12.5mm) and antennal appearance. The extensive coating of the base of the dark fuscous antennae with bronzy fuscous scales (one-tenth in the male and one-quarter in the female) rules out *C. frischella* and *C. alcyonipennella*. *Coleophora mayrella* is similar, but the white-ringed antennae are coated by scales for the first two-fifths of their length.

The case itself is trivalved, meaning the anal end appears divided into three sections when viewed end on as in the left hand photo. *C. frischella* cases may also be found on red clover (although white clover is their usual foodplant). The case of *frischella* is covered by a floret of clover which is barely modified. If in doubt the larvae should be bred through to confirm identification.

Larval cases are hard to find in the field. The best method is to collect a number of red clover flower-heads, put them in a clear tub, and watch out for the larval cases climbing up the sides of the tub. One may also see larvae of *Grapholita compositella* emerging in the same way (p.148).

# Mompha bradleyi

| | |
|---|---|
| Momphidae | 40.007 *Mompha bradleyi* Riedl, 1965 |
| Foodplant | Great willowherb (*Epilobium hirsutum*). |
| Life cycle | Larva: May to July. Adult: late-August to early June. |
| Distribution | Local in England and Wales. Unrecorded in Scotland and Ireland. Local in VC58, 59, 60. |
| Photo details | Feeding signs from Chorlton, Manchester VC59; 21.08.16 (BS). |

The presence of the larva of this species can be detected by looking for a gall within the stem of great willowherb. This will usually be in the upper parts of the plant affecting the main stem or one of the larger side-branches and is usually quite visible in July and August. Close inspection will usually reveal a partial exit-hole at the lower aspect of the gall. This hole is approx. 1.5mm in diameter. The epidermis is left just intact, giving the exit hole a silvery appearance.

If the gall is opened one may see the dark-headed, yellow larva within the chamber. By August one is more likely to find that the larva has finished feeding and has already spun the thick, white pupal cocoon within the chamber as in the photo on the second from left below.

This species is a recent arrival into the area, with the first Cheshire and Lancashire records dating from 2011, since when it has moved northwards into VC60, and become locally common in the south of the region. Care does need to be taken when identifying the adult, as *Mompha bradleyi* can easily be mistaken for *M. divisella*. At present *divisella* is not known from this region, but as many of the *Mompha* species are spreading north it seems reasonably likely that it will turn up at some point soon. *M. divisella* tends to show more white at the base of the forewing than *bradleyi*, although dissection is only way to be certain of the identification of trapped moths.

# Mompha terminella

| | |
|---|---|
| Momphidae | 40.014 *Mompha terminella* (Humphreys and Westwood, 1845) |
| Foodplant | Enchanter's-nightshade (*Circaea lutetiana*). |
| Life cycle | Larva: August to September. Adult: July to August. |
| Distribution | Local in England and Wales. Few records in Scotland and Ireland. Local in VC60. Unrecorded in VC58, 59. |
| Photo details | Feeding signs from Gait Barrows, Lancashire VC60; 08.08.16 (BS). |

This single brooded species may be swept by day and will occasionally come to light. However it is much more easily encountered in its early stages by searching for their leaf-mines on enchanter's-nightshade in late summer.

The distinctive mine is remarkably convoluted at the outset, with the larva creating a number of rings around the egg site. It then widens into blotch feeding where frass is laid down in a broad band. The larva has a creamy coloured appearance, with a pale brown head and prothoracic plate, and may move to another leaf during its development.

The only possible confusion species on enchanter's-nightshade is *M. langiella* (p.107), which mines a little earlier in the year and has a dark-headed larva with a dark prothoracic plate.

*Mompha terminella* overwinters in the pupal stage, and this takes place within a thick white cocoon. The cocoon may be formed under the leaf, in leaf litter, or occasionally within the leaf itself. My experience is that this species is quite easy to rear in captivity, as three larvae collected in 2015 all gave rise to adults the following year. They were kept over winter in an 7cm x 7cm plastic pot, with a small amount of dry soil and a couple of dried *Circaea* leaves amongst which to pupate. The pot was left undisturbed in the shed, with adults emerging in June.

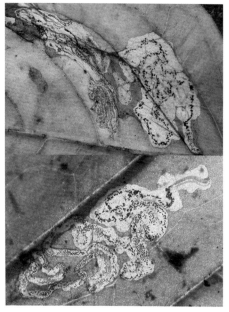

# Amblyptilia acanthadactyla

| | |
|---|---|
| Pterophoridae | 45.010 *Amblyptilia acanthadactyla* (Hübner, [1813]) |
| Foodplant | Cranesbill (*Geranium* spp.), cross-leaved heath (*Erica tetralix*), hedge woundwort (*Stachys sylvatica*) etc. |
| Life cycle | Larva: June, August. Adult: July, mid-August to early May. |
| Distribution | Common throughout British Isles. |
| | Common in VC58, 59, 60. |
| Photo details | Feeding signs from Chorlton, Manchester VC59; 03.08.15 (BS). |

*Amblyptilia acanthadactyla* is a plume moth that has become increasingly common in the last few decades, particularly in gardens, where the larvae have been noted to feed on a wider variety of foodplants than previously recognised.

I commonly find this larva in the garden on plants of the cranesbill family, such as herb robert and various cultivated *Geranium* ssp. Other plants such as hedge woundwort are also used.

The eggs are laid singly close to the flower-heads. The early instar larva has a definite pinkish hue, gradually becoming green by the final instar. The presence of the larva may be suspected by noting the petals of the flower being spun together. Frass, silk, and holes in the petals may be additional signs of larval feeding.

Once feeding is complete, the larva pupates on the stem just below the flower-head. The second generation of adults emerge from late summer onwards and overwinter in this stage.

There is a similar species, *Amblyptilia punctidactyla*. The larvae are very similar and mainly feed on hedge woundwort. The adults are generally darker and a little larger and are usually found in damp, shady places.

# Acleris hastiana

| | |
|---|---|
| Tortricidae | 49.080 *Acleris hastiana* (Linnaeus, 1758) |
| Foodplant | Sallows (*Salix* spp.), white poplar (*Populus alba*) and bog-myrtle (*Myrica gale*). |
| Life cycle | Larva: April to June, July to October. Adult: June to July, August to April. |
| Distribution | Widely distributed throughout British Isles. Common in VC58, 59, 60. |
| Photo details | Feeding signs from Rixton, Warrington VC59; 24.8.16 (BS). |

The adult of this species is remarkably variable, with over eighty different forms found in the British Isles. Although the forewing pattern varies, each individual tends to fall into one of three different types. Individuals may be plain, or may have transverse or longitudinal markings. The adult shown is obviously an example of the latter. The basic shape of the forewing is constant, as is the presence of small scale-tufts on the forewings.

*Acleris cristana* is similar, although can be differentiated from *hastiana* due to its more concave costa, and the presence of large scale tufts in the centre of the forewing. At present *cristana*, a feeder on blackthorn, hawthorn, rowan and apple, is unrecorded from Lancashire and Cheshire.

The larva of *hastiana* feeds on various species of *Salix*, favouring saplings, and spinning a few of the terminal leaves together, often fastening them to the stem.

The early instar larva is greyish green with a dark head. Later instars see the abdomen becoming light green, whilst the head and prothoracic plate varies between light green and brownish-green. The larva is quite easy to rear, particularly as the adult will emerge in the same season, by keeping it in a clear plastic pot, and every few days cleaning out the frass and providing a fresh leaf or two.

# *Eucosma cana*

| | |
|---|---|
| Tortricidae | 49.265 *Eucosma cana* (Haworth, 1881) |
| Foodplant | Common Knapweed (*Centaurea nigra*), thistles (*Cirsium vulgare*, *Carduus* spp.). |
| Life cycle | Larva: August to April. Adult: June to early August. |
| Distribution | Widely distributed and common throughout British Isles. Common in VC58, 59, 60. |
| Photo details | Feeding signs from Rixton, Warrington VC59; 31.08.16 (BS). |

The larva of this species can be commonest in the heads of spear thistle (*Cirsium vulgare*). However to open the drying flower-heads can be a painful business. An easier option is to look for the heads of common knapweed where *E. cana* may also be common. The larva feeds within the base of the flower-head, eating pith and seeds forming a frass filled cavity that may include the upper part of the stem, as in the photo below. The larva will be full-fed in autumn. Usually it vacates the flower-head to overwinter in a silken cocoon amongst the leaf litter; occasionally it remains in the flower-head. If rearing, keep outside over winter in a small netted pot with leaf litter.

Identifying which knapweed heads are tenanted is a bit of a hit and miss affair. There may be a little bit of thickening of the stem just below the flower-head. That is far from being 100% reliable but it gives a clue as to which ones may be worth further investigation. Also, where one flower-head is tenanted, many of the neighbouring plants will be too. Dipteran larvae, as well as the orange larva of *Eucosma hohenwartiana* (p.148) and the white *Metzneria metzneriella* larva (p.34), can also be found tenanting knapweed flower-heads.

# Cydia pomonella

| | |
|---|---|
| Tortricidae | 49.338 Codling Moth *Cydia pomonella* (Linnaeus, 1758) |
| Foodplant | Apple (*Malus* spp.), other fruit (plum, pear, quince etc). |
| Life cycle | Larva: August to April. Adult: May to August. |
| Distribution | Common in England and Wales; less so in Scotland and Ireland. Common in VC58, 59, 60. |
| Photo details | Feeding signs from Chorlton, Manchester VC59; 30.08.16 (BS). |

Whilst obviously not a favourite with gardeners and commercial orchards, *Cydia pomonella* is quite an attractive tortricid moth, and it can be good to look out for signs of the larva so as to know which apples to avoid! Signs of its presence are the frass accumulating at a large, untidy and uneven hole at one end of the apple. There may be a similar hole roughly on the opposite side of the apple. Infected fruit tends to fall earlier, so it is worth checking the apples on the ground before looking at those on the tree. If one carefully opens the fruit in half, feeding signs will be quite apparent, with a frass stained chamber and tunnels formed throughout the fruit. To find the larva you may need to open the core itself. In the main photo below, the larva can just be seen tunnelling into the core. The larva attains its pinkish hue as it becomes full-fed. On completion of feeding, the larva leaves the fruit to spin a cocoon amongst plant debris, pupating in the spring.

In common with the rearing of other overwintering tortricid larva, it is advisable to keep the cocoons outside in a netted pot with leaves and other plant debris, to maximise the chances of successful emergence.

Other fruit can also used by this species such as pears, plums, peaches, figs, walnuts and quinces. Its vernacular name, the Codling Moth, refers to an old name for a variety of apple.

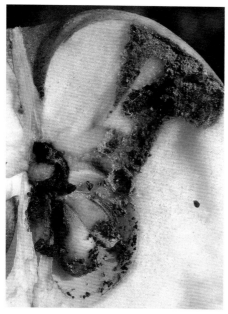

# Pammene aurana

| | |
|---|---|
| Tortricidae | 49.379 *Pammene aurana* (Fabricius, 1775) |
| Foodplant | Hogweed (*Heracleum sphondylium*). |
| Life cycle | Larva: August to April. Adult: June to July. |
| Distribution | Common in British Isles. |
| | Common in VC58, 59, 60. |
| Photo details | Feeding signs from Carrington Moss, Trafford VC58; 27.08.12 (BS). |

The adult moth is commonly found on hogweed flowers in summer. It is a reasonably distinctive tortricid moth with its two bright orange patches on each chocolate-brown forewing, although care should be taken to ensure that it is not confused with *Phaulernis fulviguttella* (p.161), which tends to be on the wing a little later and generally favours angelica.

The larvae feed on the seeds of hogweed as in the top left-hand photo below.

If one is hoping to find the larva, then clearly it is best to check at a site where the adult is known. Probably the best way to then find the larva is to collect a bunch of seeds, and examine them individually. A pair of seeds spun together, holes in the seeds and the presence of pale brown frass may suggest seeds that are worth examining a little closer. Open the seed up carefully and hopefully a larva will be revealed within feeding between layers of the seed. If no larva is immediately apparent within the seeds, it is best to hang on to the seeds for a few weeks and re-examine for feeding signs. If you are fortunate, the larva may leave its feeding place and wander on the inside of the container, giving away its presence.

In the wild, the larvae continue feeding amongst the seeds on the umbel until full-fed in autumn, at which point they descend to the ground to construct a cocoon in the earth to overwinter.

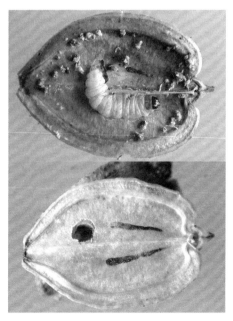

# *Phycitodes maritima*

Pyralidae          62.057 *Phycitodes maritima* (Tengström, 1848)
Foodplant          Ragwort (*Senecio jacobaea*), yarrow (*Achillea millefolium*).
Life cycle         Larva: July to April. Adult: May to August.
Distribution    .    Local throughout British Isles.
                   Local in VC58, 59, 60.
Photo details      Feeding signs from Chorlton, Manchester VC59; 03.08.15 (BS).

*Phycitodes maritima* and *saxicola* adults are inseparable other than by dissection. One advantage therefore, of looking for the larvae, is the comparative ease of identification. Both larvae feed on members of the Asteraceae family, with ragwort or yarrow the usual choice.

The larvae of *P. maritima* have a reddish-brown colouration, often with a greenish tinge. The black prothoracic plate is divided medially and the head is dark brown. The larva of *P. saxicola* differs markedly. This has a pale abdomen with pinkish dorsal and subdorsal stripes, a pale brown head, and a pale prothoracic plate with a dark line along the thoracic edge of the plate. The larva of *saxicola* can be seen on page 24.

Larvae of *maritima* can be found feeding, usually in twos or threes, in a web amongst the flowers of the foodplant, spinning together a bunch of flower-heads with frass and silk appearing obvious as in the photo below. If recording this species on the basis of ragwort or yarrow spinnings, make sure that the culprit is not the green larva of *Epiphyas postvittana* (p.211), as this can feed in similar but smaller spinnings at the tips of these flowers.

The larvae overwinter, and so are best reared by keeping outside in a netted pot containing other plant debris, in a sheltered spot, and regularly checked for adult emergence from May onwards.

# *Pyrausta aurata*

| | |
|---|---|
| Crambidae | 63.006 *Pyrausta aurata* (Scopoli, 1763) |
| Foodplant | Marjoram (*Origanum vulgare*), mint (*Mentha* spp.), clary (*Salvia* spp.), calamint (*Clinopodium* spp.). |
| Life cycle | Larva: June-July, August-Sept. Adult: May-June, mid-July to early Sept. |
| Distribution | Common in England, Wales. Scarce in Scotland. Unrecorded in Ireland. Common in VC58, 59, 60. |
| Photo details | Feeding signs from Chorlton, Manchester VC59; 03.08.15 (BS). |

I find this species commonly on marjoram in the garden. The initial larval feeding is under a single leaf, although it is much easier to detect when later forming a web amongst the leaves and flowers of various forms of Lamiaceae. The web is quite notable as the foliage is drawn together, feeding damage can be seen and on careful inspection, the larva can usually be seen sitting within the spinning.

The larva is initially dark green with a divided pale green dorsal stripe, and conspicuous large, dark pinaculae. As the larva becomes full-fed, the dark green turns to dark pink as in the photos below right. Pupation occurs within a tough cocoon, often found in openings in nearby woody vegetation. Goater (1986) notes cocoons may also be found in old flower-heads.

The adult has a lovely reddish purple forewing with variable golden markings, although the large gold spot near the costa is a consistent feature. The hindwing contains a broad golden yellow cross-line, which helps to separate this species from the generally larger *Pyrausta purpuralis*. The hindwing of the latter species bears a creamy yellow cross-line. The larva of *P. purpuralis* feeds between spun leaves of thyme and mint between June and September.

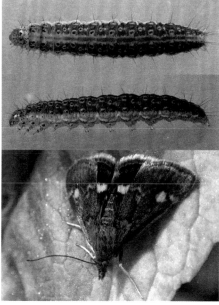

# A selection of micro-moth larvae from summer and autumn

14.010 *Bucculatrix ulmella* - oak 7, 9-10.
18.001 *Plutella xylostella* - crucifers 6-7, 8-9.
35.010 *Aproaerema anthyllidella* - clover 4-5, 7.
35.035 *Chrysoesthia drurella* - orache, etc. 7-8, 9-5.
39.001 *Blastodacna hellerella* - in haws 9-10.

45.044 *Emmelina monodactyla* - bindweed 6-8.
49.083 *Acleris ferrugana* - oak 5-6, 8.
49.266 *Eucosma hohenwartiana* - knapweed, etc. 8-5.
49.347 *Grapholita compositella* - clover, etc. 6-7, 8-4.
62.007 *Cryptoblabes bistriga* - oak 8-10.

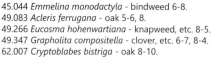

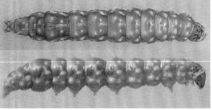

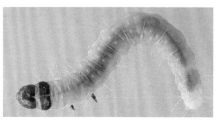

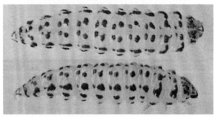

# SEPTEMBER FIELD TIPS

September and the arrival of autumn mark a change in fortune for the entomologist interested in the early stages, as all of a sudden the number of microlepidoptera larvae again escalates. Tutt (1901) was of similar opinion when he wrote that "September, dependent upon meteorological conditions, may be, and sometimes is, one of the most interesting months to the field lepidopterist."

Many species can be found feeding in seed-heads and in fruit such as apples, hawthorn berries and rose-hips. Leaf-mines abound in much greater numbers than their first generation earlier in the year, and some of these, such as *Acrolepia autumnitella* and many of the *Caloptilia* species, will result in adult emergence before the onset of winter.

150. *Stigmella oxyacanthella*
151. *Roeslerstammia erxlebella*
152. *Bucculatrix cidarella*
153. *Caloptilia stigmatella*
154. *Parornix scoticella*
155. *Phyllonorycter rajella*
156. *Swammerdamia caesiella*
157. *Swammerdamia pyrella*
158. *Acrolepia autumnitella*
159. *Carpatolechia notatella*
160. *Carpatolechia proximella*
161. *Phaulernis fulviguttella*
162. *Acleris notana*
163. *Hedya atropunctana*
164. *Epinotia tetraquetrana*
165. *Pammene fasciana*
166. *Anania coronata*
167. *Udea prunalis*

*Delamere Forest, Cheshire, 4th September 2016*

# *Stigmella oxyacanthella*

| | |
|---|---|
| Nepticulidae | 4.026 *Stigmella oxyacanthella* (Stainton, 1854) |
| Foodplant | Hawthorn (*Crataegus* spp.), apple (*Malus* spp.), pear (*Pyrus* spp.). |
| Life cycle | Larva: September to November. Adult: June. |
| Distribution | Common and widespread throughout British Isles. Common in VC58, 59, 60. |
| Photo details | Mines on hawthorn from Chorlton, Manchester VC59; 28.09.15 (BS). |

This leaf-miner, commonly found on hawthorn, is an easy one to identify when tenanted, although less so when vacated. The larva is bright green with a pale brown head. The only miner of hawthorn that looks at all similar is *S. crataegella* (p.114), as this latter species also has a bright green larva (with a greenish head), but is present in late June-July and never as late as September.

The initial mine of *oxyacanthella* starts as a long, slender gallery. This contains linear frass and often follows the path of the midrib or the leaf edge. The mine then abruptly widens, as the larva begins to fill it with coiled reddish-brown frass. Finally, there is a short stretch of mining where the frass is again contracted into a narrow line, prior to the larva leaving the leaf. It does so by making a slit on the upperside of the leaf, before constructing the dark brown cocoon on detritus or on the soil surface in which the pupa overwinters.

The adult is rarely seen and only likely to be encountered if reared through. It has an orange head, white eyecaps, and deep purple-fuscous forewings.

I have reared this species a couple of times by keeping the leaf in an 8cm x 8cm clear plastic pot until the cocoon is formed, and then removing excess plant material to prevent mould. The pot was then kept in the shed, with a clear id label. Emergence was in late May.

# *Roeslerstammia erxlebella*

Roeslerstammiidae 13.002 *Roeslerstammia erxlebella* (Fabricius, 1787)
Foodplant        Lime (*Tilia* spp.), birch (*Betula* spp.).
Life cycle       Larva: July, September-October. Adult: May-June, August-September.
Distribution     Local in Great Britain. Locally common in South. Absent from Ireland.
                 Common in VC58; local in VC59, 60.
Photo details    Leaf-mine from Chorlton, Manchester VC59; 20.10.13 (BS).

The most reliable way to record this moth is by looking for the larval feeding signs on lime. The first instar mines the very tip of the lime leaf and this can be clearly detected by standing under the tree, looking upwards where the pale tips of the mined leaves stands out. On leaving the mine, the white larva has a dark head and prothoracic plate (photo middle, left). It continues to feed from the underside making small holes in the leaf. As it develops the larva becomes creamy white with a brown head. The gut-line is visible, giving the larva a greenish tinge when feeding. The body is markedly constricted between the abdominal segments, each displaying a number of long hairs. Colourless pinaculae are present. Pupation is in a silken cocoon under a turned down leaf edge.

The early instar *erxlebella* larva below was found in mid-September on the underside of a lime leaf, (with a *Bucculatrix thoracella* larva also feeding on the same leaf).

Larvae may also be noted descending on silken threads from lime.

I have also found a larva feeding on beech (larva below, left). This is an unusual foodplant for this species, and seems to be previously unrecorded. This record was from Dunham Massey in VC58, a site with plentiful lime, so it is possible the larva was windswept onto beech after leaving its mine. Nevertheless it continued to eat beech up to pupation, and gave rise to the adult moth below.

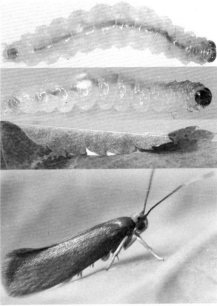

# Bucculatrix cidarella

Bucculatricidae    14.008 *Bucculatrix cidarella* (Zeller, 1839)
Foodplant    Alder (*Alnus glutinosa*), bog myrtle (*Myrica gale*).
Life cycle    Larva: August to September. Adult: May to June.
Distribution    Widespread and fairly common throughout British Isles.
   Common in VC58; local in VC59, 60.
Photo details    Larva beaten from alder, from Chorlton, Manchester VC59; 28.09.15 (BS).

I have never yet managed to find a tenanted mine of this species. Fortunately vacated ones are usually good enough to record the presence of the species. The larvae mine alder leaves in late summer for the first couple of instars before leaving the mine to feed on the leaf surface. The short gallery mine is relatively narrow and packed with black frass. The *cidarella* larval exit hole is on the upperside of the leaf, whereas for the alder-feeding nepticulid species it is on the underside.

Probably the easiest way to find the larvae is to look for them on the underside of leaves in their external feeding phase eating out characteristic windows, or to beat alder over a beating tray or upturned umbrella. If using the beating method, try and avoid excess force which will damage the plant, and ideally return the many other invertebrates obtained to their host plant, once the tray or umbrella has been checked for interesting larvae. Keep an eye out for the nepticulid *Bohemannia quadrimaculella* as this moth may also be obtained by beating alder branches in late summer (July to August is the likeliest time to find *quadrimaculella*).

Once feeding is complete the larva makes a delicately ribbed, buff coloured cocoon on plant material or detritus. Pupation occurs within the cocoon before the onset of winter.

Although usually univoltine, favourable seasons may see a small second generation in August.

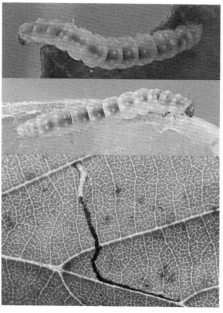

# *Caloptilia stigmatella*

| | |
|---|---|
| Gracillariidae | 15.010 *Caloptilia stigmatella* (Fabricius, 1781) |
| Foodplant | Sallows, willows (*Salix* spp.), poplars (*Populus* spp.). |
| Life cycle | Larva: May to June, late July to October. Adult: September to May, late June to mid-August. |
| Distribution | Common and widespread throughout British Isles. Common in VC58, 59, 60. |
| Photo details | Feeding signs from Irlam Moss, Salford VC59; 13.09.15 (BS). |

Adult moths of the *Caloptilia* genus are quite distinctive when at rest, because of their characteristic posture. They appear to sit upright, as their relatively long forelegs are held straight below the thorax. Of this genus, *stigmatella* is one of the easier moths to identify to species level because of the creamy triangular costal blotch against a reddish-brown forewing.

Larval feeding occurs on sallows, willows, poplars and aspen, and rarely on birch. An initial gallery mine leads to a blotch, the lower epidermis of which is brown, as in the right-hand leaf in the bottom left photo, and it is possible to mistake this for an early *Phyllonorycter* mine. On leaving the mine, the larva rolls two or three successive cones on the same or neighbouring leaves, feeding within. The larva itself is pale green and featureless, in common with other *Caloptilia* larvae. On completion of feeding the larva finds a spot on the underside of a nearby leaf and forms a pale green membranous cocoon within which it pupates, as in the top left photograph.

Similar *Caloptilia* feeding signs can be seen on field maple (*C. semifascia*), azalea (*azaleella*), sycamore (*rufipennella*), ash (*cuculipennella* and *Gracillaria syringella*) alder (*elongella* and *falconipennella*), birch (*populetorum* and *betulicola*) and oak (*robustella* and *alchimiella*).

# *Parornix scoticella*

| | |
|---|---|
| Gracillariidae | 15.030 *Parornix scoticella* (Stainton, 1850) |
| Foodplant | Rowan (*Sorbus aucuparia*), whitebeam (*Sorbus aria*). |
| Life cycle | Larva: mid-August to early October. Adult: probably late June to July. |
| Distribution | Widespread throughout British Isles. |
| | Local in VC58, 59, 60. |
| Photo details | Feeding signs from Great Wood, Broadbottom VC58; 20.09.15 (BS). |

According to the Cheshire and Lancashire records, this species seems to be univoltine in our region, with larval feeding signs recorded from mid-August onwards. Further south, the moth is bivoltine, with mines occurring in July and then again in August to September, and with the two generations of adults emerging in May and August.

Eggs are laid on the underside of the leaf of the foodplant. In addition to rowan and whitebeam, this species is also known to utilise apple and wild service-tree.

On hatching, the larva makes an initial broad gallery in the lower epidermis, which is then extended into a blotch mine. This is brown underneath, which should serve to separate it from small *Phyllonorycter* mines. The larva then moves across to another of the leaflets on rowan, causing the leaf to fold over. It feeds below a dense silken pad within the fold. The species is easiest to detect during this stage, although these larval signs are a little less obvious on whitebeam. Once feeding is complete, the larva will then leave this leaflet to pupate within a buff-coloured cocoon. This can be formed either on the ground, or in the folded edge of a leaf.

The larva has a brown head with dark spots laterally, and the four black spots on the prothoracic plate that are typical of *Parornix* larvae.

# Phyllonorycter rajella

Gracillariidae    15.067 *Phyllonorycter rajella* (Linnaeus, 1758)
Foodplant    Alder (*Alnus glutinosa*), other *Alnus* spp.
Life cycle    Larva: July, Sept. to Oct. Adult: May, Aug. Occasional 3rd generation.
Distribution    Common throughout British Isles.
   Common in VC58, 59, 60.
Photo details    Leaf-mine on alder from Chorlton, Manchester VC59; 20.09.16 (BS).

Alder is a good source of *Phyllonorycter* leaf-mines and all five British species can be found here in Lancashire and Cheshire.

*Phyllonorycter rajella* is the commonest of the five, and can be found wherever the foodplant is present, even on unusual varieties such as the cut-leaf alder in the top right photo. The mine of *rajella* is usually quite small, nestling against the midrib and showing a discoloured patch on the upperside of the leaf. Turn the leaf over and you will see that the underside has a strong central crease when fully developed, and sometimes a reddish tinge. The larva is white to pale green, with a pale brown head. Many mines may be found on a single leaf.

*P. froelichiella* also mines the underside of alder leaves, typified by a smooth lower epidermis and around 25mm in length (p.212). The larva is grey, unlike the other alder *Phyllonorycter* larvae.

*P. klemannella* feeding results in a small mine on the underside of alder, usually away from the midrib, often rounded in shape and without a strong, central crease (p.212).

A fourth species, *P. stettinensis*, is easy to identify as it is the only upperside alder miner (p.194).

Lastly there is *Phyllonorycter strigulatella* (p.212). This is found only on grey alder (*Alnus incana*). The larva forms an extended reddish underside mine between two veins.

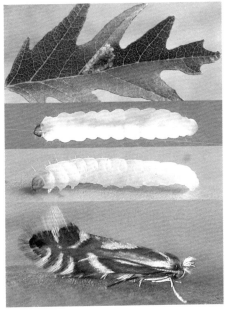

155

# Swammerdamia caesiella

| Yponomeutidae | 16.015 *Swammerdamia caesiella* (Hübner, 1796) |
| Foodplant | Birch (*Betula* spp.). |
| Life cycle | Larva: July, September. Adult: May to June, late July to August. |
| Distribution | Common throughout British Isles. |
| | Common in VC58, 59, 60. |
| Photo details | Feeding signs from Little Woolden Moss, Salford VC59; 26.09.15 (BS). |

The larval stage of this species can be found on birch trees in heath and woodland. I have found it particularly common on saplings in the mosses of Greater Manchester, and also at Lindow Common in Wilmslow (VC58).

The adult is attracted to light, but is not very easy to identify even when fresh, as the grey forewings and white head are shared by most *Swammerdamia* species. The posture, with head down and abdomen raised is typical of the group. The larva, on the other hand, presents no difficulties in identification.

The larva is pale green, with darker green dorsal and dorsolateral lines, as well as transverse dark green lines between the segments. Each abdominal segment contains a pair of tiny black spots either side of the dorsal line. The head and the divided prothoracic plate are brown.

Initial larval feeding is in a tiny leaf-mine on birch. On leaving the mine, the larva then spins a silken web on the upper surface of the birch leaf. These feeding signs are particularly noticeable on an autumn morning, when droplets of dew attach themselves to the web.

From beneath this web, the larva feeds on the upper epidermis of birch, causing a windowing effect. Pupation occurs within a dense white cocoon, usually spun on detritus within the ground.

# Swammerdamia pyrella

| | |
|---|---|
| Yponomeutidae | 16.017 *Swammerdamia pyrella* (Villers, 1789) |
| Foodplant | Hawthorn (*Crataegus* spp.), apple (*Malus* spp.), pear (*Pyrus* spp.) etc. |
| Life cycle | Larva: July, September-October. Adult: May, mid-July to early September. |
| Distribution | Common in England and Wales. Local in Scotland and Ireland. |
| | Common in VC58, 59, 60. |
| Photo details | Feeding signs on apple from Chorlton, Manchester VC59; 20.10.07 (BS). |

If looking for leaf-miners on hawthorn or apple, you may come across this very smart larva feeding under a slight web on the upper surface of one of the leaves, nibbling away at the upper epidermis, leaving bare patches on the leaf surface. The yellow larva has quite distinctive reddish-brown stripes, giving it a latticed appearance. The larva of *Choreutis pariana* also feeds in a web on the same range of foodplants. However the larva of *pariana* (p.95) has black spots and lacks the stripes of *pyrella*. It also leaves more obvious skeletonised patches on the leaf.

*S. pyrella* larva may occasionally be found late in the year. For instance, the occupied larval web pictured below left was found on cherry in late October. When feeding is complete, the larva falls to the ground. It spins a dense white cocoon and pupates within, overwintering in this stage.

The moth can be found in hedgerows, gardens, heathland, woodland and woodland.

The adults are readily attracted to light, but can be difficult to identify in these circumstances as there are a number of similar close relatives with grey forewings and white heads. A notable identification feature of *pyrella* is the copper tinge at the tips of the forewings, but this can be difficult to see in worn individuals. On the other hand, if freshly emerged, the feature can be very clear, as in the photo below.

157

# Acrolepia autumnitella

Glyphipterigidae   19.014 *Acrolepia autumnitella* Curtis, 1838
Foodplant   Bittersweet (*Solanum dulcamara*), deadly nightshade (*Atropa belladonna*).
Life cycle   Larva: June and September. Adult: July to August, October to early June.
Distribution   Common in S Eng., Wales. Local in N Eng., Ireland. No Scottish records. Common in VC58, 59, 60.
Photo details   Feeding signs on bittersweet, Rixton, Warrington VC59; 13.09.16 (BS).

Previously considered a moth of southern England, the first records of this species in all three vice-counties of Lancashire and Cheshire were around the recent turn of the century, (VC59 in 1999, VC58 in 2000, and VC60 in 2003). Since then the moth has become much more widespread, and one is likely to find the mines wherever the foodplant, chiefly bittersweet, occurs. This is particularly so in shaded damp woodlands.

The presence of this species is shown by large, untidy, translucent blotches on bittersweet leaves. The pale larva may be seen feeding between the upper and lower epidermis, occasionally with the tip of the abdomen protruding from the mine, ensuring that most of the frass is expelled. Any remaining frass within the mine is green in colour. The larva can switch leaves during feeding.

The only other lepidopterous miner on bittersweet, *Scrobipalpa costella* (p.178), makes small dark mines, with dark brown frass lining the margins of the mine. Unlike the larva of *autumnitella*, which is whitish green with a pale brown head, *costella* is grey, with a dark grey thorax, dark brown head and reddish subdorsal lines.

Once feeding is complete, the *autumnitella* larva spins a delicate brown network cocoon on the ground and pupates within. Emergence is rapid, and the adult overwinters.

# *Carpatolechia notatella*

| | |
|---|---|
| Gelechiidae | 35.150 *Carpatolechia notatella* (Hübner, [1813]) |
| Foodplant | Goat willow (*Salix caprea*) and other *Salix* spp. |
| Life cycle | Larva: August to mid-October. Adult: May to early August. |
| Distribution | Widespread and fairly common in British Isles. |
| | Local in VC58, 59, 60. |
| Photo details | Feeding signs from Irlam Moss, Salford VC59; 13.09.15 (BS). |

This moth tends not to wander too far from its habitats of woodland, heathland, sheltered moorland, scrub and fens, and so will rarely be found in garden traps. Unfortunately, even when trapped, adults of this genus are not easy to identify.

A much more reliable way to record the species, is by looking for the larval feeding signs on sallow. Look for two leaves spun together, one partially covering the other. The area of the upper leaf that overlays the other, is marked brown on the upperside, showing where feeding has occurred. If one opens up the spinning it can be very difficult to find the larva as it feeds under the downy hairs on the underside of the leaf supplemented by a layer of silk. Holding the leaf up to the light, as in the photo on the bottom left, should reveal the presence of the larva. The larva itself is pale green with a pale green-brown head and small black pinaculae. It does not seem to be particularly variable in appearance.

The species overwinters as a pupa, in captivity within a cocoon formed between two leaves, or amongst detritus on the ground in its natural habitat.

Care needs to be taken when identifying the adult. Similar to other gelechiids of the *Carpatolechia* genus, the adult is darker than *C. proximella* (p.160) and lacks the raised scales of *C. fugitivella*.

# Carpatolechia proximella

| | |
|---|---|
| Gelechiidae | 35.151 *Carpatolechia proximella* (Hübner, 1796) |
| Foodplant | Birch (*Betula* spp.), alder (*Alnus* spp.). |
| Life cycle | Larva: August to September. Adult: May to June. |
| Distribution | Common throughout British Isles. |
| | Common in VC58, 59, 60. |
| Photo details | Feeding signs from Little Woolden Moss, Salford VC59; 13.09.15 (BS). |

Although *Carpatolechia proximella* can be found in all types of habitats where the foodplants occur, I have found it particularly common in our heaths and mosses, such as at Lindow Common and Irlam Moss. It is also present amongst the larger birch trees in mature woodland, such as at Healey Dell in Rochdale and Rossendale, and at Gait Barrows. The moth seems to have a preference for areas where birch naturally occurs, rather than in areas of amenity planting.

The larva feeds within a fully or partially folded leaf of birch, or occasionally alder. Closure of the leaf is by thick silken sutures, each composed of many strands, which pull the leaf together. Even when the leaf is fully folded, these thick strands of silk will usually be partially visible.

If one opens the leaf to search for the larva, be careful it doesn't wriggle away on to the ground as soon as it is exposed, as it can be rather lively. Keep a hand or better still, a container, beneath the leaf. The larva itself is pale green with black pinacula. The head of the final instar larva is yellowish brown. Earlier instars may have the head, thoracic legs, prothoracic plate and anal plate marked with dark brown.

The moth is quite easy to rear. Keep the larva in a clear plastic pot, with a few leaves. When full-fed provide dry leaves and a small amount of dry, sterile soil, and keep in a shed or similar.

# Phaulernis fulviguttella

| | |
|---|---|
| Epermeniidae | 47.001 *Phaulernis fulviguttella* (Zeller, 1839) |
| Foodplant | Angelica (*Angelica sylvestris*), hogweed (*Heracleum sphondylium*). |
| Life cycle | Larva: September to October. Adult: July to August. |
| Distribution | Widespread and locally common throughout British Isles. Local in VC58. Scarce in VC59, 60. |
| Photo details | Feeding signs from Hurst Clough, Tameside VC58; 20.9.15 (BS). |

This moth bears a superficial similarity to the tortrix moth *Pammene aurana*, whose life cycle is also closely connected to umbellifers. Whereas *P. aurana* is more likely found on hogweed flowers, *P. fulviguttella* is more closely connected to angelica, and adults may be found on the flower-heads in summer. The yellow spots on the forewing are smaller than those of *aurana*.

Larvae can be found feeding within the seed-heads from September. The larva spins a few seeds together and feeds within the web. These spinnings are quite evident on damp September mornings when droplets of dew adhere to the silken strands. Once you have found one spinning it can be relatively easy to locate a few more. The larva itself is not particularly distinctive. It is cream-coloured with greyish pinaculae and two faint subdorsal lines.

The orange pupa overwinters within a flimsy cocoon amongst detritus in the wild. A small amount of dry, sterile soil and a few dry leaves should provide the same function in captivity.

Rearing seems straightforward as three larvae gave rise to three moths the following August. The only cautions are to remove frass and change foodplant regularly to avoid mould development.

The species appears to be particularly scarce in Lancashire, with no VC59 record since 1953. It was recorded at Gait Barrows in 2016, which was the first VC60 record for over 200 years.

# *Acleris notana*

| | |
|---|---|
| Tortricidae | 49.084 *Acleria notana* (Donovan, 1806) |
| Foodplant | Birch (*Betula* spp.), alder (*Alnus glutinosa*), bog myrtle (*Myrica gale*). |
| Life cycle | Larva: May, Aug-Sept. Adult: mid-June to early Aug, Sept. to mid-April. |
| Distribution | Widely distributed throughout British Isles. Common in VC58, 59, 60. |
| Photo details | Feeding signs from Chorlton, Manchester VC59; 05.09.15 (BS). |

As separation of the adult moth from its close relative *Acleris ferrugana*, an oak feeder, is by dissection only, an easier way to record *notana* (or *ferrugana*) is to look for the feeding signs. Both moths are bivoltine, and the autumn generation of larvae will give rise to adults before the end of the season. Both species overwinter as adults.

*Acleris notana* is a birch feeder (although rarely may also be found on alder and bog myrtle). The larvae make untidy spinnings on the leaves, often spinning a bunch together as in the photo below. The larva is green, with some variation in the colour of head and prothoracic plate from brown to black. Pupation is in the larval habitation.

*Acleris ferrugana* (p.148) feeds between two oak leaves spun together, with the upperside of the top leaf discoloured as the lower epidermis is consumed. The larva is similar to *notana*.

If one wishes to determine the identity of trapped moths of the *notana/ferrugana* pair, then a useful characteristic to look for is a prominent patch of raised black scales at about one-third length of the forewing from the head. The presence of these suggests *ferrugana*. The scales may be dislodged, and there is variation, but this feature at least provides a guide as to which individual moths may warrant closer examination.

# Hedya atropunctana

| | |
|---|---|
| Tortricidae | 49.159 *Hedya atropunctana* (Zetterstedt, 1839) |
| Foodplant | Birch (*Betula* spp.), willows (*Salix* spp.), bog myrtle (*Myrica gale*). |
| Life cycle | Larva: August to October. Adult: late May to July. |
| Distribution | Widespread but local in British Isles. |
| | Local in VC58, 59, 60. |
| Photo details | Feeding signs from Little Woolden Moss, Salford VC59; 05.09.16 (BS). |

*Hedya atropunctana* larvae on birch make a very secure spinning of a single leaf, or sometimes spinning one leaf to another, to create a pod in which to feed. In each case, a large quantity of silk is used, giving the spinning the appearance of one likely to contain a spider. The spinning is so secure, that a little force must be used to open up the leaf. Doing so should reveal a greyish green larva with a black head and prothoracic plate. The larva feeds on the upper epidermis of the spun leaf, and will move to a fresh leaf when the first is exhausted. Personal experience is that this species has quite a high parasitisation rate, and this can be obvious when opening the pod, as small parasitoid larvae may be seen extruding from the *atropunctana* larva.

When feeding is complete, the larva constructs a cocoon amongst leaf litter on the ground. In captivity, it makes a partial cut in a dried leaf and then folds the leaf at the cut, making its cocoon within. It seems likely that the larva will exhibit similar behaviour in the wild. The species overwinters in the pupal stage.

The adult has a definite pink tinge when newly emerged. As can be seen in the photo below, there is a dark transverse fascia across the forewing. There is a pink square-shaped blotch on the costa before this, and a round black spot after the fascia, half way across the width of the forewing.

163

# Epinotia tetraquetrana

| | |
|---|---|
| Tortricidae | 49.245 *Epinotia tetraquetrana* (Haworth, 1811) |
| Foodplant | Birch (*Betula* spp.), alder (*Alnus glutinosa*). |
| Life cycle | Larva: July to October. Adult: April to mid-June. |
| Distribution | Widely distributed throughout British Isles. Locally common in VC58, 59, 60. |
| Photo details | Feeding signs from Little Woolden Moss, Salford VC59; 27.09.15 (BS). |

The adult moth can be beaten from birch in summer. It is quite a variable species with some individuals well-marked, and others virtually melanic, as in the reared example pictured below.

The larvae are easiest to find by examining the leaves of birch saplings on heaths and mosses. One may find a turned over leaf edge, a little similar, although less tidy, than that created by the birch *Parornix* species. Under this leaf edge one will find a larva feeding under a silken web as in the lower picture on the left (showing a penultimate instar). Larval descriptions suggest possible pink subdorsal lines (Bland, ed., 2015). This has been a prominent feature on the larvae I have found.

Following the egg's hatching, the larva bores into a twig and begins feeding within. However feeding signs at this stage are very hard to find. There is a very subtle swelling of the inhabited twig with a small entrance hole at one end. In the photo the hole is at the top of the mined portion of twig. One may be alerted to the presence of this affected twig, by finding an occupied leaf-fold and then examining neighbouring twigs for signs of previous tenancy.

The larva pupates in October and overwinters in this stage. Pupation is within a silken cocoon amongst leaf litter. I reared this species in an 8cm x 8cm plastic pot with a few old birch leaves. It formed the cocoon between these leaves, pupated over winter, and emerged at the end of May.

# *Pammene fasciana*

| | |
|---|---|
| Tortricidae | 49.367 *Pammene fasciana* (Linnaeus, 1761) |
| Foodplant | Oak (*Quercus* spp.), sweet chestnut (*Castanea sativa*). |
| Life cycle | Larva: July to April. Adult: May to August. |
| Distribution | Widespread in British Isles, although more local in Scotland and Ireland. Common in VC58, 59, 60. |
| Photo details | Feeding signs on oak from Chorlton, Manchester VC59; 19.09.15 (BS). |

If it is a good year for acorns, then it is likely to be a good year to look for larvae of acorn-feeding micros too. Locally the easiest to find seems to be the tortricid *Pammene fasciana*. I found four of these feeding in acorns, in Chorlton, Manchester in September 2015.

The larva lives inside the acorn hollowing out the kernel. Its presence is obvious because of an exit hole about 2-3mm in diameter. Frass is expelled through this. There is often plenty of silk around the hole, and the acorn may be spun onto an adjoining leaf, possibly for some degree of protection. The larva may also be found in some of the oak-galls.

*Pammene fasciana* is a distinctive larva, with dark brown pinaculae and dark posterior edging to the prothoracic plate. It will at times lie outside the acorn, as in the third photo below. Otherwise, pop a tenanted acorn into a specimen pot, and you will probably find that the larva has exited the acorn within a few days, allowing identification to be made.

Other common acorn feeders include *Cydia splendana* (p.24) and *Blastobasis lacticolella* (p.24), so it is necessary to get a view of the larva to identify the species responsible for the feeding signs.

Alternatively, place a selection of tenanted acorns collected in autumn in a netted flower-pot, and see what emerges in spring.

# *Anania coronata*

| Crambidae | 63.018 *Anania coronata* (Hufnagel, 1767) |
|---|---|
| Foodplant | Elder (*Sambucus nigra*). |
| Life cycle | Larva: August to May. Adult: June to August. |
| Distribution | Common in England and Wales. Local in Scotland and Ireland. Common in VC58, 59, 60. |
| Photo details | Feeding signs from Irlam Moss, Salford VC59; 26.09.15 (BS). |

Quite a common species and a very nicely marked one. I was having trouble finding the larvae of this species so reared a batch through from ova laid by a female *P. coronata* visiting the moth trap on 10th July 2014. The larvae fed on elder and made distinctive spinnings on the underside of fresh leaves. The spinnings cause a tenting of the upperside of the leaf. Larval feeding also means the leaf may contain a few large holes. The larvae frequently moved from one leaf to another to continue feeding. The larva itself is pale green, with two whitish subdorsal stripes and a pale head. Generally, the appearance changes little throughout the larval development, although as feeding becomes complete, the larva attains a pinkish hue.

Once I got my eye in from the feeding signs exhibited by the larvae reared from ova, it became fairly easy to detect this species in the larval form by looking for the tenting of the leaf.

The species overwinters in the larval stage. A silken cocoon is spun amongst leaf litter, bark or dead wood. The larvae obtained from ova were kept in the shed in a plastic container with a few side-holes, and plenty of suitable material for overwintering, with pupation occurring in spring within the cocoon. Eventually the first of many adults emerged on 3rd July 2015, almost one year after the eggs were laid.

# Udea prunalis

| | |
|---|---|
| Crambidae | 63.034 *Udea prunalis* ([Denis & Schiffermüller], 1775) |
| Foodplant | Blackthorn (*Prunus spinosa*). See notes below on other foodplants. |
| Life cycle | Larva: September to May. Adult: late June to August. |
| Distribution | Common throughout most of British Isles. |
| | Common in VC58, 59, 60. |
| Photo details | Feeding signs from Frodsham, Cheshire VC58; 19.09.15 (BS). |

The early instar larvae can be found feeding on blackthorn in autumn. It feeds under a thick silken web on the underside of blackthorn leaves, small blotches being visible on the upperside, a little like the feeding signs of *Coleophora anatipennella*. At this stage the larva is only 5mm long (bottom, left). It is greenish white, with a black head, and pale prolegs and thoracic legs. There is a slight hint of subdorsal pale stripes. The larva overwinters within the silken hibernaculum. I have also found the early instar on elm, with the same signs as on blackthorn.

Thanks to Steve Hind for the information within this tip, and for finding the larva that was subsequently reared, following overwintering in a shed. The larva emerged from its hibernaculum on 15th April (top, right) and lost the black head on 23rd April. The larva continued to feed on blackthorn leaves and fed until 10th May. It then spun a few leaves together and pupated in a silken cocoon within the spinning. The moth emerged on 11th June.

Interestingly, Goater (1986) does not mention blackthorn among the foodplants, listing herbaceous and woody plants such as deadnettle, woundwort, nettle, dog's mercury, honeysuckle, bramble, elder and elm as hostplants in spring. The larva is stated to be found living under the leaves which it spins together.

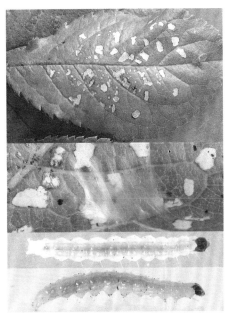 

# A selection of leaf-mines from autumn (1)

4.004 *Stigmella tiliae* - lime 7, 9-10.
4.010 *S. microtheriella* - hazel, hornbeam 6-7, 9-11.
4.014 *Stigmella catharticella* - buckthorn 6-7, 9-10.
4.024 *Stigmella magdalenae* - rowan 7-8.
4.030 *Stigmella hybnerella* - hawthorn 5-6, 8-9.

4.032 *S. floslactella* - hazel, hornbeam 6-7, 9-11.
4.039 *Stigmella trimaculella* - poplar 6-7, 9-10.
4.043 *Stigmella lemniscella* - elm 7, 9-10.
4.054 *Stigmella perpygmaeella* - hawthorn 7,10.
4.055 *Stigmella hemargyrella* - beech 6, 8-9.

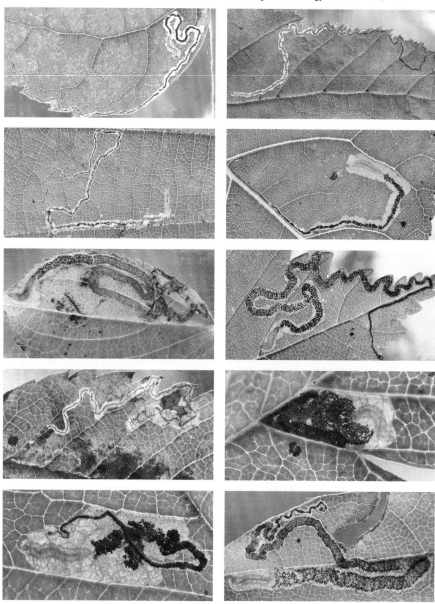

# OCTOBER FIELD TIPS

Although summer has now passed, October remains a very productive month to search for early stages of the microlepidoptera. The fruit and seeds of autumn can house a number of larvae, although the feeding signs may take some searching for. Much more obvious are the leaf-mining species on broad-leaved trees. These are particularly numerous in this month, and make it possible to record 30-50 species in a productive day. This month is particularly good for leaf-mines of the Nepticulidae, as most will still be tenanted by the larva, making identification easier. When looking for these leaf-mines, keep an eye out for any spinnings or signs of larval feeding on the leaves, as other species may also be detected.

170. *Stigmella tityrella*
171. *Ectoedemia occultella*
172. *Caloptilia elongella*
173. *Parornix devoniella*
174. *Phyllonorycter schreberella*
175. *Phyllonorycter tristrigella*
176. *Leucoptera malifoliella*
177. *Carcina quercana*
178. *Scrobipalpa costella*
179. *Coleophora gryphipennella*
180. *Elachista gangabella*
181. *Pseudargyrotoza conwagana*
182. *Ancylis mitterbacheriana*
183. *Grapholita janthinana*
184. *Pammene aurita*
185. *Strophedra weirana*

*Little Budworth Common, Cheshire, 25th October 2015*

# *Stigmella tityrella*

| Nepticulidae | 4.034 *Stigmella tityrella* (Stainton, 1854) |
| --- | --- |
| Foodplant | Beech (*Fagus sylvatica*). |
| Life cycle | Larva: June-July, Sepember-October. Adult: April-May, July-August. |
| Distribution | Common in England and Wales; less so in Scotland and Ireland. Common in VC58, 59, 60. |
| Photo details | Leaf-mine from Little Budworth Common, Cheshire VC58; 25.10.15 (BS). |

This leaf-miner is very common on beech, so much so that it is hard to find a beech tree unaffected by this species. The mine is serpentine, often incorporating many S-shaped bends.

The egg is laid on the underside of the leaf, typically in the angle between the midrib and a vein. Like other nepticulid species the egg is shiny black, and by using a hand-lens, the egg can be seen at the start of the mine. The initial mine contains a thin line of frass, which later becomes widely dispersed. Unlike *S. tityrella's* fellow beech leaf-miner *Stigmella hemargyrella* (p.168), the mine does not contain a section of coiled frass. The latter species usually lays its egg away from the midrib, and this may be on either side of the leaf.

As the *tityrella* mine progresses, a number of 180 degree changes in direction are made in an area between two veins. Towards the end of October, larvae may still be found actively feeding, even in leaves that have fallen to the ground. Their presence may be obvious by the development of green islands within the leaf. When feeding is complete, the dark-headed yellow larva leaves via a slit made on the upper surface of the leaf.

It then goes on to construct a white cocoon covered with flossy silken fibres. This is quite different to the pale yellow cocoon of *hemargyrella*, which lacks this flossy coating.

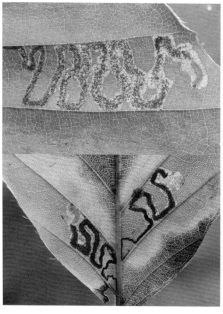

# Ectoedemia occultella

| | |
|---|---|
| Nepticulidae | 4.099 *Ectoedemia occultella* (Linnaeus, 1767) |
| Foodplant | Birch (*Betula* spp.). |
| Life cycle | Larva: August to October. Adult: June to July. |
| Distribution | Widespread and common throughout British Isles. Common in VC58, 59, 60. |
| Photo details | Leaf-mine from Chorlton, Manchester VC59; 22.10.11 (BS). |

The egg of *E. occultella* is laid on the underside of a leaf. Each mine then begins as a round dark brown spot with no obvious gallery. There may be many on a single leaf. The discolouration of the leaf is not caused by the presence of frass, but by damage to the leaf tissue sustained during the early feeding. As the larva continues to feed, the mine extends to become a translucent blotch surrounding the original dark spot. Observing the larva within the mine is sometimes difficult, as it can only be seen in the pale blotch, and it retreats beneath the dark spot when not feeding. The larva is pale green with a brown head, and has small brown spots on the venter (the underside of the larva). When feeding within the mine, the larva remains venter upwards.

After feeding is complete, the larva vacates the mine and forms a brown cocoon on the surface of the ground. If rearing, *Ectoedemia* species are best overwintered outside.

The moth is sexually dimorphic. The female has a yellowish head and collar, whereas the male, pictured below, has a blackish head and collar, often containing a few fuscous scales.

The other *Ectoedemia* species on birch, *Ectoedemia minimella*, (also found on hazel), is less common in the region. The yellow larva feeds in a large irregular blotch with dispersed frass, which begins with a very convoluted early gallery (p.130).

# Caloptilia elongella

| | |
|---|---|
| Gracillariidae | 15.004 *Caloptilia elongella* (Linnaeus, 1761) |
| Foodplant | Alder (*Alnus* spp.). |
| Life cycle | Larva: May-July, August-October. Adult: September-May, June-August. |
| Distribution | Common and widespread throughout British Isles. |
| | Common in VC58, 59, 60. |
| Photo details | Feeding signs from Rivacre Valley, Wirral VC58; 10.10.15 (BS). |

The life cycle of this species seems to differ from that given in other texts. Generally, the larval stage is given as May and July. However within the north-west (and likely elsewhere), there is a large autumn generation of larvae, with tenanted mines recorded as late as mid-November. The leaf-mine below from mid-October, gave rise to an adult moth, emerging on 19th November. I'm unsure if this represents a third generation or an extended second generation.

The larva initially feeds in a small gallery, leading to a whitish blotch on the upper surface. This blotch becomes contracted as feeding progresses. The final feeding stage involves half, or even the whole leaf, being longitudinally spun with the pale green larva feeding within.

The adult moth is very similar to that of *Caloptilia betulicola*, but can be separated with care. In *elongella*, the trochanter (upper area) of the hindleg is yellowish-buff. In *betulicola*, it is white.

There is another *Caloptilia* species on alder, *C. falconipennella*, which is locally recorded in southern England. At present there is no definite record of this within the region, although undoubtedly it is worth looking out for. The mining stages in July and August differ considerably from *elongella*. There is a small initial gallery leading to a brown blotch at the leaf margin, followed by two or three folds, similar to a *Parornix* species, at the leaf edge.

# *Parornix devoniella*

| Gracillariidae | 15.029 *Parornix devoniella* (Stainton, 1850) |
| Foodplant | Hazel (*Corylus avellana*). |
| Life cycle | Larva: July, September to October. Adult: May and August. |
| Distribution | Widespread throughout British Isles. |
| | Common in VC58, 59, 60. |
| Photo details | Feeding signs from Rivacre Valley, Wirral VC58; 10.10.15 (BS). |

Feeding on hazel, the larva may go through all the stages of its life-cycle on the same leaf.

The ova giving rise to the overwintering generation is laid in August on the underside of the leaf. On hatching the tiny larva forms a gallery mine in the lower epidermis which is extended to a small square area (occasionally triangular), turning the underside brown. The browning of the underside, and the squarish nature of this mine, should be enough to separate the mine from that of *Phyllonorycter nicellii*. *P. nicellii* forms a much longer, rectangular, tentiform mine between two veins which is greenish on the underside (p.212).

Following the mining stage, the larva goes on to make two or three folds, often on the same leaf as the initial mine, and usually on the upper surface. Within this fold the larva feeds on the inner surface of the leaf. A much smaller fold is made when the larva is full-fed, as it goes on to pupate in an ochreous cocoon, under the edge of a leaf, sometimes amongst the leaf-litter.

Other *Parornix* species to be found in the region, all with similar life histories, are *anglicella* on hawthorn (p.10), *betulae* (p.133) and *loganella* on birch, *scoticella* on Sorbus (p.154), and *finitimella* and *torquillella* on blackthorn. The latter two can be separated by larval appearance. *P.finitimella* has the legs ringed black, whereas *torquillella* legs are concolourous with the body.

# *Phyllonorycter schreberella*

| | |
|---|---|
| Gracillariidae | 15.074 *Phyllonorycter schreberella* (Fabricius, 1781) |
| Foodplant | Elm (*Ulmus* spp.). |
| Life cycle | Larva: July, September to October. Adult: May and August. |
| Distribution | Local in England and Wales. Unrecorded in Scotland and Ireland. Local in VC58, 59. Unrecorded in VC60 since 19th Century. |
| Photo details | Leaf-mine on elm from Rivacre Valley, Wirral VC58; 10.10.15 (BS). |

The less common of the two elm-mining *Phyllonorycter* species in our region, *schreberella* becomes even scarcer as one moves north, with over 100 records in Cheshire and only one very old report from north Lancashire. The species favours the smaller leaved elms, avoiding wych elm. The larval mine is on the underside of the leaf, and may be square or oval with several long central creases. The mine may cross a vein, and results in the leaf becoming contorted. The upper surface of the leaf-mine often shows a small green patch of uneaten parenchyma.

The larva is amber coloured with a dark brown head, unlike the larva of *tristrigella*, which is whitish green. However exposing the larva to confirm identity is not really required as it will be unable to develop further if removed, and the two mines can easily be separated from each other (see page 175).

Pupation occurs in a tough greenish cocoon, similar to that of *Phyllonorycter tristrigella*. Both species overwinter in this stage.

The adult is one of the more distinctive *Phyllonorycter* species, and cannot really be confused with any other, particularly when freshly emerged. It has a black head, a silvery thorax and silver fascia, the first two of which are unbroken.

# *Phyllonorycter tristrigella*

Yponomeutidae  15.078 *Phyllonorycter tristrigella* (Haworth, 1828)
Foodplant  Elm (*Ulmus* spp.).
Life cycle  Larva: July, September to October. Adult: May and August.
Distribution  Common in England and Wales. Local in Scotland. Unrecorded in Ireland. Common in VC58, 59, 60.
Photo details  Leaf-mine on elm from Rivacre Valley, Wirral VC58; 10.10.15 (BS).

The larval stage of this species can be commonly found on elm leaves, including wych elm, throughout the region. The pale whitish green larvae form long, tubular mines on the underside of the leaf between two veins, often reaching from close to the leaf edge to the midrib. There are numerous creases in the lower epidermis. These have the effect of contracting the mine, and pulling the veins on either side of the mine tightly together. Pupation occurs in a tough greenish brown cocoon, a little broader than that of *schreberella*. The cocoon is strongly attached to the lower epidermis of the mine. The cocoon of *P. schreberella*, in contrast, is only lightly attached to the uneaten area of the upper surface of the mine and even more loosely to the lower epidermis.

The adult moth is variable in the intensity of its markings. The one pictured here is quite a dark individual. Fresh moths can be identified, although care is required to separate *tristrigella* from the hazel miner *P. nicellii*, and the alder miners *P froelichiella*, *P. klemannella* and *P. stettinensis*, all of which can be found throughout Lancashire and Cheshire.

Rearing *Phyllonorycter* moths is not difficult. Placing some of the leaves in an old stocking in a sheltered spot and bringing them inside in spring can be very rewarding and allows one to see these beautifully marked species at their best.

# *Leucoptera malifoliella*

| | |
|---|---|
| Lyonetiidae | 21.008 *Leucoptera malifoliella* (Costa, [1836]) |
| Foodplant | Hawthorn (*Crataegus* spp.), apple (*Malus* spp.), pear (*Pyrus* spp.), etc. |
| Life cycle | Larva: August to October. Adult: June and July. |
| Distribution | Local in England, Wales. Scarce in Scotland and Ireland. Widespread in VC58, 59, 60. |
| Photo details | Feeding signs on hawthorn from St Helens VC59; 01.10.15 (BS). |

In addition to the foodplants listed above, this species has also been recorded mining leaves of rowan, blackthorn, quince and Cotoneaster spp.

The larva mines a single leaf, initially forming a circular blotch with the frass filling this circle and being attached to the upper cuticle. The final instar sees the larva extending this blotch, and depositing frass in a more random manner. The larva should now be quite visible within the pale areas of the blotch. The dark prothoracic plate is evident within the mine.

The mine below was found on 1.10.15 when just the initial circular mine was present, and the larva could not be seen. The photograph was taken 4 days later after the blotch had been extended. The larva exited the mine on 10.10.15, constructing the fairly elaborate cocoon the following day at a leaf edge. The species overwinters in the pupal stage.

Although the species has quite a wide distribution locally and nationally, its occurrence is quite erratic. It may be seem to be absent for a few years, before occurring in relative profusion. This cyclical variation is possibly related to parasitisation.

There are two other members of the genus found locally. *L. laburnella* forms a larger blotch on laburnum in summer (p.186). *L. spartifoliella* mines broom and is described elsewhere (p.103).

# Carcina quercana

| | |
|---|---|
| Peleopodidae | 31.001 *Carcina quercana* (Fabricius, 1775) |
| Foodplant | Oak (*Quercus* spp.), beech (*Fagus sylvatica*). |
| Life cycle | Larva: September to June. Adult: July and August. |
| Distribution | Common in England, Wales and Ireland. Local in Scotland. Common in VC58, 59, 60. |
| Photo details | Feeding signs from Little Budworth Common VC58; 25.10.15 (BS). |

This common moth flies at dusk, but is easily disturbed from trees where it will rest during the day. It is a frequent visitor to light traps, and a well-marked one with its pink and yellow markings and notably long antennae.

The larvae can be found in autumn in oak and beech woods, and favour these foodplants, although it has also been recorded on sweet chestnut, sycamore, rose, apple and bramble.

In autumn, the larva can be located by looking for a brown patch on a leaf where the lower epidermis has been consumed. When not feeding, or when disturbed, the 4mm larva can be found on the underside of this leaf beneath a dense silken patch on one side of the midrib. It may be difficult to make out the larva within the spinning, but holding it up to the light should confirm its presence, as in the bottom left photo, where the larva is to the right of the pale patch.

In spring, the larva recommences feeding under a lighter silken web. It may attain a length of 17mm. When fully grown, the larva is green with two longitudinal subdorsal white lines as in the larva below right.

Pupation takes place on the underside of the leaf, beneath a silken membrane, somewhat similar to those formed by *Caloptilia* larvae.

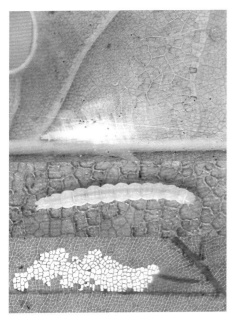

# Scrobipalpa costella

| | |
|---|---|
| Gelechiidae | 35.123 *Scrobipalpa costella* (Humphreys & Westwood, 1845) |
| Foodplant | Bittersweet (*Solanum dulcamara*). |
| Life cycle | Larva: May, August to October. Adult: June, September to June. |
| Distribution | Widely distributed in England and Wales. Local in Scotland and Ireland. Common in VC58, 59, 60. |
| Photo details | Leaf-mines from Collyhurst, Manchester VC59; 01.10.16 (BS). |

The larval signs of this species seem to be reasonably local in our area, as many seemingly suitable patches of bittersweet can be checked and yet the only lepidopterous miner present is often *Acrolepia autumnitella*. However if one strikes lucky and *costella* is present, then it may be so in large numbers, with many larvae mining a single leaf, as in the photo on the bottom left.

The young larvae begin mining the midrib, and from there extend their mines to form an untidy blotch within the leaf containing dark brown frass (unlike *autumnitella* mines, p.158). Larvae may also be found feeding within the stem, feeding externally between spun leaves, and in the berries. The first two of these methods were also noted at the site where these photos were obtained.

The larva has a dark brown to black head and prothoracic plate. The first two thoracic segments are purplish brown. The pale grey abdomen bears pale pink or brown subdorsal and dorsal lines. These turn notably reddish prior to pupation, as in the example below.

The exact phenology of the various stages of this species still seems incompletely understood. It was formerly thought that the adult moth overwintered, but it is now felt likely that the species may also be able to overwinter as a larva. In the colony photographed below in early October, there was a wide variety of larval instars, with pre-pupal larvae as well as early instar mines.

# Coleophora gryphipennella

| | |
|---|---|
| Coleophoridae | 37.006 *Coleophora gryphipennella* (Hübner, 1796) |
| Foodplant | Rose (*Rosa* spp.). |
| Life cycle | Larva: September to May. Adult: Late June to July |
| Distribution | Common in British Isles, although more local in N Scotland and Ireland. Common in VC58, 59, 60. |
| Photo details | Case from Gait Barrows VC60; 18.10.15 (BS). Adult (Oliver Wadsworth). |

Autumn is the likeliest time to record this species, although one may be more successful in rearing cases found in spring, when the larva has already overwintered.

The presence of a case may be noted by locating pale blotches on rose leaves with a small circular hole in the lower epidermis. This hole allows the mining larva to enter the underside of the leaf from the safety of its case.

The case is constructed from the margin of a rose leaf, resulting in the case having the same serrated edge as the leaf and it may construct three or four cases during its development.

The species hibernates as a partially-fed larva, completing its feeding in the spring. It makes a final case before searching for a pupation site, usually on a stem of the foodplant. Pupation occurs within the case.

The chances of successful rearing of this species, as with most of the other Coleophoridae, can be enhanced by keeping the case outside overwinter and during the pupal stage. Probably the best way to do so is to sleeve a portion of the foodplant containing the case with some fine netting (such as stocking material), and to ensure that this is securely tied around the stem to prevent the larva leaving, and to reduce the chances of predators entering.

# *Elachista gangabella*

| | |
|---|---|
| Elachistidae | 38.015 *Elachista gangabella* Zeller, 1850 |
| Foodplant | False brome (*Brachypodium sylvaticum*). |
| Life cycle | Larva: August to April. Adult: May to June. |
| Distribution | Local in England, Wales and Ireland. Unrecorded in Scotland. Local in VC60. Unrecorded from VC58, 59. |
| Photo details | Leaf-mines from Gait Barrows, Lancashire VC60. 18.10.15 (BS). |

*Elachista* mines on grasses are never particularly easy to find, but spring is generally the most productive time for searching. An exception to this is *Elachista gangabella*. It has a slightly odd distribution in that it is commonest in southern England, absent from much of the Midlands to south Lancashire, south Yorkshire and Cheshire, but with records from north Lancashire, Cumbria and the north-east of England. The species frequents shady woodland where the foodplant is found.

Where they occur, the mines can be quite common on false brome. They have also been recorded on cock's-foot (*Dactylis glomerata*) and soft-grass (*Holcus* spp.). The mines are quite conspicuous, with a large pale blotch in the blade of the leaf. Within this, the larva constructs a silken tube containing some frass.

The larva is olive-green when feeding, but greyish, as below, when feeding is complete. The head and prothoracic plate are orange-brown.

The species overwinters as a full-fed larva inside the mine. The larva leaves the mine in spring and pupates, forming an orange-brown pupa which is lightly spun onto dead vegetation.

To rear this species it is advisable to keep the plant material outside over winter and to bring inside from early May, keeping a close watch for emergence.

# Pseudargyrotoza conwagana

| | |
|---|---|
| Tortricidae | 49.091 *Pseudargyrotoza conwagana* (Fabricius, 1775) |
| Foodplant | Ash (*Fraxinus excelsior*), privet (*Ligustrum* spp.). |
| Life cycle | Larva: August to October. Adult: May to July. |
| Distribution | Widely distributed and common throughout British Isles. Common in VC58, 59, 60. |
| Photo details | Feeding signs from Chorlton, Manchester VC59. 17.10.15 (BS). |

This beautifully marked moth can be abundant wherever ash or uncut privet are found.

Keep an eye out when around ash in autumn, and one may see the larva dangling from a silken thread below an ash tree. Although fairly plain, it is quite a distinctive larva with an unusual arrangement of spots, so can be definitely identified to species.

Alternatively, the larvae can be located by looking for small round holes in the keys, the larvae feeding on the seeds within. This hole allows it to expel frass, and eventually to leave the key when feeding is complete. Opening up the key should show obvious signs of feeding where the seed has been partially or wholly consumed, and some frass will still be present even if the larva has already departed.

Larvae can also be found by putting a randomly selected bunch of ash keys in a clear plastic container, and waiting for them to emerge and crawl up the sides of the container. Remove the lid for a minute or so each day to reduce the risk of mould development.

Larvae also use the berries of privet. On the continent, berries of lilac and barberry have also been noted as food material.

The species overwinters in the pupal stage within a white cocoon formed on the ground.

# Ancylis mitterbacheriana

| | |
|---|---|
| Tortricidae | 49.216 *Ancylis mitterbacheriana* ([Denis & Schiffermüller], 1775) |
| Foodplant | Oak (*Quercus* spp.), beech (*Fagus sylvatica*), sweet chestnut (*Castanea*). |
| Life cycle | Larva: August to October. Adult: May to July. |
| Distribution | Widespread but local in British Isles. |
| | Local in VC58, 60. Not recorded in VC59 since around 1900. |
| Photo details | Feeding signs from Gait Barrows, Lancashire VC60; 18.10.15 (BS). |
| | Adult (Chris Manley). |

The larva of this species of deciduous woodland feeds on the upper epidermis of either oak, beech, or sweet chestnut (in decreasing order of their frequency) from within the protection of a folded leaf. The two sides of the leaf are tightly pulled together by thick silken sutures, and then sealed along the leaf edges to form a pod. The whole of the inside of this pod is consumed, and frass is deposited within. The larva can then move to a further leaf and repeat the process.

The larval colour varies between brown and green, with very prominent pale pinaculae, and a prothoracic plate marked with black patches. When full-fed, it forms a cocoon in its pod and hibernates within, pupating in spring.

Within Cheshire and Lancashire, other Ancylis species found feeding in pods include *geminana* and *diminutana* on sallow, *badiana* on clover, *unculana*, *obtusana* and *apicella* on buckthorn and alder buckthorn, and *myrtillana* on bilberry.

As the larvae of these species overwinter, it is better to keep them outside until spring, either netted on the foodplant itself, or with the tenanted pod kept in a flowerpot protected by netting. Personal experience is that *mitterbacheriana* larvae seem vulnerable to high rates of parasitism.

| | |
|---|---|
| Tortricidae | 49.359 *Grapholia janthinana* (Duponchel, 1835) |
| Foodplant | Hawthorn (*Crataegus* spp.). |
| Life cycle | Larva: September to May. Adult: mid-June to early August. |
| Distribution | Common in England and Wales. Local in Ireland and southern Scotland. Common in VC58, 59, 60. |
| Photo details | Feeding signs from St Helens, Lancashire VC59; 01.10.15 (BS). |

If one can find two hawthorn berries (haws) spun together, with a small amount of silk and some frass present, then one can be almost certain to have detected the feeding signs of *janthinana*. To observe the larva, one can carefully attempt to open up the haw or just stick them in a pot. Within a few days the larva is likely to have exited the haw and will be found crawling up the sides of the pot.

Earlier instar larvae are pinkish but with a dark brown head and prothoracic plate. Final instar larvae are salmon-pink, with a light brown head and prothoracic plate. The larva overwinters.

The feeding signs should be contrasted with that of *Blastodacna hellerella*, which makes a hole in the side of the haw without attaching it to a neighbour. The larva of *hellerella* is a darker pink with reddish lateral spots and dark brown anal plate and thoracic legs (p.148). Other species feeding in haws include *Blastobasis lacticolella* and various diptera. I have found one other Lepidoptera larva in haws (yellow abdomen, black head). I suspected early instar *Ditula angustiorana*, but was unable to rear through to confirm identity. I have also found a couple of early instar *Acrobasis advenella* larvae attached to the haw in October, although did not observe any definite feeding. These *advenella* larvae successfully overwintered and developed into adults.

# Pammene aurita

| | |
|---|---|
| Tortricidae | 49.376 *Pammene aurita* Razowski, 1991 |
| Foodplant | Sycamore (*Acer pseudoplatanus*). |
| Life cycle | Larva: August to September. Adult: July to August. |
| Distribution | Locally common in S. England, Wales. Unrecorded in Scotland, Ireland. Local in VC58, 59, 60. |
| Photo details | Feeding signs from Chorlton, Manchester VC59; 12.10.15 (BS). |

*P. aurita* larvae feed on sycamore seeds. Searching through the keys may reveal some tenanted or (more likely) vacated and frass-filled, as the hole is made shortly before the larva leaves the key.

It is possible that similar neat 2mm diameter exit-holes may be made by *Pammene regiana* larvae, although I am unsure whether it makes such a neat exit-hole. I can find no reference to this.

One may find a larva dangling from the keys, or perhaps crawling down the trunk. Below is a larva I found in 2006, in a cocoon amongst detritus under the tree where the keys below were found. The head is darker than that of *P. regiana*. The adult was reared to confirm identity.

There is an interesting account of the first finding of the larvae of *Pammene aurantiana* (now *aurita*), by S. Wakely in The Entomologist's Record (Vol 72, 15/11/60). Wakely reports finding the larvae, as well as *P. regiana* larvae, in sycamore keys in Surrey during September and October. He documents successful rearing by drilling small holes at half-inch depth in soft wood, and by hand placing the larvae head first into these holes. He found the larvae stayed put and sealed off the end prior to pupation. Others formed cocoons in tissue paper. In its natural habitat, the pupation site is unknown. Wakely suggests that they may pupate beneath sycamore bark in the manner of *regiana*. If so, I am surprised never to have found any overwintering in this manner.

# *Strophedra weirana*

| | |
|---|---|
| Tortricidae | 49.381 *Strophedra weirana* (Douglas, 1850) |
| Foodplant | Beech (*Fagus sylvatica*). |
| Life cycle | Larva: August to October. Adult: June. |
| Distribution | Locally common in S. England, Wales. Unrecorded in Scotland, Ireland. Local in VC58, 60. Unrecorded in VC 59. |
| Photo details | Feeding signs from Little Budworth Common VC58; 26.09.15 (BS). |

This moth has a largely southern distribution, but has been found at a number of sites in Cheshire and at a single site in north Lancashire. It is worth looking for throughout the whole of our region, as its feeding signs are probably more distinctive than the dark, minimally marked adult moth.

The larvae feed in autumn between two beech leaves, one lightly spun on top of the other. The larva feeds on the lower surface of the upper leaf, leaving a tell-tale brown discolouration of the top leaf. The expelled frass is laid down around the larva and is later used to line a white, silken, pupal cocoon formed in the feeding place, as in the photos below.

The feeding signs could potentially be confused with *Acleris sparsana*, which may also feed between flatly-spun beech leaves. However these feed earlier in the year, so will be vacant when *weirana* is feeding, and will show no evidence of a frass-coated cocoon. If *sparsana* larva is present, this is quite different too, being green with a light brown head.

The closely related species *Strophedra nitidana*, and the gelechiid *Teleoides luculella*, feed in a similar manner to *weirana*, but on oak, also forming a frass-coated cocoon between two flatly spun oak leaves. *Strophedra nitidana* appears to be currently absent from our region, although there is a historical north Lancashire record from the 19th Century.

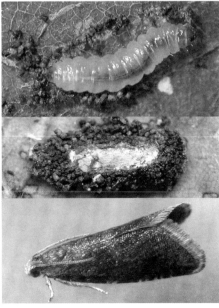

# A selection of leaf-mines from autumn (2)

4.060 *Stigmella ruficapitella* - oak 6-7, 9-10.
4.062 *S. samiatella* - sweet chestnut, oak 6-7, 9-10.
4.063 *Stigmella roborella* - oak 6-7, 10-11.
4.089 *Ectoedemia albifasciella* - oak 8-10.
4.091 *Ectoedemia heringi* - oak 10-11.

4.094 *Ectoedemia angulifasciella* - rose 9-11.
4.095 *Ectoedemia atricollis* - hawthorn, apple, etc. 8-4.
10.002 *Tischeria dodonaea* - oak 9-4.
21.004 *Leucoptera laburnella* - laburnum 6-7, 9.
49.280 *Gypsonoma oppressana* - poplar 9-5.

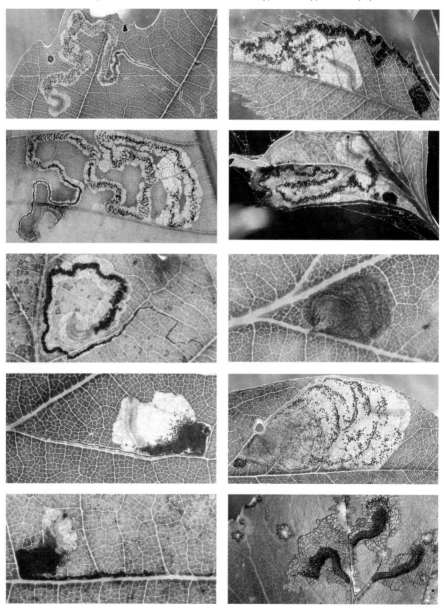

# NOVEMBER FIELD TIPS

Early November can still be a good time to search for the leaf-mining species, particularly those feeding within 'green islands' in leaves, such as *Ectoedemia argyropeza* on aspen. Larval feeding seems to induce the area around the mine to remain photosynthetically active, thus maintaining the nutritional value of that particular area.

The distinctiveness of these islands means that nepticulid and *Phyllonorycter* species can be searched for with relative ease, even when the leaves have fallen to the ground.

Many larvae overwinter full-fed, but most will by now have entered their cocoons thus making it hard to locate them. Even if the larvae cannot be found, their feeding signs may remain visible, as with the signs of *Coleophora artemisicolella* on mugwort.

188. *Stigmella atricapitella*
189. *Ectoedemia intimella*
190. *Ectoedemia argyropeza*
191. *Ectoedemia subbimaculella*
192. *Tischeria ekebladella*
193. *Gracillaria syringella*
194. *Phyllonorycter stettinensis*
195. *Phyllonorycter joannisi*
196. *Scrobipalpa acuminatella*
197. *Coleophora artemisicolella*
198. *Ancylis badiana*
199. *Gypsonoma dealbana*

*Lindow Common, Wilmslow, Cheshire, 14th November 2015*

# Stigmella atricapitella

Nepticulidae     4.061 *Stigmella atricapitella* (Haworth, 1828)
Foodplant     Oak (*Quercus* spp.).
Life cycle     Larva: June-July and Sept-Nov. Adult: May-June and Aug-Sept.
Distribution     Widespread and common throughout British Isles.
    Common in VC58, 59, 60.
Photo details     Leaf-mine from Chorlton, Manchester VC59; 01.11.13 (BS).

The early stages of the *Stigmella* species on oak represent quite a difficult identification challenge, and in some cases rearing through to the adult stage is the only way to be certain of the species. As a result, it is the case that some of the historical records for these species are somewhat unreliable, particularly where they relate to vacated mines. *S. atricapitella* is one of the less tricky to identify. It is a bivoltine species, with tenanted mines present up to the middle of November.

To try and identify the leaf-mine, it is essential that one first determines if the shiny black egg at the start of the gallery is on the under or upperside of the leaf. In *atricapitella*, the egg is typically on the underside. The yellow larva has a brown head with conspicuous black prothoracic sclerites. These are the two triangular markings just behind the head – see larval photo below.

Of the other species, *Stigmella ruficapitella* (p.186) lays its egg on the upperside of the leaf. The yellow larva has a pale brown head, with pale brown prothoracic sclerites.

*S. roborella* (p.186), *S. svenssoni* and *S. samiatella* (p.186) are less common in our counties. Their eggs are usually laid on the underside, but occasionally on the upper, usually away from the leaf margin. *S. basiguttella* mines are packed with green frass. *S. suberivora* is found on holm oak. The latter two have not yet been found in this region.

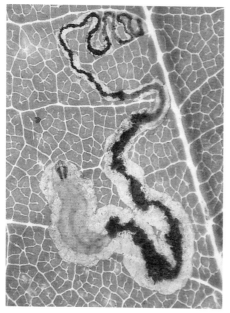

# *Ectoedemia intimella*

| | |
|---|---|
| Nepticulidae | 4.082 *Ectoedemia intimella* (Zeller, 1848) |
| Foodplant | Goat willow (*Salix caprea*) or other *Salix* spp. |
| Life cycle | Larva: July to November. Adult: June. |
| Distribution | Widely distributed throughout British Isles. Local in VC58, 59, 60. |
| Photo details | Leaf-mine from Flixton, Manchester VC59; 09.11.08 (BS). |

This species can be found whilst the leaves are still on the tree, or by looking for green islands in the fallen leaves below sallow trees.

It is one of the later leaf-miners to look for, as its early larval stages are quite inconspicuous. The larva first mines the midrib, leaving a slightly blackish discolouration on the mined portion. The more obvious signs of mining only occur from the end of October onwards, when, after reaching approximately one third of the way up the midrib, the larva branches out into the leaf blade. The larva mines out a blotch, usually with a double line of frass at the start of the blotch. The larva may retreat back into the midrib when not feeding, so take care in dismissing an *E. intimella* leaf-mine as vacated if the blotch is fairly small and there is no sign of a slit in the leaf. The larva continues to extend the blotch, laying down frass randomly within it.

On completion of feeding, the larva spins a reddish-brown cocoon amongst the leaf-litter, and pupates within, spending the winter in this stage before emergence in June.

Some mines of *Stigmella salicis* on sallow can look a little like that of *E. intimella*, as the gallery mine formed by *salicis* may sometimes form a false blotch close to the midrib. However closer inspection will reveal that the midrib itself has not been mined.

 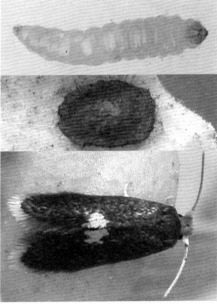

# *Ectoedemia argyropeza*

| | |
|---|---|
| Nepticulidae | 4.085 *Ectoedemia argyropeza* (Zeller, 1839) |
| Foodplant | Aspen (*Populus tremula*). |
| Life cycle | Larva: September to November. Adult: May to June. |
| Distribution | Locally common throughout British Isles. |
| | Local in VC58, 59. Unrecorded in VC60. |
| Photo details | Feeding signs from St Helens, Lancashire VC59; 03.11.15 (BS). |

Searching for this leaf-mine on aspen is more likely to be successful if concentrating on the fallen leaves, rather than those still on the tree. Look for leaves containing conspicuous green patches. Closer inspection should reveal a small mined area, between two veins at the base of the midrib. Initial mining is within the petiole below the leaf blade. causing it to swell and become a little discoloured. When the larva enters the leaf, it initially makes two lines of frass, but later deposits frass in a more random pattern. When still small, the larva will retreat back into the petiole when it is not feeding.

The larva feeds ventral side upwards. The ventral side bears a chain of brown spots on the thoracic segments and a dark brown thoracic plate. These markings can be seen on the larva within the mine. When full-fed, the larva leaves its mine and forms a cocoon amongst the soil and detritus.

The green islands that form on tenanted aspen leaves are also found on leaves of other species tenanted by microlepidoptera larvae, and appear linked to the presence of symbiotic *Wolbachia* bacteria. Kaiser et al (2010) demonstrated the presence of *Wolbachia* bacteria on *Phyllonorycter blancardella* larvae, and that antibiotics used to kill the bacteria also reduced the green islands and adversely affected adult emergence.

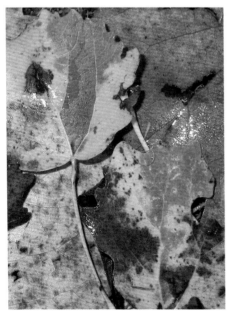

# Ectoedemia subbimaculella

Nepticulidae      4.090 *Ectoedemia subbimaculella* (Haworth, 1828)
Foodplant         Oak (*Quercus* spp.).
Life cycle        Larva: October to November. Adult: June to July.
Distribution      Widespread throughout British Isles.
                  Common in VC58, 59, 60.
Photo details     Feeding signs from Chorlton, Manchester VC59; 12.11.16 (BS).

This species appears late in the season, with tenanted mines present into the second half of November, It is easy to identify, even when vacated, as the underside of the blotch-mine contains a conspicuous slit to facilitate frass removal. Mines are usually formed in the angle between the midrib and a major vein. The greenish larva has a dark brown head and prothoracic plate. To rear, leave the larvae outside overwinter in a netted pot, and adults should emerge the following June.

The main confusion species on oak in November is *E. heringi* (p.186). The mine is similar to that of *subbimaculella*, but lacks the slit. The larval head colour of *heringi* varies from pale to chestnut brown. This species is much less common throughout the region, particularly in Lancashire.

Other *Ectoedemia* found on oak include the common *E. albifasciella* which feeds in a blotch, usually away from the midrib, in August and September (p.186). *E. heringella* feeds on holm oak. *E. quinquella* feeds in a contorted gallery, and many may be found on the same leaf. *E. heckfordi* (discovered in 2004) makes a large blotch close to the edge of the leaf, containing two frass lines and a green larva. There are two further species, *E. atrifrontella* and *E. longicaudella*, that mine the bark of oak trees. Other than *albifasciella*, these other *Ectoedemia* are as yet unrecorded in Lancashire and Cheshire.

# Tischeria ekebladella

Tischeriidae     10.001 *Tischeria ekebladella* (Bjerkander, 1795)
Foodplant     Oak (*Quercus* spp.), sweet chestnut (*Castanea sativa*).
Life cycle     Larva: September to November. Adult: late May to mid-July.
Distribution     Common throughout British Isles.
            Common in VC58, 59, 60.
Photo details     Leaf-mine on oak from Lindow Common, Wilmslow VC58; 14.11.15 (BS)

The larvae slowly feed within their mines on oak during the autumn, forming creamy blotches on the upper surface of oak leaves. The blotch is slowly extended outwards, leaving a slightly darker centre. I find the shape of the mines a little like a miniature fried egg. There is a slit on the edge of the mine to allow expulsion of frass.

Holding the leaf up to the light should reveal the larva within. If feeding is complete, one will see the larva curled in a c shape in a circular chamber in the centre of the mine. Overwintering occurs in this stage, with pupation occurring in spring within this chamber. The yellow larva has swollen thoracic segments, a pale brown head, and a dark brown anal plate. The head is extremely flattened, presumably aiding its passage beneath the upper surface of the leaf. There are no prolegs or obvious thoracic legs. Close examination shows tiny projections beneath the thoracic segments in place of functioning legs.

In warmer years, leaf-mines may develop earlier and go on to produce adults in August.

A much rarer species in our region is *T. dodonaea*. This also mines the upperside of oak leaves in autumn, forming brown blotches containing concentric rings. As with *ekebladella*, the larva of *dodonaea* overwinters within a circular chamber.

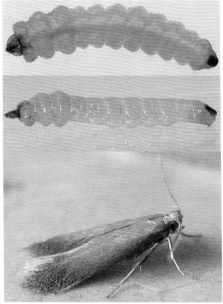

# Gracillaria syringella

| | |
|---|---|
| Gracillariidae | 15.014 *Gracillaria syringella* (Fabricius, 1794) |
| Foodplant | Privet (*Ligustrum*), lilac (*Syringa*) and ash (*Fraxinus excelsior*). |
| Life cycle | Larva: July, September. Adult: April to June, August to September. |
| Distribution | Common throughout British Isles. |
| | Common in VC58, 59, 60. |
| Photo details | Feeding signs from Chorlton, Manchester VC59; 07.11.16 (BS). |

Feeding signs of this species can be found through much of the year. The leaf-folds can be tenanted well into the second half of November.

Early instar larvae mine the leaves of the foodplant. Each mine may affect up to half of the leaf and will contain a number of larvae. Frass is randomly deposited throughout the mine. The leaf becomes increasingly distorted and turns brown as the larva continues to feed. Later in the larval development, a couple of untidy, brown folds with copious frass are formed, with a number of larvae feeding communally in each.

The larva is greyish white, with a green gut-line and a pale brown head. The thoracic legs and prolegs are concolourous with the abdomen. Pupation occurs within a greyish-white membranous cocoon, which may be formed amongst the leaf-litter or occasionally on the underside of a leaf.

This species can be easily reared in captivity, particularly from the leaf-fold stage. The cocoons will be formed along the edge of the pot, and keeping it in a cool place overwinter should be sufficient to allow the adults to emerge in early spring.

*Caloptilia cuculipennella*, a much scarcer moth, shares the same foodplants, but has a silvery-grey mine rather than brown, and the cocoon is clearly different (see p.118).

# Phyllonorycter stettinensis

Gracillariidae    15.079 *Phyllonorycter stettinensis* (Nicelli, 1852)
Foodplant         Alder (*Alnus* spp.).
Life cycle        Larva: July and October to November. Adult: May and August.
Distribution      Common in England and Wales. Local in Scotland. Unrecorded in Ireland.
                  Common in VC58, 59; local in VC60.
Photo details     Leaf-mine from Flixton, Manchester VC59; 21.10.16 (BS).

One of four *Phyllonorycter* species that can be found on common alder, *P. stettinensis* can easily be differentiated from the other three by the fact that it is the only one that mines the upper side of the leaf. The initial mine is pale green, becoming browner as the larva feeds within. The mine, which is usually situated over a vein, becomes contracted and a central crease becomes apparent. As in the left hand photo below, one may often find a number of mines on a single leaf. If you hold it up to the light, the larvae or pupal cocoons should be evident.

The larva is yellowish white, with similarly coloured thoracic legs and a brown head. As with other *Phyllonorycter* larvae, the thoracic segments are the widest, with gradual tapering towards the anal plate. The relative width of the thoracic segments is more pronounced in the early instars.

*Gracillariidae* larvae are characterised by hypermetamorphosis, meaning that there is a distinct change in terms of structure and feeding habits between early and late instars. The first two instars are extremely flattened, with mouthparts adapted for sap feeding from the epidermal cells. Later instars (as shown here) are more rounded in shape and have thoracic legs and prolegs (absent in the early instars). The head becomes rounder, as with the larva below, and the new mouth parts allow chewing in this, the tissue-feeding phase, as parenchyma is consumed (Emmet et al, 1985).

# Phyllonorycter joannisi

| | |
|---|---|
| Gracillariidae | 15.085 *Phyllonorycter joannisi* (Le Marchand, 1936) |
| Foodplant | Norway Maple (*Acer platanoides*). |
| Life cycle | Larva: July and October to November. Adult: May and August. |
| Distribution | Common in England and Wales. Unrecorded in Scotland and Ireland. Common in VC 58, 59, 60. |
| Photo details | Leaf-mine from Chorlton, Manchester VC59; 07.11.16 (BS). |

As long as there are leaves on the trees one may find the mines of *Phyllonorycter* species. Even when the leaves have fallen, the leaves below may be checked for the presence of the mines, meaning that this genus can be recorded throughout November and December.

*Phyllonorycter joannisi* mines are found on the leaves of Norway Maple. The upperside becomes progressively discoloured as the larva feeds, as in the top photos below. The large whitish mine is situated on the underside of the leaf between two veins. There is no strong central crease, but instead the mine is characterised by a number of very small creases.

As with most *Phyllonorycter* moths, it is easiest to rear the adults from the first generation. Nevertheless, keeping the autumn mines over winter can also be quite successful, particularly if the mines are kept with a few other leaves, netted and secured, and secured in a sheltered spot.

Three *Phyllonorycter* species mine *Acer* leaves. All the adults have white forewings with three fascia, the first (nearest the head) being weakly marked. The fascia of *joannisi* are darker than those of *P. acerifoliella*, a field maple miner, while *P. geniculella*, a miner of sycamore, differs in that the second fascia is acutely angled with the apex of the chevron running into the third fascia. The mines of *P. acerifoliella* and *P. geniculella* are featured on p.212.

# Scrobipalpa acuminatella

| | |
|---|---|
| Gelechiidae | 35.109 *Scrobipalpa acuminatella* (Sircom, 1850) |
| Foodplant | Thistles (*Carduus* and *Cirsium* spp.). |
| Life cycle | Larva: July and September to November. Adult: May to June and August. |
| Distribution | Common throughout British Isles. |
| | Common in VC 58, 59, 60. |
| Photo details | Feeding signs from Stretford, Manchester VC59; 2.11.15 (BS). |

The larvae of this gelechiid moth can be found in summer and autumn, feeding within large blotch mines on the lower leaves of thistle plants growing in meadows, field edges and disturbed ground. Emmet and Langmaid (2002) give the usual larval feeding periods as July to September, and in reality November is not the best time to look for this species, yet it is certainly a possibility. The larva photographed below left, was found in a creeping thistle mine at the end of October on the edge of a football field in a small scrap of south-facing vegetation against a low wall. I have also found the mines at the edge of a field, again south-facing, in early November, with adult emergence confirming the identity.

The mine and larval appearance are distinctive enough to allow identification to be made from this stage of the life cycle. Within the tenanted mine, one may see the larva resting against the midrib within the leaf. As the blotch is extended, becoming slightly inflated, frass is deposited in a few clumps within the mine. The younger larva is greenish yellow with a blackish brown head. As it develops, the anterior part of each segment becomes increasingly bright pink.

Pupation occurs outside the mine in the leaf litter. The adult is relatively plain, having brown forewings with a few subtle orange streaks running along the veins.

# Coleophora artemisicolella

| | |
|---|---|
| Coleophoridae | 37.090 *Coleophora artemisicolella* Bruand, [1855] |
| Foodplant | Mugwort (*Artemesia vulgaris*). |
| Life cycle | Larva: August to May. Adult: July to August. |
| Distribution | Local in England and Wales. |
| | Local in VC 58, 59, 60. |
| Photo details | Feeding signs from Irlam Moss, Salford VC59; 02.11.15 (BS). |

The feeding signs of this species are most obvious around this time of year, although it may be too late to find any cases as these will be already at the base of the plant ready to overwinter. If you look on mugwort flowers, you may see numerous small holes in the seeds. These are made as the larva feeds, moving from seed to seed. This *Coleophora* can therefore easily be recorded throughout the winter. Where they occur, the holes will usually be present in large numbers.

If a site has been discovered where the larval presence has been confirmed, one may wish to return the following September to look a bit closer for active larval cases. The larva forms a case of silk, but encloses it in an excavated seed-head, meaning camouflage is excellent. The tenanted seed-heads tend to be a bit browner, and larvae in these cases may be found on the side of another seed-head actively feeding, or occasionally feeding on a leaf of the plant.

One may also find the cases by gently beating the plant over an upturned umbrella. Leave the seed-heads for a short time and some will start to move. Alternatively, collect the seed-heads displaced by beating and put them in a pot and wait for tenanted ones to climb up the sides.

To rear, one will need to keep the larvae outside over winter and spring before adult emergence in summer. This can be done by potting and netting some cases on a small mugwort plant.

# Ancylis badiana

| | |
|---|---|
| Tortricidae | 49.214 *Ancylis badiana* ([Denis & Schiffermüller], 1775) |
| Foodplant | Clover (*Trifolium* spp.), vetch (*Lathyrus* and *Vicia*). |
| Life cycle | Larva: June-July, September-April. Adult: late April-June, July-early Sept. |
| Distribution | Common throughout British Isles. |
| | Common in VC 58, 59, 60. |
| Photo details | Feeding signs from Chorlton, Manchester VC59; 23.10.15 (BS). |

One of the commoner of this large genus of tortricid moths, *Ancylis badiana* can be found in meadows, uncultivated ground, and clearings in woods throughout the region wherever the food-plants occur.

Careful searching, particularly in an area where the adult moth is frequently found, will usually produce evidence of the larva on clover or vetch. Developing a familiarity with the feeding signs and the larval appearance, means that when recording on other sites at a time of year where the adults are no longer flying, it can still be possible to record the presence of this species.

The feeding signs are probably more conspicuous on clover than on vetch. The larva folds a leaf of clover, usually down the middle, and tightly seals the edges with silk, feeding within. This causes patches of the leaf to turn yellowish white. The larvae can also be found feeding on various vetches, where they may make a spinning between two leaves.

Larvae feed in two generations; in early summer and again in autumn. The autumn larvae overwinter full-fed, and pupate in spring in the feeding place. The larva is yellowish brown, with large dark spots on the lateral edges of the prothoracic plate, and also on the anal plate. The head is pale brown, thoracic legs are dark brown.

# *Gypsonoma dealbana*

| | |
|---|---|
| Tortricidae | 49.279 *Gypsonoma dealbana* (Frölich, 1828) |
| Foodplant | Oak (*Quercus* spp.), willow (Salix spp.), hawthorn (Crataegus spp.) etc. |
| Life cycle | Larva: September to May. Adult: early June to late August. |
| Distribution | Common throughout most of British Isles; local in Scotland. |
| | Common in VC 58, 59, 60. |
| Photo details | Feeding signs from Chorlton, Manchester VC59; 12.11.16 (BS). |

Larval feeding signs of this tortricid moth can commonly be found in autumn on the leaves of a number of different tree species. Oak, sallow and hazel are often used. The larva feeds on the underside of the leaf, beneath a layer of silk, coated in frass. The frass will usually be arranged in a funnel shape. As the larva feeds on the lower epidermis, it creates a windowing effect which can be seen on the upperside of the leaf, meaning that the presence of the species can be detected as long as the leaves stay on the tree, which in the case of oak may well be until late November. The photos of feeding signs at the bottom of the page, show underside (left) and upperside (right).

Larvae can be found in spring, feeding on buds, catkins and leaves of the same foodplants. The larva is pale grey, with a blackish brown head, prothoracic plate and thoracic legs

This adult is similar to other *Gypsonoma* species and identification may be a little tricky. Look for the creamy-white patch on the front of the face around the palps of *dealbana*. In *G. aceriana* this is pale fuscous, whereas in *G. sociana* this is pure white.

Similar early feeding signs may be found on poplars, created by the larva of *Gypsonoma oppressana* (p.186). In some cases, there may be a number of larvae feeding on the same leaf. The larva of *oppressana* is brown with a blackish head, so quite distinguishable than that of *dealbana*.

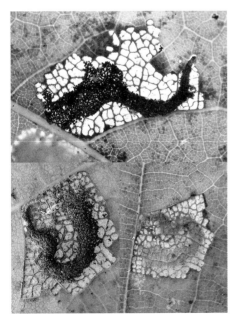

# A selection of larval cases from autumn and winter

7.001 *Nemophora degeerella* (photo: Tina Schulz) ?-4.
8.001 *Incurvaria pectinea* - birch, hazel, lime, etc. 6-9.
12.027 *Tinea pellionella* - wool, hair, etc. all year.
35.037 *Thiotricha subocellea* - marjoram, mint 8-11*.
37.009 *Coleophora milvipennis* - birch 8-5.

37.012 *Coleophora limosipennella* - elm 9-7.
37.038 *Coleophora lineolea* - woundwort, etc. 9-6.
37.063 *Coleophora albicosta* - gorse 8-4.
37.069 *Coleophora caespititiella* - rushes 8-4.
37.070 *Coleophora tamesis* - jointed rush 8-5.

*As yet unrecorded in Lancashire or Cheshire, although scattered distribution in UK suggests it could be present.

# DECEMBER FIELD TIPS

At the end of the year, there is much to be done in terms of sorting out the year's findings. Identifications may need to be confirmed, records should be completed and sent to the county recorders, and any larvae or pupae collected in the previous twelve months should be readied for the oncoming winter, placing them outside as appropriate. Don't forget to include specimen information in the larval container, particularly if rearing a number of species, to help clarify the newly emerged moth's identity.

It is still possible to make new finds for the year. Trees and shrubs in sheltered spots may keep their leaves well into December, giving the opportunity to collect *Phyllonorycter* mines after pupation has occurred.

202. *Stigmella aurella*
203. *Ectoedemia septembrella*
204. *Taleporia tubulosa*
205. *Psyche casta*
206. *Phyllonorycter heegeriella*
207. *Phyllonorycter oxyacanthae*
208. *Argyresthia trifasciata*
209. *Coleophora pyrrhulipennella*
210. *Coleophora argentula*
211. *Epiphyas postvittana*

*Tatton Park, Cheshire, 29th December 2015*

# Stigmella aurella

| Nepticulidae | 4.045 *Stigmella aurella* (Fabricius, 1775) |
|---|---|
| Foodplant | Bramble (*Rubus* spp.), avens (*Geum* spp.). |
| Life cycle | Larva: Throughout the year. Adult: April to Sept in 3 or more generations. |
| Distribution | Common throughout British Isles. |
| | Common in VC58, 59, 60. |
| Photo details | Leaf-mines from Rixton, Warrington VC59; 7.12.15 (BS). |

Certainly one of the easiest leaf-miners to find throughout the country. Tenanted mines can also be found at any time, as generations are many and overlap. The mines are long and serpentine, crossing veins and often the midrib. The frass is of varying thickness, but usually the typical *aurella* mine will include at least one section where the width of the line of frass is relatively broad. On leaving its mine, the yellow larva spins a pale brown cocoon on the detritus below.

Despite the mines being extremely common, one is unlikely to find the adults unless rearing through. When freshly emerged, the base of the forewings is golden brown, and the apex has a violet sheen, There is a broad cream-coloured metallic fascia across the wings. The head is orange, aiding differentiation from the black-headed moth *Stigmella splendidissimella*, the mines of which are found on the same foodplant. *S. splendidissimella* mines are similar to *aurella* but feature a narrow frass line for the entire length of the mine. However as *aurella* mines may occasionally do the same, rearing to adult is essential if one is to record *splendidissimella*.

*S. auromarginella* makes a similar mine to *aurella* but is limited to a few sites in Dorset and the Burren (in Ireland). *Ectoedemia erythrogenella* and *E. rubivora*.are blotch miners on bramble. Both are mainly S. England species, although *rubivora* has also been recorded in Yorkshire.

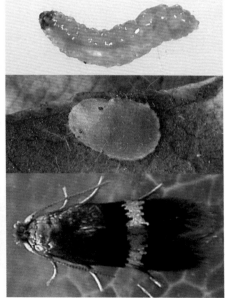

# *Ectoedemia septembrella*

| | |
|---|---|
| Nepticulidae | 4.078 *Ectoedemia septembrella* (Stainton, 1849) |
| Foodplant | St John's-wort (*Hypericum* spp.). |
| Life cycle | Larva: July-October in two generations. Adult: May to June and August. |
| Distribution | Widespread and locally common throughout British Isles. |
| | Common in VC58, 59, 60. |
| Photo details | Leaf-mines from Rochdale, Lancashire VC59; 25.12.15 and 22.8.15 (BS). |

Shrubs of St John's-wort (*Hypericum* spp.) are often found growing over garden walls and in supermarket car parks, and are a good source of *Ectoedemia septembrella* mines. This nepticulid is unusual amongst its close relatives in that it feeds and pupates all within a single leaf. The larva makes a long, slender gallery ending in a blotch, usually with some reddish-staining. The frass itself may be reddish at the start of the mine, later becoming blackish.

Feeding is complete by December, the larva then spinning a pupal cocoon within the leaf in an inflated, silk-lined chamber. Pupation takes place within this cocoon and the adult emerges the following spring.

Successful emergence will usually follow if the mines are kept in an air-tight pot in a cool place. Alternatively, the mined leaves can be placed into a pot (large yoghurt pots are ideal for this purpose), with stocking material secured over the top, and kept in a sheltered spot within the garden. This should be brought into the shed, or similar environment, in spring.

The larva can also be found on native *Hypericum* plants such as *H. perforatum*.

There is a further generation in summer, with mines in July and August and the adults flying from August to September.

# *Taleporia tubulosa*

| | |
|---|---|
| Psychidae | 11.006 *Taleporia tubulosa* (Retzius, 1783) |
| Foodplant | Lichens and decaying plant matter. |
| Life cycle | Larva: Aug-April, sometimes over two years. Adult: May to June. |
| Distribution | Local in England and southern Scotland. |
| | Local in VC58. Unrecorded in VC59, 60 (see below). |
| Photo details | Larval case from Little Budworth Common, VC58; 05.12.15 (BS). |

This psychid appears to be very scarce in the north of the region. Whereas it has been recorded from around twenty sites in Cheshire, there is only one possible (historical) record from south Lancashire (VC59). Hopefully there are sites waiting to be discovered. However the case is so distinctive this is perhaps unlikely. The case is long and cylindrical, tapering to a point, and becoming triangular in cross-section at the tip. The larval case is a little similar to that formed by the Land Caddis (*Enoicyla pusilla*).

The larva begins feeding on lichens on tree trunks, fence posts or similar, in autumn. Winter is spent amongst the leaf-litter on the woodland floor. The larva ascends the trunk, post, etc. again from April onwards, and pupates in this position. The fully developed case may be up to 20mm in length, and is covered with fragments of lichen and algae which make it slightly less conspicuous.

The adults emerge in May and June. The male has a full set of wings, whereas the female (below right) is completely apterous (without wings), and never ventures far from the case.

Following emergence the case remains securely in place upon the tree, usually with the pupal exuvia protruding from the lower end. This makes it a good species to look for in December, when evidence of other micro-moths may be a little thin on the ground.

# *Psyche casta*

| | |
|---|---|
| Psychidae | 11.012 *Psyche casta* (Pallas, 1767) |
| Foodplant | Grass, lichens and decaying plant matter. |
| Life cycle | Larva: August-May. Adult: May to June. |
| Distribution | Occurs throughout British Isles, more commonly in the south. Local in VC58, 59, 60. |
| Photo details | Larval case from Little Budworth Common, VC58; 05.12.15 (BS). Female (David Shenton). |

The adult *Psyche casta* is rarely seen, meaning the easiest way to record the species is to look for the larval case. It may be found near the base of a fence post or on the trunk of a tree although the only cases found at this time of year are likely to be vacated. Overwintering larvae (in their cases) will be situated amongst the leaf litter until spring, with the adults emerging from May.

The male has broad, featureless, dark brown wings and impressively feathered antennae. It is very rarely attracted to light. The female is apterous (bottom, right).

On emergence, the female stays in its case only protruding enough to allow mating to occur. The resultant eggs are laid within the case. The tiny larvae hatch in August and initially produce their own cases constructed from pieces of the maternal case, to which they remain attached. As the larvae increase in size, they disperse, and form larger cases from longitudinally arranged sections of grass stems. These pieces each extend beyond the length of the larva and are slightly splayed out at the rear end of the case.

Other old, vacated Psychid cases which may be found on trees and posts in December include *Narycia duplicella* (p.26) and *Luffia ferchaultella* (p42).

# *Phyllonorycter heegeriella*

| | |
|---|---|
| Gracillariidae | 15.036 *Phyllonorycter heegeriella* (Zeller, 1846) |
| Foodplant | Oak (*Quercus* spp.). |
| Life cycle | Larva: July and September to October. Adult: May and August. |
| Distribution | Widespread throughout British Isles. |
| | Local in VC58. Records from VC59, 60 are unconfirmed. |
| Photo details | Leaf-mines from Flint, Flintshire, Wales VC51; 07.12.13 (BS). |

*Phyllonorycter heegeriella* mines are worth looking for on oak saplings in sheltered spots, even in early winter, as in the example below, taken from North Wales. The mines appeared very good candidates for *heegeriella*. Fortunately rearing was successful and identity was confirmed.

This moth was previously thought to be reasonably widespread throughout the region with a number of records in all three of our Vice-Counties. These records were mostly based on leaf-mines alone, no adults having been reared in Lancashire and just three in Cheshire. Those recorded without rearing are now considered unconfirmed, in line with the National Micro-moth Recording guidelines (Langmaid et al, 2016). Nevertheless, there are certain features that suggest the possibility of *heegeriella* mines. Likely candidates can then be collected and reared.

The typical *heegeriella* mine is less than 10mm in length and is often formed at the tip of a lobe, causing it to fold over. There are numerous small creases on the underside of the mine. Often there are a number of *heegeriella* mines on the same leaf. However, if only one small mine is found amongst other larger mines, I would be concerned about the possibility that the small mine may be an aberrant mine from another species, perhaps from a larva that had failed to fully develop.

The adult differs from the similar *P. harrisella*, by the presence of a dark-bordered basal streak.

# *Phyllonorycter oxyacanthae*

| | |
|---|---|
| Gracillariidae | 15.043 *Phyllonorycter oxyacanthae* (Frey, 1856) |
| Foodplant | Hawthorn (*Crataegus* spp.), pear (*Pyrus* spp.), quince (*Cydonia oblonga*). |
| Life cycle | Larva: July and September to October. Adult: May and August. |
| Distribution | Common throughout British Isles. |
| | Common in VC58, 59, 60. |
| Photo details | Leaf-mines from Rixton, Warrington VC59; 7.12.15 (BS). |

Mines of this species may be found on hawthorn, throughout autumn and early winter. Even after the leaves have fallen, collecting a handful of fallen hawthorn leaves and overwintering them in a netted pot outside in a sheltered location, is likely to give rise to adults in the spring. Make sure that no other leaves, particularly from rowan and apple which can give rise to very similar species, have been mixed up with the hawthorn leaves as confusion and errors may result.

Rearing is the easiest way of identifying the adult moths, as there are no consistent external differences between *oxyacanthae* and its close relatives *P. sorbi* and *P. mespilella*. Any that turn up at light traps require dissection if to be identified to species level.

The larva is greenish yellow, with a pale brown head. It mines the underside of the leaf, usually in a lobe as in the photos below. The mine becomes contracted and contains many small creases. It is initially pale green, but does become browner with age. Take care to avoid confusing the mine of this species with that of *Parornix anglicella* (p.10). The latter species makes a much smaller underside mine on hawthorn, which is brown throughout its development. One may also find cones on the leaf lobes where the *anglicella* larva has continued to feed. The *anglicella* larva has the four black prothoracic spots typical of the genus.

# *Argyresthia trifasciata*

| | |
|---|---|
| Argyresthiidae | 20.005 *Argyresthia trifasciata* Staudinger, 1871 |
| Foodplant | Cypress (*Chamaecyparis, Cupressocyparis*), juniper (*Juniperus* spp.). |
| Life cycle | Larva: November to February. Adult: May to early July. |
| Distribution | Widely distributed in British Isles. Common in England and Wales. Common in VC58, 59, 60. |
| Photo details | Leaf-mine from Chorlton, Manchester VC59; 06.12.14 (BS). |

A native of France and Switzerland, this moth is a relatively recent arrival in this country. The first UK record of *Argyresthia trifasciata* was in Hampstead, London in 1982, and was first recorded from Cheshire and Lancashire in 1999 and 2000 respectively. It seems likely to have been imported with cypresses and junipers (Emmet, 1982), and is now common in gardens throughout the region, particularly where cypresses occur.

The mines can easily be found on *Leylandii* cypresses, as patches of the shoot appear bleached. Closer inspection may reveal dark brown frass around the shoot and a larva within this discoloured section. The mines become brownish with time.

It can be difficult to separate old mines of this species from those of *Argyresthia cupressella* which may be locally common on *Leylandii* cypresses and will also turn brown with age. The timing of the two does differ however with *cupressella* larva being active in April and May. Also *trifasciata* larvae have a dark brown to black head, whereas that of *cupressella* is light brown.

The adult *trifasciata* is a very distinctive moth with its three transverse white fascia on a brassy brown forewing, although very worn specimens might possibly be mistaken for one of the *Phyllonorycter* species. The adult moth is attracted to light.

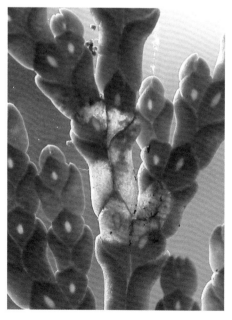

# Coleophora pyrrhulipennella

| | |
|---|---|
| Coleophoridae | 37.055 *Coleophora pyrrhulipennella* Zeller, 1839 |
| Foodplant | Heather (*Calluna vulgaris*), bell heather (*Erica cinerea*). |
| Life cycle | Larva: September to May. Adult: June to July. |
| Distribution | Widespread throughout British Isles.<br>Local in VC58, 59, 60. |
| Photo details | Larval case from Little Budworth Common VC58; 05.12.15 (BS).<br>Adult (Chris Manley). |

The first instars of this species begin feeding by grazing on the undersides of the leaflets of heather. A case is constructed from the remnants of the ova and silken spinning. Feeding then continues from within this case, on the leaves and flowers of the foodplant. The larva is brown, with the head, prothoracic plate and thoracic legs all black. The fully developed case is glossy black and 9mm long. It has a ventral keel just over half-way along the case.

On completion of feeding in May, the larva fixes the case to the stem, often right at the tip, in full sunshine and pupates in this position. Cases may be found by sweeping the heather in spring. Adults can be disturbed during the day from their resting position amongst the foodplants.

When looking for this species in autumn or winter, one may either find the empty cases vacated by the adults that have emerged that summer, or the overwintering larvae in fully-formed cases. If kept in captivity, the cases will hopefully begin to move in spring as they awake from their winter diapause. It is essential to keep the cases outside if one wishes to rear the adult. Probably the best way to do so is to keep it on a netted section of the foodplant, with the base of the netting tightly secured to keep the larva within and predators out.

# Coleophora argentula

| | |
|---|---|
| Coleophoridae | 37.102 *Coleophora argentula* (Stephens, 1834) |
| Foodplant | Yarrow (*Achillea millefolium*), sneezewort (*Achillea ptarmica*). |
| Life cycle | Larva: September to May. Adult: late June to mid-August. |
| Distribution | Local in Great Britain; more common in south. Unrecorded from Ireland. Local in VC58, 59. Very local in VC60. |
| Photo details | Larval case from St Helens, Lancashire VC59; 07.12.15 (BS). |

One is only likely to encounter the adults of this attractive Coleophorid by rearing from the larval cases. The larvae begin feeding in early September on withered flowers and seeds. Like other members of the genus, the later instars feed from the protection of a case. This is fully developed by the end of September. It is a brown, cylindrical construction with a grainy appearance from its coating of tiny fragments of plant material and is typically 5.5-6mm in length. The anal end of the case is trivalved. These cases can be quite plentiful amongst the dried flower-heads of yarrow, from autumn onwards.

To rear the adults, the cases will need to be kept outside over winter. I used a small yoghurt pot with the bottom cut out and placed it within some fine netting, such as a stocking, with a knot tied at the lower end. Some yarrow heads, cleared of spiders and containing cases, were placed into the yoghurt pot with some sterile moss and a few dry leaves. A knot was then tied at the top of the stocking which was then secured onto a lower branch deep in the heart of a garden shrub, offering protection from the worst of the elements. The majority of cases successfully gave rise to adults.

The forewings of the adult moth are pale brown with white lines along the veins and a few scattered dark spots. The white antennae are ringed for most of their length.

# *Epiphyas postvittana*

| | |
|---|---|
| Tortricidae | 49.039 Light Brown Apple Moth *Epiphyas postvittana* (Walker, 1863) |
| Foodplant | Extremely polyphagous (see below). |
| Life cycle | Larva: Throughout the year in 2-3 generations. Adult: April to November. |
| Distribution | Common in England and Wales. Local in Scotland and Ireland. Common in VC58, 59, 60. |
| Photo details | Feeding signs on rose from Chorlton, Manchester VC59; 29.12.15 (BS). |

Seemingly introduced from the Antipodes on horticultural stock, the larvae of this species are extremely polyphagous. Despite the vernacular name, the larvae are certainly not restricted to apple and can be found on virtually any garden plant, and are also found much further afield than the garden, such as on the broom plants of Ainsdale and Formby on the Lancashire coast.

The presence of the larva may be indicated by a tight spinning in the leaves or flowers of the affected plant. In making its spinning, the larva produces copious amounts of silk, and this can help in differentiating it from other species. For instance, the spinnings of *postvittana* on broom contain much more silk than those of *Agonopterix assimilella* (p.49) on the same plant.

The larva of *postvittana* is usually green with a few small black spots on the green or pale brown head. Occasionally, larvae may have more of a yellowish, brownish, or even pinkish tinge. I have often found the species feeding on the leaves and flowers in ragwort heads, and those doing so seem to take on a yellowish colour, presumably from their consumption of the flowers

The species can be continuously brooded throughout the year and larvae may be found at any time. Other foodplants include privet, geranium, lavender, ivy, rose, honeysuckle, St John's-wort, willow-herbs, teasel heads, hazel catkins and brambles. There are many, many more.

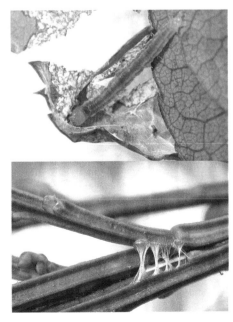
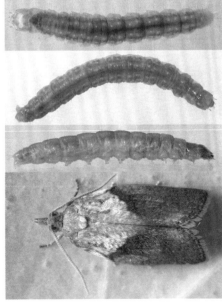

# A selection of *Phyllonorycter* mines

15.039 *P quercifoliella*. - oak 7-8, 9-10.
15.064 *P. coryli* - hazel 7, 9-10.
15.066 *P. strigulatella* - grey alder 7, 9-10.
15.073 *P. lautella* - oak 7, 9-10.
15.076 *P. emberizaepenella* - snowberry, etc. 7, 9-10

15.080 *P. froelichiella* - alder 9-10.
15.081 *P. nicellii* - hazel 9-10.
15.082 *P. klemannella* - alder 9-10.
15.084 *P. acerifoliella* - field maple 7, 10.
15.086 *P. geniculella* - sycamore 7, 10.

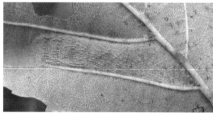

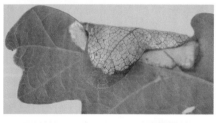

# References and further reading

Agassiz, D. J. L., Beavan, S. D. & Heckford, R. J., 2013. *A Checklist of the Lepidoptera of the British Isles*. Royal Entomological Society, St Albans.

Bland, K. P. (Ed.), 2015. T*he Moths and Butterflies of Great Britain and Ireland*, Vol. **5** (Pts 1 & 2). Brill, Leiden.

Clifton, J. & Wheeler, J., 2012. *Conifer Moths of the British Isles*. Clifton and Wheeler, Dorchester.

Dunn, T. C., 1991. *An Investigation into an insect epidemic on Harnisha Hill, County Durham* . Vasculum **76**: 33-36.

Emmet, A. M., 1982. *Argyresthia trifasciata* Staudinger, 1871 (Lep.: Yponomeutidae) in Britain.  The Entomologist's Record and Journal of Variation **94**: 180-182.

Emmet, A. M. (Ed.), 1988. *A Field Guide to the Smaller British Lepidoptera* (2nd Edition). British Entomological and Natural History Society, London.

Emmet, A. M. (Ed.), 1996. *The Moths and Butterflies of Great Britain and Ireland*, Vol. **3**. Harley Books, Colchester.

Emmet, A. M. & Langmaid, J. R. (Eds.), 2002. *The Moths and Butterflies of Great Britain and Ireland*, Vol. **4** (Part 1 & 2). Harley Books, Colchester.

Goater, B., 1986. *British Pyralid Moths*. Harley Books, Colchester.

Hart, C., 2011. *British Plume Moths. A guide to their identification and biology*. British Entomological and Natural History Society, Reading.

Heath, J. (Ed.), 1976. *The Moths and Butterflies of Great Britain and Ireland*, Vol. **1.** Harley Books, London.

Heath, J. & Emmet, A. M. (Eds.), 1985. *The Moths and Butterflies of Great Britain and Ireland*, Vol. **2**. Harley Books, Colchester.

Jordan, M. P., Langmaid, J. R. & Doorenweerd, C., 2016. Morphological difference between upperside and underside leaf-mining larvae of *Phyllocnistis unipunctella* (Stephens, 1834) (Lep,: Gracillariidae) and its changing phenology. The Entomologist's Record and Journal of Variation **128**: 121-127.

Kaiser, W., Huguet, E., Casas, J., Commin, C. & Giron, D., 2010. Plant green-island phenotype induced by leaf-miners is mediated by bacterial symbionts. Proc. Of the Royal Society B: Biol. Sci. **277**: 2311–2319.

Langmaid, J. R., Palmer, S. M., Parsons, M. S. & Young, M. R., 2016. Micro-moth Grading Guidelines. http://www.mothscount.org/text/73/guidance_notes.html

Manley, C., 2015. *British Moths* (2nd Edition). Bloomsbury, London.

van Nieukerken, E. J. (Ed.), 2016. Nepticulidae and Opostegidae of the world, version 2.0. Scratchpads, biodiversity online. http://nepticuloidea.info/

Patocka, J. & Turcani, M., 2005. *Lepidoptera Pupae*. Central European Species. Apollo, Copenhagen, Denmark.

Sterling, P., Parsons,  M. & Lewington, R., 2012. *Field Guide to the Micro-moths of Great Britain and Ireland*. British Wildlife Publishing, Dorset.

Tutt, J. W., 1994 (reprint). *Practical Hints for the Field Lepidopterist* (Vols. **1-3**, 1901-1905). British Entomological and Natural History Society, London.

Watson, H. C., 1852. *Cybele Britannica* (Vol. **3**). Longman and Co., London.

# Index of featured species (scientific names)

| | |
|---|---|
| Acleris ferrugana | 148 |
| Acleris hastiana | 142 |
| Acleris notana | 162 |
| Acleris rhombana | 96 |
| Acleris sparsana | 129 |
| Acrobasis advenella | 96 |
| Acrobasis consociella | 112 |
| Acrocercops brongniardella | 100 |
| Acrolepia autumnitella | 158 |
| Adaina microdactyla | 21 |
| Agonopterix angelicella | 82 |
| Agonopterix arenella | 7 |
| Agonopterix assimilella | 49 |
| Agonopterix carduella | 94 |
| Agonopterix heracliana | 9, 104 |
| Agonopterix kaekeritziana | 94 |
| Agonopterix nervosa | 94 |
| Agonopterix ocellana | 94 |
| Agonopterix propinquella | 135 |
| Agonopterix scopariella | 94 |
| Agriphila straminella | 56 |
| Alucita hexadactyla | 108 |
| Amblyptilia acanthadactyla | 141 |
| Anacampsis blattariella | 10, 94 |
| Anacampsis populella | 84 |
| Anania coronata | 166 |
| Anania crocealis | 113 |
| Anania hortulata | 24 |
| Anarsia spartiella | 95 |
| Ancylis badiana | 198 |
| Ancylis mitterbacheriana | 182 |
| Anthophila fabriciana | 7, 87 |
| Aphelia paleana | 95 |
| Aphomia sociella | 24 |
| Apodia bifractella | 19 |
| Apotomis turbidana | 96 |
| Aproaerema anthyllidella | 148 |
| Archips podana | 95 |
| Argyresthia albistria | 56 |
| Argyresthia bonnetella | 56 |
| Argyresthia cupressella | 63 |
| Argyresthia dilectella | 62 |
| Argyresthia goedartella | 47 |
| Argyresthia pygmaeella | 78 |
| Argyresthia retinella | 79 |
| Argyresthia trifasciata | 208 |
| Aspilapteryx tringipennella | 60 |
| Athrips mouffetella | 95 |
| Bedellia somnulentella | 134 |
| Blastobasis adustella | 36 |
| Blastobasis lacticolella | 11, 24 |
| Blastodacna hellerella | 148 |
| Bohemannia pulverosella | 98 |
| Bucculatrix cidarella | 152 |
| Bucculatrix maritima | 59 |
| Bucculatrix nigricomella | 6, 44 |
| Bucculatrix thoracella | 15 |
| Bucculatrix ulmella | 148 |
| Callisto denticulella | 119 |
| Caloptilia cuculipennella | 118 |
| Caloptilia elongella | 172 |
| Caloptilia populetorum | 132 |
| Caloptilia rufipennella | 10 |
| Caloptilia stigmatella | 153 |
| Cameraria ohridella | 114 |
| Carcina quercana | 177 |
| Carpatolechia alburnella | 95 |
| Carpatolechia notatella | 159 |
| Carpatolechia proximella | 160 |
| Caryocolum fraternella | 95 |
| Caryocolum tricolorella | 51 |
| Caryocolum viscariella | 65 |
| Cataclysta lemnata | 55 |
| Cedestis subfasciella | 30 |
| Celypha lacunana | 96 |
| Choreutis pariana | 95 |
| Chrysoesthia drurella | 114, 148 |
| Chrysoesthia sexguttella | 136 |
| Chrysoteuchia culmella | 24 |
| Cnephasia asseclana | 96 |
| Cnephasia stephensiana | 96 |
| Cochylis roseana | 52 |
| Coleophora albicosta | 200 |
| Coleophora albidella | 38 |
| Coleophora albitarsella | 38 |
| Coleophora alticolella | 20 |
| Coleophora argentula | 210 |
| Coleophora artemisicolella | 197 |
| Coleophora betulella | 38 |
| Coleophora caespititiella | 200 |
| Coleophora deauratella | 138 |
| Coleophora discordella | 38 |
| Coleophora flavipennella | 38 |
| Coleophora gryphipennella | 179 |
| Coleophora juncicolella | 68 |
| Coleophora laricella | 38 |
| Coleophora limosipennella | 200 |
| Coleophora lineolea | 200 |
| Coleophora lusciniaepennella | 38 |
| Coleophora lutipennella | 38 |
| Coleophora milvipennis | 130, 200 |
| Coleophora otidipennella | 10 |
| Coleophora paripennella | 69 |
| Coleophora peribenanderi | 105 |
| Coleophora pyrrhulipennella | 209 |
| Coleophora serratella | 38 |

| | |
|---|---|
| Coleophora striatipennella | 124 |
| Coleophora tamesis | 200 |
| Coleophora trifolii | 137 |
| Coptotriche marginea | 14 |
| Crambus lathoniellus | 7, 56 |
| Cryptoblabes bistriga | 148 |
| Cydia pomonella | 144 |
| Cydia splendana | 24 |
| Depressaria daucella | 83 |
| Depressaria radiella | 17 |
| Dichrorampha simpliciana | 11 |
| Diplodoma laichartingella | 38 |
| Ditula angustiorana | 56 |
| Diurnea fagella | 7, 123 |
| Dyseriocrania subpurpurella | 114 |
| Ectoedemia albifasciella | 186 |
| Ectoedemia angulifasciella | 186 |
| Ectoedemia argyropeza | 190 |
| Ectoedemia atricollis | 186 |
| Ectoedemia heringi | 186 |
| Ectoedemia intimella | 189 |
| Ectoedemia louisella | 117 |
| Ectoedemia minimella | 130 |
| Ectoedemia occultella | 171 |
| Ectoedemia septembrella | 203 |
| Ectoedemia subbimaculella | 191 |
| Elachista argentella | 7 |
| Elachista cinereopunctella | 71 |
| Elachista gangabella | 180 |
| Elachista maculicerusella | 70 |
| Elophila nymphaeata | 73 |
| Emmelina monodactyla | 148 |
| Endothenia gentianaeana | 53 |
| Endothenia marginana | 24 |
| Epermenia chaerophyllella | 110 |
| Epiblema scutulana | 56 |
| Epinotia brunnichana | 90 |
| Epinotia immundana | 22 |
| Epinotia ramella | 54 |
| Epinotia solandriana | 96 |
| Epinotia sordidana | 89 |
| Epinotia tetraquetrana | 164 |
| Epiphyas postvittana | 211 |
| Eriocrania cicatricella | 74 |
| Eriocrania salopiella | 74 |
| Eriocrania sangii | 76 |
| Eriocrania semipurpurella | 74 |
| Eriocrania sparrmannella | 74 |
| Eriocrania unimaculella | 74 |
| Esperia sulphurella | 16 |
| Eucosma cana | 143 |
| Eucosma hohenwartiana | 148 |
| Eudemis profundana | 88 |
| Eudonia mercurella | 56 |
| Evergestis forficalis | 96 |
| Exoteleia dodecella | 67 |
| Glyphipterix fuscoviridella | 48 |
| Glyphipterix haworthana | 61 |
| Glyphipterix simpliciella | 32 |
| Gracillaria syringella | 193 |
| Grapholita compositella | 148 |
| Grapholita janthinana | 183 |
| Grapholita lunulana | 24 |
| Gypsonoma aceriana | 91 |
| Gypsonoma dealbana | 199 |
| Gypsonoma oppressana | 186 |
| Hedya atropunctana | 163 |
| Hedya nubiferana | 56 |
| Helcystogramma rufescens | 64 |
| Heliozela hammoniella | 130 |
| Heliozela resplendella | 99 |
| Heliozela sericiella | 114 |
| Hypatima rhomboidella | 95 |
| Incurvaria pectinea | 114, 200 |
| Lampronia fuscatella | 41 |
| Lathronympha strigana | 92 |
| Leucoptera laburnella | 186 |
| Leucoptera malifoliella | 176 |
| Leucoptera spartifoliella | 103 |
| Limnaecia phragmitella | 33 |
| Lozotaenia forsterana | 24 |
| Luffia ferchaultella | 42 |
| Lyonetia clerkella | 122 |
| Metzneria lappella | 18 |
| Metzneria metzneriella | 34 |
| Mirificarma mulinella | 7 |
| Mompha bradleyi | 139 |
| Mompha conturbatella | 86 |
| Mompha epilobiella | 106 |
| Mompha langiella | 12, 107 |
| Mompha locupletella | 7 |
| Mompha miscella | 114 |
| Mompha raschkiella | 126 |
| Mompha subbistrigella | 125 |
| Mompha terminella | 140 |
| Morophaga choragella | 6, 56 |
| Myelois circumvoluta | 37 |
| Narycia duplicella | 26 |
| Nemapogon clematella | 58 |
| Nemophora degeerella | 200 |
| Neofaculta ericetella | 24 |
| Ocnerostoma piniariella | 31 |
| Oidaematophorus lithodactyla | 7, 109 |
| Pammene aurana | 145 |
| Pammene aurita | 184 |
| Pammene fasciana | 165 |
| Pammene regiana | 23 |
| Pandemis cerasana | 7 |

Paracrania chrysolepidella 6
Paraswammerdamia nebulella 94
Parornix anglicella 6, 10
Parornix betulae 133
Parornix devoniella 173
Parornix scoticella 154
Phaulernis fulviguttella 161
Phycitodes maritima 146
Phycitodes saxicola 24
Phyllocnistis unipunctella 121
Phyllonorycter acerifoliella 212
Phyllonorycter coryli 212
Phyllonorycter corylifoliella 120
Phyllonorycter emberizaepenella 212
Phyllonorycter froelichiella 212
Phyllonorycter geniculella 212
Phyllonorycter harrisella 45
Phyllonorycter heegeriella 206
Phyllonorycter joannisi 195
Phyllonorycter klemannella 212
Phyllonorycter lautella 212
Phyllonorycter leucographella 29
Phyllonorycter nicellii 212
Phyllonorycter oxyacanthae 207
Phyllonorycter quercifoliella 212
Phyllonorycter rajella 155
Phyllonorycter schreberella 174
Phyllonorycter sorbi 12
Phyllonorycter stettinensis 194
Phyllonorycter strigulatella 212
Phyllonorycter trifasciella 46
Phyllonorycter tristrigella 6, 175
Phyllopòria bistrigella 130
Platyptilia gonodactyla 72
Pleuroptya ruralis 93
Plutella xylostella 148
Prays fraxinella 80
Prochoreutis myllerana 128
Pseudargyrotoza conwagana 181
Psyche casta 205
Psychoides filicivora 28
Psychoides verhuella 43
Ptycholoma lecheana 95
Pyrausta aurata 147
Rhopobota naevana 111
Roeslerstammia erxlebella 151
Scrobipalpa acuminatella 196
Scrobipalpa costella 178
Scrobipalpa instabilella 50
Scythropia crataegella 81
Spuleria flavicaput 35
Stenoptilia zophodactylus 127
Stigmella anomalella 11
Stigmella atricapitella 188

Stigmella aurella 202
Stigmella betulicola 130
Stigmella catharticella 168
Stigmella confusella 130
Stigmella continuella 130
Stigmella crataegella 114
Stigmella floslactella 168
Stigmella hemargyrella 168
Stigmella hybnerella 6, 168
Stigmella lapponica 130
Stigmella lemniscella 168
Stigmella luteella 130
Stigmella magdalenae 168
Stigmella microtheriella 168
Stigmella nylandriella 116
Stigmella oxyacanthella 150
Stigmella perpygmaeella 168
Stigmella plagicolella 114
Stigmella roborella 186
Stigmella ruficapitella 186
Stigmella sakhalinella 130
Stigmella samiatella 186
Stigmella sorbi 114
Stigmella speciosa 114
Stigmella tiliae 168
Stigmella tityrella 170
Stigmella trimaculella 168
Strophedra weirana 185
Swammerdamia caesiella 156
Swammerdamia pyrella 157
Syndemis musculana 56
Tachystola acroxantha 6
Taleporia tubulosa 204
Teleiodes sequax 85
Teleiodes vulgella 66
Thiotricha subocellea 200
Tinea pellionella 200
Tischeria dodonaea 186
Tischeria ekebladella 6, 192
Tortricodes alternella 95
Tortrix viridana 96
Triaxomera parasitella 27
Trifurcula immundella 40
Udea lutealis 96
Udea prunalis 167
Yponomeuta cagnagella 94
Yponomeuta evonymella 101
Yponomeuta plumbella 102
Ypsolopha dentella 77
Ypsolopha parenthesella 94
Ypsolopha scabrella 94
Ypsolopha ustella 6

# Foodplant Index

Acer campestre     117, 129
Acer platanoides     195
Acer pseudoplatanus     23, 129, 184
Achillea millefolium     146, 210
Achillea ptarmica     210
Alder     22, 38, 89, 99, 152, 155
    160, 162, 164, 172, 194, 212
Alnus glutinosa     22, 89, 152, 155, 162
    164
Alnus spp.     99, 160, 172, 194
Angelica     82, 110, 161
Angelica sylvestris     82, 110, 161
Anthriscus sylvestris     104
Apple     95, 98, 119, 120, 122
    144, 150, 157, 176, 186
Arctium lappa     18
Arctium spp.     105
Arrhenatherum elatius     64
Artemesia vulgaris     197
Ash     80, 118, 181, 193
Aspen     84, 190
Asplenium ceterach     43
Asplenium scolopendrium     43
Asplenium spp.     43
Aster tripolium     19, 59
Atriplex portulacoides     50
Atriplex spp.     136
Atropa belladonna     158
Avens     202

Beech     123, 129, 168, 170
    177, 182, 185
Bell Heather     68, 209
Betony     24
Betula spp.     41, 47, 54, 76, 79, 90
    122, 132, 133, 151, 156
    160, 162, 163, 164, 171
Bilberry     111
Bindweeds     134, 148
Birch     38, 41, 47, 54, 56, 76, 79, 90
    94, 95, 122, 130, 132, 133, 151, 156
    160, 162, 163, 164, 171, 200
Bird Cherry     101
Bird's-foot Trefoil     38
Bittersweet     158, 178
Black Poplar     91, 121
Blackstonia perfoliata     127
Blackthorn     56, 66, 81, 114, 167
Bog-Myrtle     142, 152, 162, 163
Brachypodium spp     64
Brachypodium sylvaticum     180
Bracket fungi     27

Bramble     14, 202
Broad-Leaved Willowherb     125
Broom     40, 49, 94, 95, 103
Buckthorn     168
Bulrush     33
Burdock     105

Calamint     147
Calluna vulgaris     68, 209
Calystegia sepium     134
Carduus spp.     37, 105, 196, 143
Carex flacca     71
Castanea sativa     165, 182, 192
Centaurea nigra     34, 69, 143
Centaurium erythraea     127
Centaury     127
Cerastium fontanum     124
Chamaecyparis     62
Chamaecyparis lawsoniana     63
Chamaecyparis spp.     208
Chamerion angustifolium     86, 126
Chenopodium spp.     136
Cherry     95
Circaea lutetiana     107, 140
Cirsium arvense     69, 135
Cirsium spp.     37, 105, 196
Cirsium vulgare     143, 135
Clary     147
Clinopodium spp.     147
Clover     148, 198
Cock's-Foot     32
Coltsfoot     72
Common Chickweed     124
Common Fleabane     19
Common Knapweed     34, 69, 143
Common Mouse-Ear     124
Common Nettle     87, 93
Common Reed     70
Convolvulus arvensis     134
Corylus avellana     123, 173
Cotoneaster     66, 81
Cottongrass     61
Cow Parsley     104
Cranesbill     141
Crataegus spp.     35, 66, 81, 120, 122
    150, 157, 176, 183
    199, 207
Creeping Thistle     69, 135
Cross-Leaved Heath     141
Crucifers     148
Cupressocyparis spp.     208
Cydonia oblonga     207

Cypress 62, 63, 208
*Cytisus scoparius* 40, 49, 103

*Dactylis glomerata* 32
*Daldinia concentrica* 16
Deadly Nightshade 158
*Dipsacus fullonum* 52, 53
Duckweed 55

Elder 166
Elm 168, 174, 175, 200
Enchanter's-Nightshade 107, 140
*Epilobium hirsutum* 106, 107, 139
*Epilobium montanum* 125
*Erica cinerea* 68, 209
*Erica tetralix* 141
*Eriophorum* spp. 61
*Euonymus europaeus* 102
*Eupatorium cannabinum* 21

*Fagus sylvatica* 123, 129,170
177, 182, 185
False Brome 180
Ferns 28
Field Maple 117, 129, 212
Field Wood-Rush 48
Firethorn 29
Fleabane 109, 113
*Fomes fomentarius* 58
*Fraxinus excelsior* 80, 118, 181, 193
Fungi 16, 58

*Geranium* spp. 141
*Geum* spp. 202
Glaucous Sedge 71
Goat Willow 159, 189
Goosefoot 136
Gorse 94, 95, 200
Grasses 24, 56, 64, 95
Great Willowherb 106, 107, 139
Greater Burdock 18
Greater Stitchwort 51
Grey Alder 212

Hart's-Tongue Fern 43
Hawthorn 35, 56, 66, 81, 94, 95
114, 120, 122, 148, 150
157, 168, 176, 183, 186, 199, 207
Hazel 94, 95, 114, 123
168, 173, 200, 212
Heather 24, 209
Hedge Woundwort 141
*Helianthemum* spp. 85
Hemlock Water-Dropwort 83

Hemp-Agrimony 21
*Heracleum sphondylium* 17, 82, 110
145, 161
Himalayan Honeysuckle 46
Hogweed 17, 82, 110, 145, 161
Holly 111
Honeysuckle 46, 77, 95, 108
Hornbeam 95, 168
Horse Chestnut 114
*Hypericum* spp. 92, 203
*Hypoxylon fuscum* 58

*Ilex aquifolium* 111
*Inula conyza* 19, 109, 113
*Ipomoea purpurea* 134
Ivy 24

*Juncus* spp. 20
Juniper 62, 63, 208
*Juniperus* spp. 62, 63, 208

Knapweed 94, 148

Laburnum 186
Larch 38, 67
*Larix decidua* 67
*Lathyrus and Vicia* 198
*Lemna* spp. 55
Lesser Stitchwort 124
*Leucanthemum vulgare* 44
*Leycesteria formosa* 46
*Leylandii* 63
Lichens 26, 42, 204, 205
*Ligustrum* spp. 193, 181
*Ligustrum vulgare* 118
Lilac 193
Lime 15, 95, 151, 168, 200
Ling 68
Lombardy Poplar 121
*Lonicera periclymenum* 46, 77, 108
*Luzula campestris* 48
*Lychnis viscaria* 65

*Malus* spp. 98, 119, 120, 122, 144
150, 157, 176
Marjoram 38, 147, 200
*Melilotus altissimus* 137
*Melilotus officinalis* 137
*Mentha* spp. 147
Mint 147, 200
Morning Glory 134
Mosses 56
Mugwort 197
*Myrica gale* 142, 152, 162, 163

| | |
|---|---|
| Nettle | 24, 87, 93 |
| Norway Maple | 195 |
| | |
| Oak | 24, 38, 45, 56, 88, 94, 95 |
| | 100, 112, 114, 123, 148 |
| | 165, 177, 182, 186, 188 |
| | 191, 192, 199, 206, 212 |
| *Oenanthe crocata* | 83 |
| *Onopordum* spp. | 37 |
| Orache | 114, 136, 148 |
| *Origanum vulgare* | 147 |
| Oxeye Daisy | 44 |
| | |
| *Pastinaca sativa* | 17 |
| Pear | 150, 157, 176, 207 |
| *Phalaris arundinacea* | 70 |
| *Phragmites* | 70 |
| Pine | 30 |
| *Pinus* spp. | 30 |
| *Pinus sylvestris* | 31, 67 |
| *Plantago lanceolata* | 60 |
| Ploughman's Spikenard | 19, 109, 113 |
| *Poa* spp. | 64 |
| Pondweed | 73 |
| Poplars | 84, 91, 153, 168, 186 |
| *Populus alba* | 142 |
| *Populus nigra* | 91, 121 |
| *Populus* spp. | 84, 91, 153 |
| *Populus tremula* | 190 |
| *Potamogeton* spp. | 73 |
| Privet | 24, 181, 193 |
| *Prunus padus* | 101 |
| *Prunus spinosa* | 66, 81, 167 |
| *Pulicaria dysenterica* | 19, 109, 113 |
| *Pyracantha* | 29 |
| *Pyrus* spp. | 150, 157, 176, 207 |
| | |
| *Quercus* spp. | 45, 88, 100, 112, 123 |
| | 165, 177, 182, 188 |
| | 191, 192, 199, 206 |
| Quince | 207 |
| | |
| Ragwort | 24, 146 |
| Red Campion | 65 |
| Red Clover | 138 |
| Reed Canary-Grass | 70 |
| Ribbed Melilot | 137 |
| Ribwort Plantain | 60 |
| Rock-Rose | 85, 114 |
| *Rosa* spp. | 179 |
| Rose | 186, 179 |
| Rosebay Willowherb | 86, 126 |
| Rowan | 66, 114, 116, 154, 168 |
| *Rubus* spp. | 14, 202 |
| | |
| Rushes | 20, 200 |
| Rustyback | 43 |
| | |
| *Salix caprea* | 159, 189 |
| *Salix* spp. | 78, 84, 142, 153 |
| | 159, 163, 189, 199 |
| Sallows | 78, 84, 95 |
| | 123, 142, 153 |
| *Salvia* spp. | 147 |
| *Sambucus nigra* | 166 |
| Scots Pine | 31, 67 |
| *Scutellaria* spp. | 128 |
| Sea Aster | 19, 59 |
| Sea-Purslane | 50 |
| *Senecio jacobaea* | 146 |
| *Silene dioica* | 65 |
| *Silene latifolia* | 65 |
| Skullcap | 128 |
| Sneezewort | 210 |
| Snowberry | 46, 212 |
| *Solanum dulcamara* | 158, 178 |
| *Sorbus aria* | 154 |
| *Sorbus aucuparia* | 66, 116, 154 |
| *Sorbus* spp. | 120 |
| Spear Thistle | 135 |
| Spindle | 94, 102 |
| Spleenwort | 43 |
| St John's-Wort | 92, 203 |
| *Stachys sylvatica* | 141 |
| *Stellaria graminea* | 124 |
| *Stellaria holostea* | 51 |
| *Stellaria media* | 124 |
| Sticky Catchfly | 65 |
| Stitchwort | 95 |
| Sweet Chestnut | 165, 182, 186, 192 |
| Sycamore | 23, 114, 129, 184, 212 |
| *Symphoricarpos albus* | 46 |
| *Syringa* | 193 |
| | |
| Tall Melilot | 137 |
| Teasel | 24, 52, 53 |
| Thistles | 37, 56, 105, 143, 196 |
| *Tilia* spp. | 15, 151 |
| *Trifolium pratense* | 138 |
| *Trifolium* spp. | 198 |
| *Tussilago farfara* | 72 |
| *Typha* spp. | 33 |
| | |
| *Ulmus* spp. | 174, 175 |
| *Urtica dioica* | 93 |
| *Urtica* spp. | 87 |
| | |
| *Vaccinium myrtillus* | 111 |
| Vetch | 24, 198 |

White Campion     65
White Poplar     142
Whitebeam     154
Wild Parsnip     17
Wild Privet     118
Willowherbs     125
Willows     38, 78, 84, 94, 123
     142, 153, 159, 163, 189, 199
Woundwort     200

Yarrow     146, 210
Yellow-Wort     127

**Ellison Printing** 59-61 High Street  Rishton  Blackburn BB1 4LD
01254 883208  www.ellisonprinting.co.uk